Ridley Scott

Ridley Scott

A Critical Filmography

WILLIAM B. PARRILL

McFarland & Company, Inc., Publishers

Jefferson, North Carolina, and London

LIBRARY OF CONGRESS CATALOGUING-IN-PUBLICATION DATA

Parrill, William.
Ridley Scott : a critical filmography / William B. Parrill.
p.   cm.
Includes bibliographical references and index.

ISBN 978-0-7864-5866-0
softcover : 50# alkaline paper ∞

1. Scott, Ridley — Criticism and interpretation.
I. Title.
PN1998.3.S393P36   2011   791.43'0233'092—dc23   2011022551

British Library cataloguing data are available

On the cover: Sigourney Weaver in the 1979 film *Alien*
(Twentieth Century–Fox/Photofest

Manufactured in the United States of America

McFarland & Company, Inc., Publishers
Box 611, Jefferson, North Carolina 28640
www.mcfarlandpub.com

Ridley Scott

Table of Contents

Preface

More than any other active film director, Ridley Scott has explained his creative process at length. His explanations are full and generous in the commentaries and featurettes included as extras on the DVD and Blu-ray editions of his films. Although he is always involved in steering the script in the direction he wants it to go, he never takes a writing credit. He is careful not to settle personal scores in public, and he almost never criticizes his actors. He is involved in the total process of filmmaking from the screenplay to the theatrical release, and sometimes for decades later. He is a workaholic who keeps his personal life private, and he never makes a sensational appearance in the tabloids. What he does is make movies.

I have privileged contemporary reviews of Scott's films. Reviewers are embroiled in the push and shove of the movies which appeared last week or two weeks ago and which are setting the standards of taste, but they are, for that reason, intensely interesting. Literary critics tend to sneer at contemporary reviewers in the belief that only idiots reviewed Herman Melville's *Moby Dick*, (1851) until they read the actual reviews, and film critics are not much different. True, the democracy of the Internet tends to flatten all taste, but even here, or even especially here, there are lessons to be learned. The criticism of Scott's films, if we include *Boy and Bicycle* and his work in advertising, is now approaching a half century and is hardly likely to diminish in the foreseeable future.

Introduction

Scott's Way

"A Director of Commercials from England"

Ridley Scott's success as a filmmaker is the result of two factors: the first is his enormous talent, and the second is his mastery of the entire process of filmmaking, including what we may call the non-artistic part, its organization and planning. In this, he resembles Stanley Kubrick, who had an encyclopedic knowledge of filmmaking, knew about camera angles, special effects techniques and apparently everything else about the making of films up to the time of their release. In the last forty years of his life, Kubrick, a meticulous craftsman, made nine films. During a comparable period of time, Scott produced more than twice that many and also did extensive work in advertising and in Scott Free, the production company he formed with his brother Tony. According to the Internet Movie Database, Scott Free has now produced, including television, more than 160 films, many of them enormously ambitious, such as the mini-series *The Pillars of the Earth* (2010), based on the Ken Follett bestseller, and with many more on the way.

Although the making and release of any big-budget commercial movie is a process which varies from one film to another, it is always more or less linear and involves four stages: pre-production (whatever happens before the actual shooting of the film begins), production (the actual shooting of the film), post-production (editing, scoring the film and generally preparing the film for its theatrical release). The final step in the process, which begins at some point before the film is actually released, is exploitation, including its advertising, its theatrical release in America and abroad, its release on DVD and Blu-ray, and eventually on cable and network television. Often recently, there has been an additional step in the process, the release of a second or third, or even fourth edition of the film.

During the silent years of filmmaking, directors were handed a script, or, more likely, a scenario or outline, sometimes on the day they were to begin shooting, and had little control over the editing of the material shot under their supervision. John

3

Introduction

Ford knew that if the studios did not have a particular shot or scene, they could not put it in the film, and all Ford students will recognize the shot of Ford sitting in his chair beside the camera, calling "cut" and putting his hand over the lens. Even so, the studio often did what they could to "improve" the film. In Ford's silent epic *The Iron Horse* (1924), close-ups of the heroine were taken out of place and inserted where the producers wanted them. In the scene of Maureen O'Hara's wedding in *How Green Was My Valley* (1941), Walter Pidgeon, the losing suitor, was shot as a small figure in the background of the joyous scene. When Ford was asked about shooting a close-up of Pidgeon, he replied in effect that the SOBs, i.e., the company editors, would just use it. Ford knew that if the studio did not have a shot, or indeed a scene, they could not use it. In some cases, additional footage was shot, usually close-ups and continuity shots. Murnau's *City Girl* (1930) was taken away from the director, re-edited and, it is universally agreed, seriously damaged in the process. In all honesty, it must be admitted that the film's ruins are still impressive. Of course, different scenes were shot in various ways for censorship restrictions, and, during the silent period, a so-called B camera was sometimes used for export and to save money. The B camera export version of Murnau's *Faust* (1926), that is, the version shot to be shown outside Germany and until recently the only version available in America, is clearly inferior to the domestic version. Ford and Murnau were among the greatest of film directors, and they worked hard to control their product, but they hardly exercised the control that Ridley Scott has managed over his long career.

Until recently, the studio's word was the end of it, but with the coming of VHS, DVD and Blu-ray, the director, occasionally even a dead director, can eventually carry the day. Sam Peckinpah's *The Wild Bunch* (1969) is a famous example of a film which was restored to the director's cut after the director's death. Peckinpah's earlier film *Major Dundee* (1965) was not so fortunate. The score was changed, but most of the original material needed for restoration had been lost. Today's studios, although still not perfect, are much better at preservation of outtakes because they know they have commercial value. At the worst, they can be used as extras on DVDs and Blu-ray editions; they may even be used for a new "extended cut" or "director's cut," or in the case of *Blade Runner*, for both.

CGI (Computer-Generated Imagery) has, for more than two decades, slowly at first and then with ever-increasing rapidity, become important in big-budget filmmaking. Originally, many producers and directors thought that the process gave "good value" and would make filmmaking more efficient and therefore cheaper. This was certainly true for filmmakers with limited budgets who used the process sparingly and effectively, but it turned out to be an illusion for studio films. In order to "juice up" their films and make them more attractive to an increasingly more sophisticated — or blasé — public who seemed to want only more and bigger explosions and more and different alien hordes, studios began to use more and more CGI. Today, the result is that actors are often reduced to caricatures of themselves. Ultimately, actors may be eliminated completely, at least in certain types of films, and images of John Wayne, composited from his films and brought to life digitally, may yet revive the western.

The coming of CGI represents the largest change in the motion picture industry since the coming of sound some fifty years earlier, and Scott's background and genius made him the perfect person to arbitrate the change. The industry was changing as *Blade Runner* was made, and it has been called the last great analog film. The potential downside of the digital revolution, at least as far as a visualist as great as Scott is concerned, is that computers do not have a mind. The images generated by a computer never produce the unexpected; they never surprise you. It can even be argued that the moiling and churning of *Blade Runner*'s troubled birth occasioned its greatness or at least allowed it and that the reason that the visuals are unlike those of any other film is that they were done on the gad, improvised by a man of genius from whatever materials happened to be at hand. And *Gladiator*, as critics have noted, took full advantage of a decade of advances in CGI. *Gladiator*, however, except for the sophistication of the images, does not look much different from the sword-and-sandal epics of thirty years or more earlier.

Inevitably, the aesthetics of film includes the means of its production. That is, the end result has always been influenced to a greater or lesser degree by the process which produced it. It is, therefore, true that as films have grown more complex, so has the process of producing them. The way a film is made — that is, the aspects which are privileged by its maker, whether or not he always controls them — profoundly influences the finished product. Although the complexity of the problems may be greater or lesser, they are basically the same whether the filmmaker is an artist or a hack. A big-budget filmmaker has all the problems of the person who animates films in his basement, and more, but filmmaking has necessarily become more impersonal, subject to greater restraints, and more difficult to control. In instances where Scott has lost control of his films, he has generally been able to reclaim it. Both *Blade Runner* and *Legend* were originally released in versions which were not approved by Scott. Even after the so-called "director's cut" of *Blade Runner* appeared, Scott continued to tinker with the film, and the director calls the most recent cut his "preferred version." The reworking of *Legend* was even more drastic. The film was taken away from him, given a new score, re-edited and shortened. Some sixteen years later, Scott restored the original score and about twenty minutes or more of film, depending upon whether the original American or export version is being compared. For nearly all his films, Scott discusses clearly what he thinks to be the merits of individual versions on DVDs and Blu-rays. But, as always, he says in effect, whichever you like is fine with him.

Scott came to the making of feature films late, and he has said that he decided early in his feature film career that he was taking too long to make a film and needed to speed up. He has said that he would like to make a film a year, but obviously he has not lived up to that goal. Considering the complexity of Scott's films and the problems associated with managing his business affairs, it is unlikely that Superman could.

Introduction

Almost all of Scott's formative years were spent in making advertisements. After his apprentice film *Boy and Bicycle* and an unsatisfactory stint in British television, he spent more than a decade in advertising, and then moved into the making of feature films under his own initiative. How many apprentice directors would have had the money—or the guts—to guarantee the completion bond on their first movie, which is exactly what Scott did with *The Duellists,* and to make a success of the project?

He is a talented artist who seems to have been born with a camera lens for an eye and a mastery of detail which have made him a formidable maker of both films and advertisements. It has also made him rich. He became progressively more efficient and, as he did, he became more ambitious and his films became more complex. The complexity included an effort to express different sides of complicated issues in order to reach the world-wide audience necessary to support such enormous films; a visual richness which attempted to make each image memorable; and an increasingly large number of scenes and characters developed not only to move the main story forward, but also to visualize relationships between people and institutions which are not necessarily the focus of the story but which place the milieu in a historical context which will make it understandable. All these objectives had, of necessity, to be achieved within the generic formulations of big-budget Hollywood films.

In his epic films—*Blade Runner, Gladiator, Kingdom of Heaven, Body of Lies,* and *Robin Hood*—scenes are short, but are generally more or less of the same length and designed to further the story. *Black Hawk Down,* although sharing some characteristics of the epics, including a large cast of characters, is more classical in form and probably should be put in a different category. Both *Black Hawk Down* and *Alien* are classical in their adherence to the unities of time, place and action, but *Black Hawk Down* has a large cast, while the cast of *Alien* consists of only the seven members of the crew of the *Nostromo,* each of whom is dispatched by the alien until finally only Ripley survives to go one on one with the critter.

Scott's difficulties in the development and filming of *Blade Runner* were apparently largely the result of inadequate preparation of the script and conflict between the director and the people working on the film, including famously the leading man, Harrison Ford. Scott frankly admits that he was used to the English system and to having his own way and that he "came a cropper" with what the Americans regarded as his dictatorial demands, including looking through the camera lens, a practice prohibited by the union. Scott maintained that he could judge whether the image was exactly the one he wanted only by examining it through the camera, and he has apparently continued to do so throughout his entire career, although the question has largely become moot because of Scott's use of his own camera. The lessons of *Blade Runner* do seem to have been useful to all concerned, and although Scott has certainly had differences of opinion with other talented people, including the celebrated playwright and filmmaker David Mamet, they seem to have been business as usual rather than a disruption of the process.

Scott apparently thinks in pictures, and has even produced an art form named after him, the Ridleygram, a sketch of only a few lines, often done on the gad, showing the organization of a shot and the movement within it. They are — and should be — treasured by people who work on his films and who are lucky enough to get one of them. Many examples of them can be seen in the "Making of" included on the DVDs and Blu-rays of his films.

Scott's ability as a visual artist was clearly god-given, but his organizational ability, his careful planning and execution of the entire process of filmmaking (from choosing a source, preparing a script, choosing the actors and talent required, calculating a budget and sticking to it, editing the film and completing the project on schedule) was largely learned through a long period of work in advertising.

Scott came to the making of feature films fully prepared. His 27-minute BBC film *Boy and Bicycle* (1965, but filmed two or three years earlier) was by any measure an apprentice film. Shorn of its context, *Boy and Bicycle* can easily be regarded as a British art film typical of the mid–1960s, and if its maker had been a New Yorker, he might easily have been regarded as disdainful of Hollywood, at least until he got an offer. Scott's first feature, *The Duellists*, which followed a dozen years later, showed the sureness of touch of a major film director. It can be argued that all his later films were a direct outgrowth of *The Duellists*. The differences have to do with budgets and the audiences to which his feature films are directed.

The real question is what happened to Scott in the long decade between *Boy and Bicycle* and *The Duellists* when he devoted himself to advertising. While it can be argued that *The Duellists* is a complete film — and it certainly is — the dozen-year interval between it and *Alien* must be regarded as a period of consolidation in which the director cast a cold eye on the entire filmmaking process. Scott already had enormous confidence in his ability to make a quality film on time and on budget — he himself guaranteed the completion bond for *The Duellists* — but he was not being given any film offers. He decided that he must initiate his own projects, and having made a sufficient amount of money from his advertising career, he was fully prepared to do so.

Although Scott knew that *The Duellists* was a quality product and was regarded as such by the studios, he was disappointed by the limited distribution the film received in America. The theater people clearly and reasonably regarded the film as an art movie of only limited appeal. Indeed, it would still be so regarded if it were released today. Scott had no interest in making low-budget films of limited appeal, but the cost of big-budget films necessitated the making of films with an international appeal. (Scott generally regards his budgets, except perhaps for some of the most recent ones, as being in the mid-range of quality films.) The question Scott asked was: What kind of a quality movie will appeal to a world-wide audience large enough to justify its enormous cost?

During his career, Scott has been able to exercise a greater control over the content of his films than almost all of the classical directors of the past, excluding only Alfred Hitchcock and perhaps one or two others. Early film directors became directors by convincing an entity or a person to give them an opportunity to make one. Essentially, they learned on the job. John Ford always spoke disparagingly of his early films, saying that he had "a good eye" and that was all he had. By this, he meant of course that he had a talent for composition within the frame, and indeed a viewing of his early films *Straight Shooting* and *Bucking Broadway* (both 1917) supports his assessment. By 1926, when shooting *Upstream,* he clearly had the ability to summarize a whole film in his mind. Charles G. Clarke, the cameraman on the film (long thought lost but recently discovered in New Zealand), said he hardly realized what was going on for three weeks "of casual filmmaking" and was amazed to discover that what he later called "quite a good picture" was finished (Eyman, 98).

Most of the later directors, at least until after World War II, worked their way up through the studio system. With the coming of television after the war, a number of top-flight directors began in television before moving into filmmaking. This group included, among others, John Frankenheimer, Sidney Lumet and Sam Peckinpah. Robert Altman made commercial films in the midwest before moving into television. Freed from the tyranny of the studio system, the new directors were more experimental and more likely to work against the prevailing grain, whatever that happened to be. While Peckinpah was a technical virtuoso, Lumet and Altman favored actors.

Recent directors have emerged from theater, animation, graphic novels, film schools and all sorts of other backgrounds. The chief difference between them and earlier directors is their mastery of a multitude of computer technologies utilized in the generation of visual images. Their deficiencies generally are in the production of emotion, character development and dramatic conflict. When well done, their best films are more likely to resemble *Memento* or the *Lord of the Rings* trilogy than *Gone with the Wind* or *A Streetcar Named Desire.*

By the time Scott finally got around to imposing himself as a maker of feature films, he had become highly successful as a maker of advertisements. Scott himself apparently does not know how many, although he generally gives the number as 2000. (Recently he has gone as high as 2600.) His career was so financially successful that it may have retarded his move into feature filmmaking. What we may call Scott's aesthetics of filmmaking has changed little since *Alien.*

According to Scott, advertising "teaches you all sorts of things you don't learn when you're in school." Film school teaches you "esoteric subjects," while what a director needs is "to somehow communicate with the audience." Scott calls the process "layering" and the end product, a film, "is like a 700-layer layer cake." What Scott learned, or rather carried over, from his work in commercial advertising, culminated in what Sammon calls "the overwhelming visual intricacy of *Blade Runner*" (Sammon, *Noir*: 41). Indeed, all of his films are visually intricate, some more, like *Kingdom of Heaven,* and some less, like *A Good Year.* Whatever the process is called, it is the single most important characteristic of all of Scott's films and what distinguishes him from the other great contemporary filmmakers.

Scott approves the actors, does some discussion and rehearsal with them for a week or so before shooting of the film starts, and, with the help of his storyboards and Ridleygrams, rapidly shoots the film. He has said that, "with me it's not endless, long, earnest discussions and constant rehearsal. We move like lightning." Of course, he makes some adjustments, but says, "I am usually flying"; "You cut to the chase much faster."

What the process means in practice is that Scott believes in the production of a crowded visual field. It is fair to say that, frame by frame, Scott's films provide more visual riches than those of any other director of big-budget feature films. Each is a vast repository of appropriate images dealing with the subject at hand. Since Scott always uses at least three cameras, he has a variety of shots to choose from. For scenes in *Robin Hood*, he is said to have used more than fifteen cameras for some battle scenes. The fact that he often switches from one camera to another enhances the visual richness of his scenes. Scott's filming is often directional; that is, the Ridleygram indicates the direction in which the scene is moving. This is not new; Scott was doing it as long ago as 1966 in "The League of Charitable Ladies" in the *Adam Adamant* series. It might be noted in passing, however, that the use of cutting in recent films has increased dramatically because of the use of additional cameras in filming and the ease of digital editing which has replaced the old cut-and-paste of earlier generations. The numerous cuts in Peckinpah's *The Wild Bunch* were long held to be the record, but that has since been surpassed by many films. But considering the number of edits in Scott's films and the individual perfection of each shot, it is hardly surprising that critics have often accused Scott of allowing the coherence of his story to get lost in the profusion of visuals.

Many great film directors have had acute visual senses and the ability to visualize both objects in motion and the relationship between them. Sergei Eisenstein could visualize whatever he wanted to, draw it, film it, edit it, and make it cohere. F.W. Murnau's intense eye for the appropriate setting can be seen in the location scenes of *Nosferatu* shown as extras on the Kino DVD. Recently, with the growing complexity of motion pictures, storyboarding has increased dramatically and it is probable that any film with a sizable budget has one or more visualists. The best person to visualize a film is the director because, even with the ubiquitous use of green screens, he is the most immediate to the shot.

Editing of big-budget films today resembles the continuity of graphic novels rather than of earlier films. It is generally directional and cuts are faster but consecutive, and the discontinuity, or surprise, of classic montage has been lost or abandoned. Eisenstein's ideas about color are, however, alive and kicking in the films of Scott, among others. According to Eisenstein, the use of the color red is not unusual until a fire breaks out; then "the gleam of a conflagration takes on a sinister character, and the colour of red becomes thematic red" (cited in Stern, *Scorsese*, 123).

Although some exceptions may be noted, Scott has little interest in building dramatic scenes, and conversations of any length are absent from his films. Conflict is generally not expressed in dialogue as much as in the counterpoint of visual images. The procession of images is not, however, the ideological point/counterpoint advocated by Eisenstein, but is at the relentless beck and call of the narrative.

Scott tells about going off to England and storyboarding all of *Alien* in less than three weeks, but it is unusual for a director to have either the talent or the ability to storyboard an entire film. Some directors will storyboard scenes they consider especially important. For example, one of the most esteemed of current directors, Martin Scorsese, storyboarded the climactic scene of *Taxi Driver* because of its importance (see Thomson, *Scorsese* 55–59).

The use of dialogue is important for Scott in order to mediate a worldwide vision of history, but artistically it is, with only rare exceptions, merely an excuse for the furtherance of the story in visual terms. The story is not carried by the language. In truth, no great film ever is, but any film buff can quote favorite lines or sometimes whole passages from favorite movies. Unlike a famous quotation from Shakespeare which retains a meaning when quoted, although not necessarily the meaning used in the play, quotations from movies, shorn of context, usually have little resonance. Even Roy Batty's famous farewell in *Blade Runner* tells us nothing that the visual overkill of the dove's mysterious appearance from nowhere and its flying off into space has not told us visually. The only passage any of my friends have been able to quote from a Ridley Scott film is Maximus's challenge to Commodus in the arena, and that was by a very bright eight-year-old. It is probable, however, that any number of women can quote passages from *Thelma & Louise*, and devotees of *Blade Runner* can quote Roy Batty's farewell.

Scott's eye is unmatched, and he can seamlessly blend together shots made thousands of miles apart, as he does at the conclusion of *Black Rain*, when, unhappy with his treatment in Japan, he shifted to the fields of California. Critics have accused him of manipulating his stories to heighten the visual impact. The explosion of the huge eighteen-wheeler filled with gasoline in *Thelma and Louise* was cited in reviews as a notable example. In other words, the explosion was put in to juice up the visual effect.

Scott has said that he always starts off every morning with "a view to doing all the storyboards ... and the board to me is absolute. It helps me think on paper. And the board helps me to say, I can chapter it ... and get on with it the next day. And no one will ever question it."

In his Blu-ray commentary on *Body of Lies*, Scott is shown before what he calls "a kind of storyboard of the whole movie" showing still shots taken by an Avid camera illustrating in sequence all the scenes of the movie. The photographs number well over two hundred, each of which has a caption at the top telling what is happening. On the right is an "Omit" group, which includes scenes which were shot but were, for one reason or another, taken out of the film, but which could be put back in. The advantage of this method is that you can consider each scene in relationship to the other scenes before and after. Theoretically at least, each individual scene may be explained as part of a sequence which might or might not be improved by putting it somewhere else. You simply rearrange the cards, consider the changes and, if you are convinced that you can improve the film, insert the changes into the film. Scott claims to be ruthless in the editing process. Sometimes, he says, "You gotta lose some of your babies."

The system has at least two disadvantages. The first is that you may lose excellent material which should be retained. In *Body of Lies*, Leonardo DiCaprio, playing an undercover secret agent in a Muslim country, has a kind of picnic with a beautiful Muslim girl, played by Golshifiteh Farahani. The scene is emotional and heartfelt, an attempted movement toward a meeting of minds over an enormous gulf, a moment of all but union. Emotionally, it is the most moving scene in the film. But Scott cut it because he considered it trapped in the intricacies of his plot and pulled down four or five of his little Avid pictures. The "before" and "after" scenes were shot to show the impossibility of the romance, and Scott considered the plot more important than the emotional content of the scene. This may seem strange since anecdotal evidence — a survey by the present writer — indicates that most viewers would have difficulty summarizing the complex plot, and the introductory and concluding sequences, although considered important by Scott for showing the difficulties the romance faces, could have been shortened or omitted completely. And anyway, why should a romance, however hopeless, be forbidden on that ground?

The second disadvantage is that important information may be mislaid along the way. In *Kingdom of Heaven*, it comes as a total surprise that where Balian (Orlando Bloom), a blacksmith by trade, takes over his inheritance, a patch of barren ground in the middle of a desert, he is able to find water where apparently no one else has found it during the past centuries. The fact that he is a hydrologist of considerable skill has apparently been mislaid somewhere along the way. Classical Hollywood filmmaking would clearly have established this fact, as well as Balian's skill as a jeweler, not once, but probably twice. The point is not that these skills are improbable, if not impossible, skills for a medieval smithy, but that the audience needs to know about them.

Of course, Scott himself is well aware of the criticism against him. He notes that he has been accused of placing too much emphasis on visuals, of being over-designed and too beautiful. He defends the use of storyboards and calls them "the first look at a film." This definition would certainly have astonished Elia Kazan or John Huston or other directors of the classical period of Hollywood filmmaking who would have considered either the script or the preliminary run-through with the actors the "first look."

As a touchstone for a mastery of "the whole motion" of filmmaking, the opening of John Huston's *Moulin Rouge* (1952) may serve as an exemplar. The Technicolor photography by Oswald Morris, which required a printing process that was so complicated and expensive that it was abandoned after Huston's *Moby Dick* (1956), is still arguably the most beautiful color film ever made. The film's reviewers recognized its beauty and favorably compared it to the Japanese film *Gate of Hell*, released contemporaneously with Huston's film and then recognized as the gold standard for film beauty.

After the credits showing examples of Henri de Toulouse-Lautrec's graphic art, the film opens with an extended sequence showing an evening at the Moulin Rouge, a huge cabaret. The time period begins with the earliest arrivals at the club while it is still daylight and continues until two o'clock or so in the morning when the club closes. Henri de Toulouse-Lautrec, seated at a small table, sketches the goings-on, drinks cognac and talks to various people, while the film documents the miscellany of dancers and patrons made famous for posterity through Lautrec's paintings and posters. The passage of time is carefully indicated: The film alternately slows down and speeds up. It shows the conflict between the entertainers, Jane Avril's singing of "April in Paris," the varied and colorful spectators, Lautrec packing away cognac and talking to a gallery owner, and ends with a rousing rendition of Jacques Offenbach's "Can-Can" and the short-legged artist limping away by himself in the early hours of the morning. The camera pans, the editing is leisurely, then frenetic, and as promised at the film's beginning, the viewers see Lautrec "and his beloved city and his time" come to life. And indeed we do, at least as far as the Moulin Rouge is concerned. Admittedly, the sequence has a problem or two which would easily have been corrected today, most notably the poor lip-synching of Zsa Zsa Gabor's Jane Avril, but overall the sequence neatly encapsulates the culmination of more than fifty years of film artistry. Alas, the rest of the film does not live up to the opening.

Although Scott's films have no extended sequence comparable to the opening of *Moulin Rouge*, he has many comparable shorter scenes. Scott's epic films contain so many scenes and characters that a seventeen-minute sequence would seem merely a vanity for him to avoid. He has, however, the devil's own ability to make memorable individual sequences which reward repeated viewing, and almost all of his films show the virtuoso's skill at shooting and editing. Examples include any number of sections of *Blade Runner*, including the opening sequence and the death of Roy Batty; the virtuoso magnificence of the wonderful pan over New York City at the beginning of *Someone to Watch Over Me*; the first gladiatorial contest in Rome in *Gladiator*; the market shoot-out at the beginning of *Hannibal* and the wonderfully decadent Florence sequences in the same film; the storm in *White Squall*; and the rescue sequence at the end of *G. I. Jane*, among others.

Scott's films generally move at an even but lively pace and he does not customarily build scenes. He does not, like classical directors, build up sequences, slow down or speed up time. His scenes and shots could almost be measured by a metronome. For example, if we compare the shootout near the beginning of *Hannibal* with the shootout at the O.K. Corral at the end of John Ford's *My Darling Clementine*, we may observe the difference. Ford begins with a geographical location showing the scene and alternately shows the combatants entering from different directions. The geographical space and the position of the players relative to each other are clear. In *Hannibal*, we have two or three brief shots and cut to the shootout. The advantage of Scott's way of filming is that it allows him to include many more scenes and characters, although sometimes with a loss of continuity. His characters are allowed to develop almost entirely through their actions, and scenes involving dialogue between more than two or three characters are both rare and short, especially in what we may call his epic films.

Richard Edlund, founder of effects house Boss Films, has stated: "There is something about serendipity and the 'happy accident' that you can't get on a computer.... [T]he computer is very precise. Every result must be thought out and programmed. It is often the unexpected happenstance that makes the shot real, and organic, and truly satisfying" (cited in Cubitt, 251). Scott's past privileges the visual arts, particularly painting, and it always looks like the past, or what we may imagine to be the past as shown in paintings and other visuals, but it is not always convincingly real. His future, which does not carry the same weight of verisimilitude, is much more convincing, even when it has, like *Blade Runner*, retreated into the present as all works of art eventually do.

Since Scott's best work tends toward complexity of the visual frame, he is most at home in the gothic. Although Scott often speeds time up, he does not usually, if ever, slow it down to increase suspense as Hitchcock does so masterfully in his best films. In *Black Hawk Down*, which may be Scott's best film, the method works perfectly. At the beginning, the editing is rather slow, at least by Scott's standards, but during the combat sequences, which occupy almost the entire film, the editing speeds up and continues at a generally rapid pace throughout the rest of the film.

Since *Blade Runner*, Scott's epic films have become progressively more complicated — more locations, more characters, more diverse points of view. *American Gangster* is said to have 360 locations and 135 speaking parts. While this is probably a record, it must certainly mean that the screenplay would be more suitable for a ten-hour film than for one lasting two and a half hours, sans credits. Scott has repeatedly stated that if a scene does not move the narrative forward, he will cut it.

Scott's response to the assertion that his epic films have too many characters and scenes would be that what is cut out of the theatrical version can be included on the DVD and Blu-ray. And indeed it can, and Scott is not the only director to do so. Additional material, which began with a trickle on VHS with directors' cuts and other material, revved up with DVDs and reached warp speed with Blu-ray, which often include not only scenes cut from the theatrical release, but also commentaries by the director and others as well as featurettes about the making of the film and, in the case of *Blade Runner*, even different cuts of the film.

The result has been the destabilization of the preferred or authorial version of the film, director's cut, preferred cut, or whatever we may choose to call it. Just as Shakespearean scholars spent the largest part of the twentieth century attempting to discover what Shakespeare wrote, they have now decided to devote their full attention to what he did not write and are examining the plays line by line to determine which of his collaborators was responsible for the changes.

Scott has not been the only director to profit from the changing technology. A new type of feature film has emerged, a kind of puzzle meant to engage the mind rather than the emotions. The Matrix trilogy, for example, privileges complexity over emotion and is clearly aimed at the DVD market where additional material can be added incrementally and the game can continue. Christopher Nolan's *Inception* is a recent example. The film's poor print reviews show that, in this instance as well as others, the on-line reviewers are ahead of the print critics.

Whatever goes wrong with Scott's films, it is never the visuals. Sometimes, however, the visuals seem at odds with the soundtrack. In *G.I. Jane*, Anne Bancroft's voice is so harsh and grating that it seems at odds not only with the visuals but with our own experience of what female Texas politicians are like. And Scott's characters do not have the rhythms of natural speech, the give and take of conversation so memorably and easily captured by David Mamet. It would be fascinating to know the exact nature of the conflict between Scott and Mamet about *Hannibal,* but it is easy enough to speculate about their differing views of film art. In general, Mamet has more interest in the conflict of character through dialogue than Scott was ever likely to allow.

At the beginning of Ford's *The Searchers*, we see a ranch home in the middle of the desert where none could have existed. Of course, Ford knows this, but he also knows that showing and depicting it as he does is part of the unity of the film, and that the whole film is of a piece. Indeed, the only scenes which seem out of place in Ford's masterpiece are the search scenes in winter in the snow which seem for indefinable artistic reasons to belong to some other and lesser film.

Scott is almost completely visual, and all of his films could be effectively shown without dialogue. They are, aesthetically, silent movies. Perhaps the best way to watch them would be on Blu-ray in a language you do not understand. Put your mind on hold and go along for the ride.

Scott's primary intellectual interest seems to be mediating history in the interests of fairness and of appealing to an international audience. Like Cecil B. DeMille, Scott has a scholar's interest in attention to detail, and he has rightly stressed his accuracy of portrayal of the way the past looked. The viewer may be confident that both the Coliseum and the gladiators shown in *Gladiator* are authentically portrayed. Scholars are, however, critical of the historical details, and the Harvard scholar chosen to edit the collection of essays entitled *Gladiator: Film and History* withdrew in despair.

If Scott loses the historical test, he wins a more important one: that of ideological fairness. Unlike directors of the past, Scott is very careful to present divergent points of view. In *Gladiator,* Maximus is not a pilgrim on the road to Christianity, but a faithful pagan. In *Kingdom of Heaven*, Scott's presentation of Saladin was not done at the expense of the story, or even as an appeal to Muslim viewers, but because the story required it in the interest of fairness.

Oddly enough, in his modern films, Scott pretty much abandons fairness for ideology. In *Thelma & Louise,* the good old boys do not get a fair chance to explain themselves. Thelma's husband and Louise's boyfriend are fair game, but the cretins are trashed. There is no appeal to language, to changing times, or to the "good old days."

Despite the explanation that they went "an insult too far," they are pure evil without even the benefit of the style or lack of it which Ford or Peckinpah would have given them.

G.I. Jane was an anachronism almost before the film was released, but the film survives as a dream of Super Woman. The SEAL program survives, but women are not a part of it. As usual, Scott examines the political ramifications of the situation, but Anne Bancroft's portrayal and ultimately her betrayal of Jane in the film are so harsh as to ruin any sympathy which might have been bestowed on her. Only the magnificent sequence at the end showing the rescue and the moving coda elevate the film to a level of greatness which clearly indicate what it could have been.

Alien exists in a different context, and Ripley is the woman Jane might have dreamed of being. Stripped to her underwear, her body is long, lanky and totally functional, equally at home in the bedroom or the machine room, a repository of authority that Thelma, Louise, and Jane can only dream of.

At the turn of the twenty-first century, Scott produced in succession a trio of films that show him in full command of his art: *Gladiator, Hannibal* and *Black Hawk Down*. The films almost seem designed to show Scott's versatility in genre films. Generically, *Gladiator* is a sword-and-sandal epic, *Hannibal* is a horror film, and *Black Hawk Down* is a war film, mission subdivision.

Gladiator revived in bravura style the sword-and-sandal genre which had been moribund for more than a third of a century. Indeed, it compares favorably with the great epics of the past, the two versions of *Ben-Hur* and Stanley Kubrick's *Spartacus*. Although it omits the persecution of the Christians — except in a sequence which was cut from the film — it depicts pagan religion favorably and presents new possibilities for the epic, an opportunity which, unfortunately, has not been realized, at least to the present, although Wolfgang Petersen's *Troy* (2004) made an attempt.

Scott has both inaugurated a franchise with *Alien* and successfully continued one with *Hannibal*. Following *The Silence of the Lambs,* one of the most critically acclaimed and popular films ever made, *Hannibal* seemed to have all the cards stacked against it. Jodie Foster, the Academy Award–winning star of the earlier film, disapproved of the script, eventually pulled out and was replaced by Julianne Moore, and *Hannibal* had a problem with the ending, but the finished film was a huge popular success. Scott emphasized the gothic elements of the story, and segments of *Hannibal*, including the magnificent Florence sequence, are worthy of Fritz Lang or F.W. Murnau.

Black Hawk Down is a war film which depicts in harrowing detail how a raid in Mogadishu by the US Special Forces went terribly wrong when a Black Hawk helicopter was shot down minutes before the extraction for which the raid was designed was to take place. The film covers some sixteen hours, but the events take place with such detail and rapidity that the images seem almost to pass by like a violent, terribly realistic dream. Mark Bowden's book about the raid was subtitled *A Story of Modern Warfare,* and Scott's great film fully deserves the accolades it received.

All of Scott's films are interesting and present sometimes difficult problems of interpretation, but when Scott is at the top of his creative form, as he is in the films discussed briefly above, he is unique: an epic filmmaker who relates us to new possibilities in history, genre and art.

Fritz Lang and Ridley Scott

METROPOLIS AND BLADE RUNNER

Richard Combs, in his review of *Black Rain*, usefully compares Scott's *Blade Runner*, *Someone to Watch Over Me* and *Black Rain*, as a group, to Fritz Lang's *Metropolis*. Indeed, the films of Scott and Lang have much in common. Despite the enormous advances in technology over the decades, filmmaking remains the same: the telling of stories through a succession of moving pictures augmented by sound. And the stories have not even changed much through the decades.

Strangely enough, the 1927 film *Metropolis* and the 1982 *Blade Runner* have, so to speak, grown up together. To date, Scott has produced five versions of *Blade Runner* and will, no doubt, produce five more if he can last another twenty-five or thirty years. Meanwhile, *Metropolis*, like a revenant in some macabre competition, has kept pace with increasingly stunning restorations of the film from the F.W. Murnau Foundation and most recently from the discovery of an admittedly cruddy 16mm print of the Holy Grail of *Metropolis* aficionados (the film which was shown at its Berlin premiere before being hacked at over and over again). The hitherto missing segments have been restored, so far as possible, and re-inserted. During the first six months of 2010, the result was released with considerable fanfare to theaters around the world and later on DVD and Blu-ray.

Linked together by McFate (to use Vladimir Nabokov's term), homage and criticism both serious and frivolous, the two films seem destined, like the workers in the endless train in Moroder's version of *Metropolis*, to be joined together as far as our limited eyes can see. Like partners in a bad twenty-five-year marriage, they exaggerate the other's presumed faults while trumpeting their own virtues. And yet, they are much more alike than different, and the likenesses are probably at least as interesting as their differences.

The similarities between the two directors are striking. Neither is much interested in actors, and both have often been criticized for neglecting them, sometimes by the actors themselves. For a long time, I thought that the restraint of Gustav Fröhlich in *Metropolis* belonged to the actor. After seeing him in Zoltan Korda's football film *Die Elf Teufel* (1927), I realized that the restraint belonged to Lang's expressionistic direction, not to the actor. And Henry Fonda's famous jibe that Lang was more interested in where the actors stood than in their acting has the ring both of legend and of truth (see McGilligan, 242–45). Lang felt that it was the picture that furnished the emotions and told the story, not the actors. Fonda certainly had a point, but then the grumpy actor did not much like John Ford's choice of actors for *Mister Roberts* either.

And no matter how much Scott praises actors, he is never quite believable. Whether or not he treats them as Hitchcock reportedly said that they should be treated, as "cattle," he has doubtlessly become more adept in the handling of actors since his celebrated set-to with Harrison Ford more than a quarter of a century ago. However, like Hitchcock, he trusts the *mise-en-scène* and the editing to tell the story.

Nothing changes so rapidly as the future, or at least as our conception of the future. The beginning of Scott's *Blade Runner* lists the location as Los Angeles in 2019. The date is now less than a decade away, and it is clear that L.A. in 2019 is unlikely to resemble the polluted hi-tech, low-life hellhole depicted in the film. And, if we need any further reminder of future uncertainty, there is always Stanley Kubrick's *2001: A Space Odyssey*, the release of which coincided with the first manned landing on the moon, to remind us. Kubrick was one of film's great visionaries, but it is fair to say that, although he got many things right, he certainly also got many things wrong. 2001 has come and gone and President Obama is cutting NASA's budget so much that there is no longer even any talk of man returning to the moon.

During the silent and the early sound periods, the screen was haunted by the contrasting images of the huge empty places of the desert and the prairie and the teeming streets of the city. It was scarcely believable that the mountains and the plains of John Ford's *The Iron Horse* could ever be overpopulated, indeed in some instances that they could ever be populated at all, at least not by any "civilized" man. The contrasting images, that of the city and that of the wilderness, haunt our imaginations still. But the plains, the rivers and the mountains have receded into both the historical and imaginary past and exist as a dream in Shane's fanciful description of "peace in the valley" (1953) or in Akira Kurosawa's fanciful depiction of peace free from machines at the conclusion of *Dreams* (1990).

Metropolis continues to dominate the discussion of the relationship between *Blade Runner* and *Metropolis*, but the connection between the two films is complex, involving as it does the often complicated differences between the two cultures, silent and sound films, differences between the two directors and the different ways the films were prepared and shot. And as time passes, the emphasis will inevitably occasionally move from one film to the other.

Although Lang always insisted that his first impression of the New York skyline inspired the filming of *Metropolis*, the truth is more complex. There is, of course, no doubt that the view of the city confirmed Lang's concept of the evolving city and stimulated his imagination. Traveling on the same boat with Lang, architect Erich Mendelson had been commissioned to report on the architecture of the "New World" for the *Berliner Tageblatt* (McGilligan, 108). The resulting book, *Amerika*, contains images interpreted as a "dramatic film" by Russian artist El Lissitzky.

Metropolis was based on a novel of the same name by Lang's then wife, Thea von Harbou. The novel, a compendium of pulp motifs, occasioned most of the criticism *Metropolis* received not only when it opened, but in the years since. Lang always regarded the ideology of the film as a means of visualizing his fantasies while at the same time acknowledging his responsibility for the film as a whole. Still, although the novel furnished the justly abused ending, it also provided the robot woman, the dance of death and the seven deadly sins, the tower of Babel and a mélange of other motifs, including the underground workers, which were reworked into memorable images mixing the modern and the medieval. In an illuminating study entitled *A Culture of Light: Cinema and Technology in 1920s Germany*, Frances Guerin discusses the aesthetics of light and darkness in Lang's films. It is no criticism of Guerin's book to point out that such a study would hardly have been possible without the splendid restorations of Lang's major films, especially *Die Nibelungen* (1924) and *Metropolis*. In the best Lang restorations, including for example the two parts of *Die Nibelungen*, Lang has a clear black and white aesthetic which carefully balances perspectives, often privileging dark foregrounded figures moving against a light background.

And what about Scott's *Blade Runner*? What Scott did was to dirty up the images of the bright city and to bring them visually closer to an imagined possible future of today. Just as Lang's film was clearly a product of the advanced technology of the period, *Blade Runner* in every frame illustrates Scott's theory of filmmaking from planning to execution. While *Blade Runner* is pre-digital — that is, it belongs to a period which was beginning to recede into the past with slow but increasing speed even as the film was being made — Scott's careful preparation, vivid imagination, strong aesthetic sense, organizational ability, and above all strong visual sense combined with his artistic and technical ability to make his visions come alive.

Amazingly, *Blade Runner* was only Scott's third feature film, but he was perfectly qualified for a large-scale, if not big-budgeted, science-fiction film. Scott had become rich making award-winning advertising films. The television ad gives the maker sixty seconds

Blade Runner (1982) design: Harrison Ford as Deckard.

18

or less to sell his product. This means that he must capture the attention of the viewer before he decides to shift to another channel. Scott succeeded through outstanding visuals and creative writing — that is, by making a little movie.

Lang's preferred form in *Metropolis*, as in all of his silent films, is allegory. The Tower of Babel, the Seven Deadly Sins, the underground workers and the lords of Metropolis, the good woman versus her evil twin, and so on, are all allegorical constructs. Scott's representations are less old-fashioned and more up-to-date, so to speak, but are allegorical nonetheless. Although Lang was the great master of film noir in both silent and sound films, the master of Metropolis is not the criminal mastermind Dr. Mabuse. Tyrell, however, is not much different from Dr. Mabuse or, for that matter, from the average mad doctor in this week's horror film. Tyrell is probably the only person in *Blade Runner* who has enough money to live wherever he wants. For whatever obscure reason — perhaps because he wants to observe his creations or to play chess with Sebastian — he chooses not to live in the comfort of the Off-World, wherever that is, but some 200 or so floors up in the heart of the polluted city.

Unlike the master of Metropolis, Tyrrell plays chess, the game of intellect, and controls replicants, but it is not clear exactly how much, if any, design work he still does, or indeed ever did. He is, nevertheless, the master of all he surveys. Quite unbelievably, many artists work on the design of hi-tech spare parts and sell them on the street. J. F. Sebastian's mechanical creatures, whatever they are, seriously resemble the automatons in Raymond Bernard's *Le jouer d'échecs* (*The Chess Player*, 1927).

The sports and pleasure model, designed apparently to entertain Off-World workers, is comparable to the evil robot who drives the rich men wild in Yoshiwara, the pleasure district of *Metropolis*. In Lang's film, the two robots, one good, the other evil, are mirror images of Hel, the lost love of the mad scientist Rotwang who had abandoned him for the master of Metropolis. Apparently the two women are exactly the same, except for the evil model's strident sexuality and destructive tendencies. This is, admittedly, a serious difference. *Blade Runner*, however, is silent on the question of the differences, if any, between individual members of the same "sports and pleasure" model type. Perhaps Deckard could simply have ordered another Rachael either with or without the same implanted memories. Besotted as he was with the present Rachael, the idea seems never to have occurred to him.

Visually, the chief difference between *Metropolis* and *Blade Runner* is not one of ideology, but Scott's use of the widescreen 2.35:1 aspect ratio. According to Scott, his filmmaking includes careful preparation, a script cast in iron, rehearsal before shooting whenever possible, and what he calls "layering": an augmentation of the visual field during shooting. Scott hates an uninteresting visual frame as intensely as Shakespeare hated a poor fifth act or Falstaff an "empty can." Visually, he is baroque, and as critics have pointed out, the story — and occasionally the actors as well — can get lost in the widescreen visuals. His visuals have every virtue except simplicity. His more complex films, such as *Kingdom of Heaven* and *Blade Runner*, gain from being watched over and over again, not only for the visuals but also for piecing together narrative strands which the viewer may have missed earlier.

While Lang and Scott both emphasize the visual, technology has, at least to some extent, limited their similarities. All of Lang's silent films were in black and white as were the best of his American film noir. When he finally began to make color films in Hollywood, his use of color was decorative rather than realistic, particularly in *Rancho Notorious* (1952), which may fairly be described as the only great indoor, expressionistic western.

Except for his apprentice film *Boy and Bicycle*, all of Scott's films are in color, and he has continued to refine the color of *Blade Runner* after more than a quarter of a century. His eye is unrivalled among present film directors. When Peter Fleming, an excellent tennis player who won many doubles tournaments with John McEnroe, was asked who the best doubles team in the world was, he is said to have replied, "John McEnroe and whoever he is playing with." The same might be said of Scott and his director of photography, whoever that might happen to be on a particular film.

Particularly to someone who has admired what Thomas Wolfe called "the dry, caked colors" of America, Scott's eye occasionally fails him. The failure is not to show something that is not American, but to show in succession landscapes and buildings which are not in proximity with each other. In both *Thelma & Louise* and *White Squall*, the juxtapositions occasionally seem wrong, at least to the admittedly imperfect eyes of the present writer.

At some point, great works of art enter into world culture and take on lives of their own. In the case of *Metropolis,* the process was aided by Giorgio Moroder's 1983 reimaging of *Metropolis*. He collected the best materials he could locate from around the world, re-edited them, colorized them, put them on steroids, and added a rock score. The result was both denounced as desecration and revered as homage.

With the help of a famous passage in Thomas Pynchon's *Gravity's Rainbow* and visual references in music videos, Moroder made *Metropolis* an open text (cf. Parrill, 251–52 for details), and Lang's film entered the world of free-fall criticism occupied by Wagner's *The Ring*, Shakespeare's *The Tempest* and a few other works central to postmodernism. What Thomas Elsaesser calls "the horizontality of meaning and the linearity of sense" of traditional criticism yielded to "the verticality of montage and the diagonal symphonies of abstraction" (*Metropolis*, 63). With Moroder's film, *Metropolis* became and will remain a visual symphony blending film, opera, set design, music video and Heaven only knows what else in the future into a dramatic phantasmagoria where the meaning is subservient to the event. *Metropolis*, unlike any other film, is free.

The game continues. A certain "Gilchrist," thousands of miles away in the wilds of New Zealand, has digitally restored Moroder's *Metropolis* and removed all the dirt and debris from the pre-digital 1983 film. The result is stunning and is currently available for purchase, under what authority I know not, from his website.

Metropolis and *Blade Runner* will move down the years, duking it out in one form or another. In this corner, we have *Metropolis*, in various versions more or less complete, and now complete if imperfect. And we also have Moroder's homage, now perfected digitally by a third hand, and even more magnificent than before. And there has been at least one new musical score for Moroder's film. And in this corner, we have five versions of *Blade Runner*, all with some degree of authority. All of them attempt in various ways to decide what man can tolerate in the decaying city and what, if anything, separates mankind from the lower orders. Of course, Darwin will decide scientifically, but artistically, at least, it will be decided at the "Thanhauser Gate," where to quote an old Firestone advertisement, "the rubber meets the road."

Advertisements

Advertising is an imperfectly understood art. While it might be argued that all arts are imperfectly understood, advertising has received little serious attention either from its audience or its makers. The attitude generally has been: If it works, it's great. What sells works and what don't sell don't work. And since "working" has been defined in terms of sales and profit, the analysis has largely been considered moot. Before the coming of radio around 1920, advertising was largely confined to inn signs, barber poles, newspapers, magazines and Sears Roebuck catalogues, and in a hit-or-miss fashion to items popularized by movies. After World War II, however, advertising reached new levels of both success and sophistication. Movie posters and previews of coming attractions continued to urge theatrical attendance. Athletes and movie stars peddled cigarettes with slogans and color pictures. New, streamlined automobiles graced the pages of *Life*, *The Saturday Evening Post* and other magazines. Movie magazines, which had been around almost since the beginning of motion pictures, continued turning out fluff, lies and glamour for an adoring public. Comic books urged young boys to hassle their parents for Red Ryder air rifles.

During the early years of television, live presentations of one sort or another filled local TV air time. The present writer remembers a jeweler who said that he would "stand on his head to please" his customers, and demonstrated the feat. The extant kinescopes of live drama often include advertisements which seem naïve today, but apparently were effective enough at the time. John Cameron Swayze's commercials for Timex watches, which debuted in 1950, retain their appeal today: "It takes a licking and keeps on ticking." And the Gillette Blue Blade ads during sporting events, particularly boxing, are fondly remembered. "Come away with me, Lucille, in my merry Oldsmobile," which dates back to 1905, was revived. Clearly, advertising was on the move.

By 1947, advertising was big enough business to catch the attention of Hollywood, via the now forgotten popular novel by Frederic Wakeman, *The Hucksters*. Apparently, Hollywood did not believe that satirizing advertising was a case of the pot calling the kettle black, at least as long as the satire was not too severe and Clark Gable was the lead. Ad man Gable, returned from the war, finds a whole new world of scummy ad men led by Sydney Greenstreet and Adolphe Menjou, two men not exactly known as straight shooters. The hard-as-nails novel was toned down to suit Gable, but even so, Gable walks out on the ad men at the end of the film. *The Hucksters* is the product of a simpler time, sort of a *Mad Men* without the sex, humor, alcohol and irony. The film still holds the interest today for its ideological content and its star power, which included Deborah Kerr—whose name the studio helpfully told the public "Rhymes with New Star." (Apparently, the only notable film about advertising to appear in the following decades was *The Sweet Smell of Success* [1957], a highly praised film produced by Burt Lancaster whose detonation at the box office seems to have deterred even the most ambitious of producers.)

Television increased both the penetration and opportunities of advertising rapidly and exponentially. Don Draper in television's *Mad Men* represents advertising's new man, a pitch man for a consumer society at a time when it seemed possible to sell anything, if only you could figure out how to do it.

Although the ultimate purpose of advertising is to sell something, the "something," whatever it is, may be approached from a variety of directions. For automobiles, the purpose is to get the would-be purchaser into the dealership where a salesman will do the actual selling. Often, prestige is the lure for selling top-of-the-line products such as luxury automobiles. A man in a doctor's outfit advertising a painkiller may be a reminder to buy the product the next time the person seeing the ad has a headache or sees the product in the drugstore or supermarket.

Scott began his career in advertising during its golden age, and his skill in directing ads pleased the corporations buying them and sold their products. After more than ten years directing advertisements, Scott began making feature films comparatively late. In the memorable words of David Thomson, he achieved an eminence and financial success in his career in advertising as a director of commercials, "many of them prizewinners, and all of them forged at that electric place where high art is now channeled into pop idioms" (*New*, 793). His financial success enabled him to put up the completion bond for his first film, *The Duellists* (1977). When he made *The Duellists*, he was already the best-known maker of advertisements in England. His 1973 Hovis wheat bread advertisement has often been chosen as the favorite English ad of all time. It has a powerful nostalgic pull, not only for the English, but for the American public as well.

Unless Raw saw a different version of the advertisement from the one available on the internet, the 29 seconds he lists as the running time is incorrect (169). The internet version runs 47 seconds and may be truncated. The ad uses the second movement of Dvořák's *New World Symphony* and a voiceover to show a young boy pushing a bicycle loaded with bread up the cobblestoned street of an English town. In a voiceover an older man opines that the climb was "like taking bread to the top of the world." After unloading the bread, the boy "takes a grand ride," if a somewhat dangerous one, down the hill. In the interior of the baker's shop, the baker puts out the bread and pours the tea. The advice which the heavily accented voice of the older man gives the boy is to "get the bread inside" him. The bread, we are told in a voiceover, is as good as it has always been. And so for that matter is the ad. According to Raw, the film was shot in Shaftesbury, Dorset, southwest England, and the man speaks with a Yorkshire accent. The second man's voice at the end of the film is that of British actor Ian Holm, who was later to play Ash in Scott's *Alien*.

As usual in Scott's ads, the visuals are more important than what is said. The ad's power comes from its nostalgia and what might be called its prestige. The nostalgic pull is so great that even an American who has never actually "seen" a cobblestoned street can feel its pull. If we combine this with the image of childhood freedom, represented by the boy's wild ride back down the street, and paradoxically with the fact that the boy is working, the representation of Hovis bread as a quality wheat bread need hardly be stated. The film is so powerful that it makes the viewer who has seen Scott's films wonder why the director has never made a personal movie, a film that grows from his personality, his experience and his deepest artistic beliefs about himself and his country. Only his apprentice film *Boy and Bicycle* seems to fill the bill, and that is obviously a minor work.

Scott's Pepsi Cola advertisement was shot in 1985 during the first season of the enormously popular TV series *Miami Vice* starring Don Johnson as Crocket and Phillip Michael Johnson as Tubbs. The ad, produced by Ridley Scott Associates, attempted to place the soft drink in the context of the lifestyles of the two main characters of the series. On the rain-slick nighttime streets of the city, the two detectives see a dancer reflected in a nightclub window. As the two men briefly question each other, a Pepsi Cola image is reflected on the car window and the ad cuts to the two actors sharing a can of Pepsi. The ad concludes, like the Hovis ad and, in all probability, most of Scott's other ads, with a voiceover, in this case notifying the viewer, "Hey, I'm everywhere, pal," and a shot of a can of Pepsi with the slogan, "Pepsi, the Choice of a New Generation."

Ironically, the producer of the television series *Crime Story* and *Miami Vice* is the film director most often compared to Scott. But unlike Scott, who gained entrance into film directing through advertising, Michael Mann took a more traditional route. Mann began his career as a writer and producer and at the time of the Pepsi ad had not yet moved into directing. He was, however, intensely interested in the "look" of his series. He wound up his visual style in *Crime Story* and put it into overdrive in *Miami Vice*. If a wise movie buff of the future were to see the Pepsi ad without any name connected to it, he would be as likely to attribute it to Mann as to Scott. Unlike Scott, Mann has generally confined himself to criminal behavior, but his *The Last of the Mohicans* (1992) is a recasting of a classical American historical novel and one of the great romantic films.

Even after what Paul Sammon calls the "travails" of *Blade Runner*, Scott's services were in demand both for advertising and filmmaking. His famous Apple Macintosh prime time television commercial (broadcast during the 1984 Superbowl game) has often been called the most famous television commercial done during the first half-century of television and unquestionably had much to do with keeping Scott in the game. The ad, which is examined in some detail by Sammon and which is widely available on the internet, echoes George Orwell's Big Brother in *1984*, identified by Sammon as IBM, and the Leni Riefenstahl films *Triumph of the Will* and *Olympia*, and who knows what else. Scott says that the ad cost only a third of the $1,000,000 it was widely reputed to have cost. Still, as ads go, it was strictly top-of-the-line both in terms of cost and creativity.

Although it would be expensive to produce, an illustrated study, either in the form of a book or Blu-ray, remains a desideratum. However much such a study might or might not tell us about Scott's film art is speculative, but it would certainly be a beautiful project. It might even tell us more than we know now about the native origins of Scott's imagery.

1

Boy and Bicycle (1962):
Playing Hooky

Version. *Boy and Bicycle* is included on the DVD version of Scott's *The Duellists* and in *Cinema 16: British Short Films* (2003). Black and white. 27 minutes. Approximately 4:3 aspect ratio. The film, although shot in 1962, was not released until 1965 after John Barry (*Thunderball, From Russia with Love*) had agreed to do the music.

Scott was a student at the Royal College of Art in London when he wrote, photographed, and directed his first film, *Boy and Bicycle*. He happened to find an old Bolex 16mm spring-wound camera, a light meter and an instruction book in a wardrobe closet, and was one of six students who made a film that year. He says that the film cost £50, "virtually shooting 1:1, or certainly no more than 3:1" (Knapp, 3). Paul M. Sammon gives the cost as £65, and writes that the BFI gave Scott another £250 to "refine" the project (*Future*, 45). Whatever the precise cost, the film was clearly inexpensive even by the standards of half a century ago. By this time, Scott, who was already in his mid-twenties, had developed an intense interest in films.

Sponsored by the British Film Institute, *Boy and Bicycle* did exactly what sponsored films should do: It enabled a young artist to show what he could do and gave him hope for the future. The 27-minute black-and-white film was shot in Billingham, an industrial town in Northeast England, and on the nearby coast. The town, which has a population of 35,000 people today, was presumably somewhat smaller when *Boy and Bicycle* was shot there. (The title is incorrectly given as *Boy on Bicycle* in the heading of the film entry in *The Ridley Scott Encyclopedia*.)

The film masterfully depicts the working-class world of a male adolescent who decides to skip school and explore the industrial seaside world of the town on his bicycle. The "boy," who is basically the only character in the film, is played by Scott's younger brother, Tony. The film opens with a shot of a one-eyed Teddy bear and a voiceover of a boy, the speaker, waking up. An argument is going on downstairs. We see a close-up of the boy watching himself in a mirror. He is concerned over the "deep personal rut" that the family is in at the same time that he attempts to convince himself that he is not worried.

The boy rides through the nearly deserted streets. At the last minute, he hears singing inside his school and decides to play hooky. He rides around the town, loiters on the beach, smokes a cigarette, attempts to convince himself that he is having fun as "the only kid" in the land who is not in school, visits a sweet shop, is chased by a dog, is rained on by a brief shower, examines the off-season amusement rides at the beach and a hut on the beach (he is chased away by a sinister old man), and returns home, we may presume, chastened. The old man is described by Sammon as "a madman," which rather overstates the evidence of the film (*Future Noir*, 45). The encounter is, however, distinctly unsettling.

Boy and Bicycle has an awesome expertise which would do credit to any filmmaker of mature years. It is impossible to tell from the film, when it is examined in the context of the period in which it appeared, its expertise and its influences, whether its maker would be likely to become a commercial filmmaker, a surrealist *à la* Buñuel, or something in between.

Swedish master Ingmar Bergman, then at the height of his reputation, is said to have been a particular favorite of Scott. The influence would seem to have been in the starkly realistic black-and-white photography, particularly of *The Virgin Spring* (1960), which Scott certainly saw not long before shooting his film, rather than in the dour Swede's religious preoccupations. Although Scott's later films, excepting only *The Duellists,* carefully disguise their literary origins, *Boy and Bicycle* clearly owes a debt to James Joyce and *A Portrait of the Artist as a Young Man*. (Philip K. Dick's novel *Do Androids Dream of Electric Sheep?*, the source of *Blade Runner*, was not generally considered a literary novel when Scott filmed it, and is hardly considered high art even today.) The black-and-white photography (done after commercial filmmaking had moved definitively to color), the realistic visuals and the voiceover clearly echo Joyce's novel, and prefigure Joseph Strick's later film versions of both *Ulysses* (1967) and *A Portrait of the Artist as a Young Man* (1977), both of which were also in black-and-white. If it is true — and it seems possible, if not probable — that Scott's early film, made for a pittance and using his younger brother as the main actor, influenced Strick's films, generally regarded as noble failures, *Boy and Bicycle* shows that Scott's distinctive visual style was present at the very beginning of his career.

In his first film, Scott already knows that a voiceover is more effective when it operates at some distance from the speaker. Stanley Kubrick, the great master of the voiceover, preferred the Olympian stance. HAL, the gabby computer in *2001: A Space Odyssey*, is sycophantic, but the viewer is hardly in doubt as to its real intentions. And the voiceover in *Barry Lyndon* tells us that everyone has been dead for a long time and that what they did had no significance anyway. A dead — or dying — man may be effectively used as a narrator, as *Double Indemnity* (1944) and *D.O.A.* (1950) demonstrate.

When *Boy and Bicycle* was made in the early 1960s, stream of consciousness was considered the central technique of modern literature, at least as compared to the literature of the past. The technique, although not abandoned and used in one way or another by most serious novelists today, was soon absorbed as simply another aspect of narration and the critics lost interest. It continues to be popular with avant-garde film-makers, who are as a group less interested in narrative than their more commercial brothers.

Stream of consciousness consists of two types of commentary: remarks on what is seen and remarks on what is running around in the narrator's mind. In special cases, it may be effective, as in *D.O.A.*, which is narrated by a dying man attempting to find out who killed him. Commercial films sometimes use it as a desperate expedient to explain what is regarded as — and what usually really is — a muddled narrative. The release version of *Blade Runner* is probably the most famous film example of this type. The problem is that movies are visual and novels are not, at least not in the same sense. If the viewer is honed in on the visual, commentary outside the narrative frame, as opposed to dialogue in the narrative proper, is often a distraction.

In addition to its distinguished literary model (James Joyce's stream of consciousness technique), the film was also indebted to the English working class films of the postwar period which introduced a new realism both in treatment and in the new breed of actors who used working class language as opposed to the King's English spoken by Gielgud, Olivier and the classical theater types. Chief among these was Albert Finney, whose portrayal of a working class roustabout in Karel Reisz's *Saturday Night and Sunday Morning* was much discussed when the film appeared in 1961, a year before *Boy and Bicycle* was filmed. Finney was to appear in *The Duellists* in 1977 and to play the genial Uncle Henry nearly thirty years later in Scott's *A Good Year* (2006).

A close study of the many literary and visual references of Scott's short film would require a long essay and would clearly indicate how successful the film is as a portrait of the artist as a young filmmaker. Even at this point in his career, however, Scott has integrated his own background and personality into the stream of consciousness with such artistry that it is difficult to distinguish his own personality from that of his chief influence, James Joyce's *Portrait of the Artist*. The relationship of the film to the mature artist will doubtlessly occupy considerable scholarly interest in the future. It is, however, to be hoped that Scott will yet revisit in his full maturity his portrayal of the young English artist in a rapidly changing society and make the English film which he has, for whatever reason, so far avoided.

Scott's original degree plan was in graphic design, but *Boy and Bicycle* got him "an admission ticket" to a television design course. In 1963, he began his association with the British Film Corporation, but his career there was not what he hoped that it would be.

2

Adam Adamant Lives! (1966): The League of Uncharitable Ladies

Version. The BBC has issued the sixteen surviving episodes of the original twenty-nine 50-minute episodes of *Adam Adamant Lives!* on Region 2 DVDs along with a fund of information about the individual episodes, including the erased ones, in a beautiful accompanying booklet with miniscule print.

Adam Adamant Lives! was a BBC television series which never quite found its mark, either with its makers or the public. The series, which lasted two seasons, was intended as light entertainment, but never quite came together as did its competition, the enormously popular and long-lived series *The Avengers,* which bids fair to run forever in one form or another and which, in its early days, furnished two "Bond girls," Diana Rigg and Honor Blackman.

Whatever the exclamatory title of the series title did, it never successfully solved its problems. The series was intended as a James Bond-lite done for television, and the opening tune apes the theme song of *Goldfinger.* The central idea is that a rich, adventurous, athletic nobleman would be frozen in a block of ice for sixty-three years before being thawed and sent out to solve problems. (It was impossible to explain how the ice remained frozen for so long or why he was not dead when it thawed.) The two leads were hardly more than adequate but in the opinion of the reviewers of the BBC-1 DVD, Gerald Harper improved during the course of the series. The female lead was never clearly enough defined for any actress to make the character believable. Additionally, the producers had problems with the permissible level of violence, and there seems to have been a constant argument about when, if, and how someone might be killed, and so on. *The Ridley Scott Encyclopedia* seems to believe that the series exemplified "the swinging sixties," but that seems to have been a heavy burden for so frail a vessel.

It is possible, but probably unlikely, that the makers of the Austin Powers movies, which began with *Austin Powers: Man of Mystery* (1997), knew the Adam Adamant series. The highly successful comic series, starring Mike Myers, chronicles the adventures of a mysterious James Bond type who is, like Adam Adamant, revived after being frozen, but who still retains the anachronistic attitudes of an earlier time.

28

Adam Adamant Lives! (1966)

Scott directed three episodes of *Adam Adamant*, but unfortunately only one of them survives: "The League of Uncharitable Ladies," broadcast on September 23, 1966. The other two episodes, "Death Begins at Seventy" and "The Resurrectionists" (both 1967), were erased. There is nothing to indicate that the two episodes, both shot quickly when the series was on the way out, were distinctive in any way. We can, however, do no more than speculate.

Since shooting the interiors was limited to two hours on the sound stage per episode, the episodes had to be efficiently shot, and creative opportunities were obviously limited. The exteriors, however, provided greater opportunities. While the interiors are well done, the opening outdoor sequence of "League" is striking and would have graced any film playing in the movie theaters the week the TV episode appeared. The episode opens in a church where a beautiful young, dark-haired woman, after either making her devotions or contemplating murder, turns away from a statue of the Virgin to the right. In sequence, Ridleygrams invariably show the direction in which the action of the scene is moving, and Scott cuts to a long, early-morning shot of a well-dressed vigorous middle-aged man with an umbrella moving sprightly through what is apparently a park, across a road and, as the camera cuts to a somewhat closer shot, through another wooded area. The woman follows the man and for some reason he speeds up a bit. He approaches two women who are collecting money for some sort of peace organization. The women are carrying small flags which have the name of their organization on them. As he stops and puts a coin in their container, the woman who has been following him stabs him from behind with one of the flags. The sequence closes with a cut to one of the flags in an interior where the murder is being investigated. The sequence is a bravura performance.

Even at this early point in his career, Scott's careful preparation and strong visual sense are apparent. Leading actress Juliet Harmer, who played Georgina Jones, the ditzy blonde who constantly followed Adam Adamant (played by Gerald Harper) around and caused a string of often unbelievable problems, says on one of the DVD featurettes, that working with Scott was the first time she had ever seen a storyboard.

Unfortunately, the series apparently did nothing to further Scott's career. The difficulty of advancing in the closed confines of the British Broadcasting Corporation would have been formidable under any circumstances, but since the series was unsuccessful both artistically and in popular appeal, his work can hardly have received the attention it deserved. Scott soon went full time into advertising, where his talent and incomparable visual skills could be richly rewarded. When he went into the making of feature films nearly a decade later, he had enough money to guarantee the completion bond for *The Duellists*, and he was on his way. No person ever came to the making of feature films better prepared.

3

The Duellists (1977): En Garde!

Version. *The Duellists* was shot in a widescreen version, 1.85:1, runs approximately 100 minutes and is rated PG. The only available version has a commentary by Scott and may be presumed to be definitive. The DVD also includes Scott's BBC apprentice film *Boy and Bicycle*.

Scott and his brother Tony moved into production in hopes of producing their own ideas for television shows. British television was, however, a small closed system, and Scott, who admits to feeling trapped in its confines, moved into advertising, hoping that his success there would allow him entry into directing. He was mistaken. After a long career in advertising in which he made thousands of advertising films, he realized that, since no one wanted to hire him to make a feature film, he would have to produce it himself. According to Scott's commentary, he decided, after four unsuccessful attempts to do a feature film, to "put his hand in his own pocket," choose a writer and have a story written. In order to save money, he decided that the story must be in the public domain. He hired Gerald Vaughan-Hughes to write a screenplay based on "the Gunpowder plot": Guy Fawkes' attempt in 1605 to blow up the House of Lords and to assassinate King James I. When Scott was unable to get financing to produce that script, Vaughan-Hughes wrote *The Duellists*, which was successfully filmed.

According to Scott's commentary, Paramount eventually agreed to a $900,000 budget, but was hesitant to proceed with shooting because of the uncertainty of the fall weather in France. Scott agreed to guarantee the completion bond himself, and despite miserable weather in all but a few days, he began the film in September and brought it in on schedule in fifty-eight days of shooting. As Scott said, "You have to be the person who is the reason for making the movie."

Joseph Conrad (1857–1924), one of the most highly regarded novelists of the twentieth century, began writing in English, his second language, after a career at sea, and won critical renown and eventually a Nobel Prize for Literature with a series of maritime adventure stories dealing with moral questions. His awkwardly elegant English prose style and his exotic settings proved a potent combination, and while he never achieved popularity remotely approaching that of his friend John Galsworthy (*The Forsyte Saga*), his sales were, considering the period and his moral earnestness, outstanding. Although he never totally abandoned stories of the sea, his later novels and stories continued his exploration of the darker sides of human behavior. His most famous work is probably his novella *Heart of Darkness*, a central work of modernism dealing with themes of colonialism and racism which became a battleground of conflicting interpretations in the late twentieth century. The most famous film version of Conrad's dark tale is Francis Ford Coppola's *Apocalypse Now* (1979), an expensive film which received enormous publicity at the time of its appearance and which holds up surprisingly well both as an allegory of the Vietnamese incursion and as a version of the Conrad tale; (Nicolas Roeg's 1993 television version has an interesting performance by John Malkovich as Kurtz.) Among other film adaptations of Conrad, three are especially notable. Maurice Tourneur, perhaps the greatest pictorialist of the silent screen, filmed *Victory* (1920), from a script by the great Jules Furthman, with Lon Chaney in a bravura performance. Carol Reed's *An Outcast of the Islands* (1951) is somber and low-key, but Richard Brooks' lavish *Lord Jim* (1965) respects the original and has an excellent performance by Peter O'Toole in the title role.

Conrad's short novel *The Duel* was serialized under the title *The Point of Honour* in *Pall Mall* magazine (January through May 1908) and was published later in the year (re-titled *The Duel*) in a Conrad collection titled *A Set of Six*. Although published later "in a small illustrated volume" under the original title, Conrad requested that the story should be published in "all the subsequent editions" of his works as *The Duel*.

According to Conrad, the story "arose from a ten-line paragraph in a small provincial journal published in the South of France." The story, which concerned the fatal outcome of "two well-known Parisian personalities," referred in passing to the "well-known fact" of two officers in Napoleon's Grand Army who had fought a series of duels in the midst of great wars and on some feeble pretext" (Conrad, II:13). Taking this hint, Conrad used his knowledge of the Napoleonic period to develop his tale. Although some critics have questioned Conrad's account of the origin of *The Duel*, and think that his complex early manhood might suggest a more personal source, there seems to be no reason to question its essential validity (but cf. Raw, 98).

Opinions of the literary merit of the story vary. Frederick R. Karl, in his massive biography of Conrad, considers the author's shorter fiction not "particularly distinguished" and in his view, "expendable" (546). According to Karl, the two duelists fighting their way through the Napoleonic wars exemplify the "Man of Destiny" theme, best exemplified of course by Napoleon himself. They attempt to give meaning to their lives by extending their duel over a sixteen-year period. At the end of the story, after D'Hubert has finally vanquished his old adversary, he feels that his life, now that it is safe, has "suddenly lost its special significance" and been "robbed of its charm" (628). Despite the fact that the career of the Emperor Napoleon might be considered, at least according to the omniscient narrator, "a duel against the whole of Europe," he did not approve of dueling among his officers. Although we need not accept Karl's interpretation completely, it is clearly true that Conrad was much more interested in providing a portrait of the period than in analyzing the psyches of the two duelists. Conrad was a master of the short novel and while *The Duel* will never be as famous as *Heart of Darkness*, it is nonetheless the work of a master.

As Roderick Davis pointed out in his detailed comparison of the novella and the film, Conrad's tale is eminently suitable for filming and, Scott might have added, for the framing of cinematic pictures. It deals with a theme of honor, has a number of vivid historical settings, does not require any large battle scenes, and has a plot which can easily be covered in a film of some 100 minutes. The problem of making a film from the story is that it has a first act and a third act and a long, essentially repetitive second act which is picturesque but does little to advance the narrative.

Keith Carradine in *The Duellists* (1977): "En garde!"

Conrad's novella is set in 1800 in Strasbourg, a garrison town, during a brief cessation of hostilities (a period which is, as Conrad notes ironically, a circumstance "so favorable to the proper appreciation of military discipline"). Lt. D'Hubert is commissioned to deliver a message to Lt. Feraud, who, detecting a perceived slight in the delivery while he is talking to a "a lady," challenges D'Hubert to a duel. Reluctantly, he agrees, and the series of duels, covering some fifteen years, begin. As they continue, the two young officers, of no special consequence or interest until then, "become objects of universal curiosity," and the justice of each contestant a matter of debate.

Unlike the story, the film begins with a striking duel in the Strasbourg countryside in which Feraud kills a man, while a young girl tending a flock of geese watches in horror. Later the same day, through a series of senseless misunderstandings, he becomes involved with Lt. D'Hubert in a duel in an alley, or city courtyard. D'Hubert has been sent by his commanding officer merely to deliver a message, but Feraud takes immediate offense. The fight is a bravura staging which takes up some two minutes of screen time. D'Hubert avoids Feraud's mad charge and the contest ends with Feraud stretched out wounded on the ground and D'Hubert defending himself from a second mad charge, that of a "pretty maid" who is enamored of Feraud. Ordinarily, this would have been the end of the affair, but through a second series of misunderstandings concerning the publicity the duel has received and Feraud's insane pride, the conflict continues.

The second fight takes place with epée in an open field near a farmhouse. Although

Feraud is injured, the combatants are not reconciled. The third fight takes place in what looks like an interior riding ring and is staged without music. The contest ends with the two men wrestling with each other before being separated. The fourth duel is fought on horseback with sabers. Feraud is unhorsed and D'Hubert exits the field with a spectacular jump over a hay wagon.

The two officers encounter each other again during Napoleon's disastrous 1812 Russian campaign. Facing death by freezing or worse, they agree to postpone their contest: D'Hubert asks courteously: "Pistols, next time?" The scene is wonderfully staged, photographed and acted and clearly shows what can be done with a large talent and a small budget. The horrors of the retreat from Moscow are portrayed as effectively as King Vidor did with an apparently unlimited budget in the Hollywood version of *War and Peace* (1956). Later, after Napoleon's defeat at Waterloo, D'Hubert, out of a quixotic sense of honor, manages to get Feraud's name removed from a list of men slated for the firing squad, even though Feraud had supported the return of the emperor.

The last duel takes place in Tours in 1814. General D'Hubert, now forty and retired, is living at a country chateau with his sister, who is planning to marry him to an eligible widow, when Feraud shows up with two down-at-the-heels companions and demands satisfaction. Annoyed and despairing at the stupidity of the request after a decade and a half of intermittent dueling, D'Hubert agrees. Lacking a second, D'Hubert is allowed to use one of the old soldiers as his second. In the pistol duel which takes place in the hills the next morning, Feraud fires both of his pistols without injuring his old enemy.

D'Hubert tells Feraud that his life is in his hands and that he never wants to see him again. In a concluding tableau imitating a romantic painting, Feraud, his life in ruins, or what he believes to be ruins, stares off into the mountainous distance. D'Hubert is now free to marry and Feraud is left to his solitary bitterness. Like Shakespeare's Othello, his occupation is gone.

Feraud is a hothead who believes himself, for some obscure reason, to have received a mortal insult and is quite willing to spend the rest of his life avenging it. Scott has in a sense stacked the cards against him by showing him killing a man in a duel at the beginning of the film. According to the arcane rules of the duel, however, a duel could be fought only between officers of equal rank and Feraud, who is intermittently outranked, is forced to endure long periods of frustration in his quixotic quest.

Unlike any of Scott's later films, which are pure Hollywood in genre and treatment, *The Duellists* has an art-house tang. Although its two stars were American, all the other casting was done in England, and the film has a distinct Brit-lit feel, sort of like a *Masterpiece Theatre* offering on steroids. At the time, Keith Carradine was a young star of impeccable credentials. The son of John Carradine (a John Ford regular perhaps best-known for his work in *The Prisoner of Shark Island* and *Stagecoach* and for decades an icon in low-budget horror movies), Keith Carradine had played the young cowboy shot on a swaying bridge by the gunman in Robert Altman's masterpiece *McCabe and Mrs. Miller* (1971) and had moved into the lead in Altman's *Thieves Like Us* (1974). Harvey

Keitel was best-known for his work with Martin Scorsese in *Mean Streets* (1973), *Alice Doesn't Live Here Any More* (1975) and *Taxi Driver* (1976). A year after *The Duellists*, Carradine and Keitel again appeared opposite each other in Alan Rudolph's underrated mood piece *Welcome to L.A.* For whatever reason, neither actor was able to sustain star billing and settled comfortably into supporting roles.

Keitel later complained that his role in *The Duellists* had been significantly altered in the editing. Scott denied the accusation, stating that Keitel "tended to milk things," and that what was cut did not change the character substantially, "and there were certainly no 'big scenes' of Harvey's that were cut" (Knapp, 9). Whatever the disagreement, it was not permanent, and Keitel and Scott were to join forces later in *Thelma & Louise,* which featured Keitel as the sympathetic policeman who attempts unsuccessfully to save the lives of the two fugitives.

The other players in *The Duellists* are almost all distinguished English representatives of the best in theater and film, both old school and new. Albert Finney's performances in *Saturday Night and Sunday Morning* (1960) and *Tom Jones* (1963) helped make working class accents and straightforward masculinity palatable in world cinema. With his contemporaries Sean Connery and Michael Caine, he introduced the world to representative but occasionally noble men whose accents were considerably wide of the British theatrical standard. According to Scott's commentary in *A Good Year*, Finney appeared in *The Duellists* without a fee. According to Knapp (7), he received a framed check for £25 inscribed, "Break glass in case of dire need." Finney was to work with Scott again some three decades later in *A Good Year,* when we may presume he received a better fee. Like Finney, both Edward Fox and John McEnery have done distinguished work in Shakespeare and Brit-lit adaptations.

The supporting players, both men and women, give strong performances. Cristina Raines was heartbreaking in *Nashville,* and Diana Quick played Julia in the television miniseries of Waugh's *Brideshead Revisited,* considered by many to be one of the best adaptations of a novel ever done.

To Scott's considerable chagrin, the critics treated *The Duellists* as an art film. Scott has said that he thought of the film as a western, but if so, the film was more stylized than even John Ford's *My Darling Clementine,* the gold standard in this regard. Unlike Ford's film, where the entire film leads up to the final confrontation, Scott's film is a series of unsatisfactory confrontations between two soldiers of the Napoleonic wars, a topic hardly designed to appeal to an American audience. The film also lacks Ford's resonance, which had the American frontier, Monument Valley and fifty years of westerns behind it.

According to *Variety*'s "Mosk," the film "delves into military codes of honor and its counterpart of violence for its own sake." What the film is actually selling, however, is "a series of carefully posed tableaus of period action and repose in colorful military days and rarely transcends this for a more robust portrayal of military life." Although Scott has "an eye for fine composition, period recreation and arresting tableaux," the film is too much taken up with surface and poses and neglects the "deeper human aspects of these two flailing men." The result is "an arty swashbuckler." Whether because of inexperience or, more likely, of budgetary restraints caused by the short shooting schedule and Scott's posting of the completion bond himself, *The Duellists*, more than any other Scott film, is composed of tableaux. Scott has stated that he patterned the tableaux after paintings and used them to indicate chapters. In later films, the shots are carefully composed but almost always in constant motion. Here, as in his later films, Scott used his so-called Ridleygrams to indicate both scene, through a vivid sketch, and movement, through the use of arrows. "After all," says Scott in his commentary, "you're doing a story in picture form."

Although Scott understandably is extremely careful in what he says in his detailed DVD commentaries, he does say that, after a few days of shooting, he became unhappy with the work of cameraman Frank Tidy—"I really wasn't getting what I wanted"—and took over looking through the camera himself, a habit which brought him into conflict with the union, but which he has continued throughout his career. Accustomed to total control of the camera through his hundreds of television commercials, he felt such control was necessary to get the precision he wanted.

The Motion Picture Guide, which was published shortly after the film appeared, states that "the main reason to see this is the fascinating attention to detail on the parts of Scott and cameraman Tidy" and that the film, like Kubrick's *Barry Lyndon*, "becomes a series of still pictures that are animated." Interestingly, the reviewer writes that Keitel, with his "Brighton Beach-Coney Island accent," is a strange choice to play Feraud. Nonetheless, with Keitel as Feraud, the film develops an implicit theme of class conflict. The elegant and sophisticated D'Hubert becomes an instant object of animosity for the unsophisticated Feraud, who can never hope to meet him as equal except in combat. D'Hubert's victory is emphasized at the film's closing in which Feraud is vanquished. The concluding shot, patterned after a nineteenth century painting, may suggest a romantic vision in the heart of that brutal man. Certainly, it softens the viewer's opinion of him. Feraud is caught in a system which neither he nor his emperor approves of but, apparently concerned over the opinion of his peers, continues to honor, if that is the word, to the end. In her review of Scott's *1492: Conquest of Paradise*, Maria Garcia wrote, certainly correctly, that D'Hubert "is hounded by the fading chivalric code he respects," and that his struggle for actualization finds expression through a "historical corollary in France's 19th century preoccupation with war and revolution." Our reaction is likely to be: enough; Feraud is an idiot; apologize and have done with the whole business.

On January 23, 2009, in a speech before the Edinburgh Film Festival, revered film producer David Puttnam urged public funding for British films carrying positive messages about the UK and its heritage. In addition to films with obvious messages such as *The Killing Fields* and *The Mission*, both of which he produced, he mentioned *The Duellists* and *Cal* as films "that adhered to some definable concept of cultural integrity" (IMDb, *The Duellists*).

4

Alien (1979): Ripley on Call

The Texts. The 1.85:1 theatrical version of *Alien,* which Scott says is his "preferred version," runs approximately 117 minutes, which is essentially the same length as the 2003 so-called "Director's Cut." "The year-long restoration process" made what Scott calls "minor adjustments" which added a little new material and omitted or edited other scenes. The differences, which are hardly significant, at least as far as interpretation is concerned, may be examined on the *Alien Quadrilogy* Blu-ray set which contains both versions, with the sections which contain differences marked. The most important changes are in a scene in which Ripley discovers Dallas and Brett being converted into alien spores.

Even before *The Duellists* was finished, Scott was looking for another project. Although he seriously considered the story of Tristan and Isolde, Scott, with the concurrence of studio head David Puttnam, eventually commissioned Gerald Vaughan-Hughes, who had written *The Duellists,* to write a screenplay. When *Star Wars* appeared, Scott was "devastated" because it took many of the "same design paths" he was considering for his medieval film, and the project was put on hold. The Vaughan-Hughes screenplay was not used for the Kevin Reynold's film version of the story (2006) and is unlikely ever to be revived (Sammon, *Close-Up,* 49).

Scott has said that *Alien* came to him out of the blue after being turned down "by about six directors." In the commentaries, everyone agreed that none of the "A level" directors they went to, including Walter Hill, Jack Clayton, Peter Yates and Robert Aldrich, wanted to do the film, which they considered "a stupid B level monster movie." Scott liked the simplicity and the energy of its story—what he calls its "thriller aspects"—and immediately accepted. He thought that the people involved had made all the characters interesting, a quality he believes is missing in many thrillers. Scott apparently did not regard *Alien,* at least initially, as science fiction, but as a shocker. Of the horror movies that Scott saw in preparation, the only one he liked was Tobe Hooper's low-budget thriller *The Texas Chain Saw Massacre* (1974). Scott spent three and a half weeks storyboarding the movie, took it back to Hollywood and, according to Scott, the studio "immediately doubled" the budget from $4.2 to 8.4 million because they could now "see" the film in their minds

The plot is strictly boiler-plate. At an unspecified time in the future, the crew of a vast but outmoded freighter spacecraft answers a distress call from a distant asteroid. The crew members are killed one at a time by a shape-shifting and very bad-tempered alien until only Ripley (Sigourney Weaver) is left to destroy — if only temporarily — the critter and to go into hyper-sleep until she reaches Earth. Even the treachery of Ash, who seeks to preserve the alien for "scientific purposes," can hardly be a surprise to a moderately sophisticated viewer. What is new is the sophistication and effectiveness of the special effects and the fact that the kick-ass hero is a woman.

In a review written some twenty-five years after the appearance of Scott's film, Roger Ebert states that the movie *Alien* most clearly resembles is Howard Hawks' *The Thing from Another World*. One of the main reasons the much-admired 1951 film has garnered so much critical attention is that, although journeyman director Christian Nyby is listed as its director, it is so much better than Nyby's other films and so much like the films of its admired producer Howard Hawks that most writers, including Ebert, list him as the film's auteur, if not as its director. The film, based upon a story entitled "Who Goes There?" by John W. Campbell, recounts the attempt of a group of scientists at a North Pole outpost to defend themselves from an alien invader. (The film also contains the answer to a famous trivia question, "Who played the Thing?" The answer, as all good trivialists know, is James Arness of *Gunsmoke* fame.)

The 1951 *Thing* is often — and with considerable justice — interpreted as a Cold War allegory. Ben Hecht, who worked with Charles Lederer on the screenplay, had been effectively banned for some time for what Todd McCarthy calls his propaganda "dedicated to forcibly removing the British from Palestine." He soon realized that the story could be turned into "an effective allegorical vehicle" poking fun at the current Cold War paranoia about Communists (473). The present writer can, however, absolutely guarantee that no single acquaintance of his who had the slightest interest in film recognized the alleged allegorical significance.

Although there are no women in Campbell's story, Hawks, who was famous for introducing strong, competent — and often professional — women into his films, created the role of Nikki especially for his then-favorite Margaret Sheridan (475). If you want to find the origin of Ripley in Scott's *Alien*, the treatment of women in the films of Howard Hawks would be an excellent place to begin. Also, the treachery of *Alien*'s Ash, a hard-core scientist who is willing to risk himself and his companions to examine the alien life form, will hardly be surprising to anyone familiar with the 1951 film.

John Carpenter's 1982 film *The Thing* starring Kurt Russell is a notable remake which updates the original while never straying far from it. Carpenter must have known Scott's *Alien*, but if so, he makes no mention of it on his commentary originally done for the release of his film on laser disc. The main differences between Hawks' film and that of Carpenter are the disappearance of the group action (which is so integral to Hawks' film) and Carpenter's darker ending. The hammy 1951 ending, in which viewers are exhorted to "watch the skies," is jettisoned for one in which the two survivors, after fashioning what is at least a bloody détente, and having nothing better to do, decide to hang out and wait to see what will happen.

The chief difference between *Alien* and Carpenter's *The Thing* is not in the acting, but in the sophistication of the special effects. The bickering over "shares" by Harry Dean Stanton and Yaphet Kotto is grating, even before the battle against the alien begins, but Keith David's Childs in Carpenter's film is also grating, and, judging by the throwaway comment by Carpenter in his commentary, the actor himself objected to it. The other characters in *The Thing* are convincing enough, and Wilford Brimley is outstanding, but Kurt Russell's performance can hardly compare to that of Sigourney Weaver's career-defining one as Ripley, nor indeed can any thrill of Carpenter's excellent film compare with the famous scene of Scott's film.

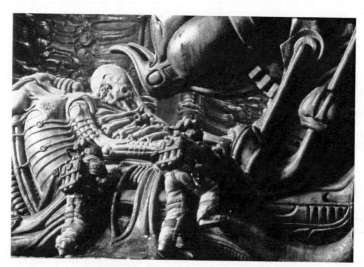

H.R. Giger design: the emergence of the alien.

Scott says that when he was shown a 1977 art book called *The Necronomicon,* he took one look and immediately decided that its author was the man he wanted to design the sets for *Alien.* Scott's choice was Swiss-born H. R. Giger, and there can be little doubt that the effectiveness of the film owes much to Giger's imaginative set designs. Giger became famous with the biomechanical dreamscapes of *The Necronomicon* (his first book). Its title comes from an imaginary book of magical spells and incantations mentioned in the horror stories of pulp writer H. P. Lovecraft. *Alien,* Giger's first film, won the artist an Academy Award for Best Achievement in Visual Effects. In addition to the films the artist himself has worked on, his designs have been widely influential and often imitated (indeed, in the opinion of some critics, plagiarized). Many of his designs may be seen on his websites.

The fantastic art of H. R. Giger imagines the merging of human and animal shapes with inanimate ones. Its effectiveness depends largely upon what might be called the plausibility of that merging. The mysterious and horrifying shapes seem to be in the process of becoming animate. This is generally most effective when the ultimate source of the image is recognizable. For example, Giger's "Hommage à Böcklin" is a haunting reimagining of German artist Arnold Böcklin's painting "Isle of the Dead," which depicts a mysterious shrouded figure arriving in a small boat at a gloomy island of lofty German trees and neo-classical abutments. The iconic image, which Böcklin painted in several versions which vary in detail, was described by the artist as a "picture to dream over."

Giger describes his *Biomechanoids* silkscreen portfolio as "a harmonious fusion of technology, mechanics and the created world" (*Portfolio*). This is precise, at least so long as the reader does not understand "harmonious" to be interpreted as "pleasurable." Giger believes, or at least pretended to believe when he did *Portfolio,* that the two worlds could be joined in a non-judgmental fashion. Scott's film, of course, will have none of that belief, nor indeed will James Cameron's *Aliens*, although the latter film plays around with the idea of the Alien as a substitute mother.

Much of the effectiveness of Scott's film depends upon the way in which Scott, with the help of Giger's visuals, depicts the alien, the other. The spaceship, named the *Nostromo* in honor of Joseph Conrad's ambitious novel of the same name, is a far cry from the immaculate space shown in Kubrick's *2001: A Space Odyssey.* George Lucas has complained that future-films always have machines which look new and unused. Of course, the future, whatever it may be, will have a mixture of new machines and old. The *Nostromo* is a working ship. Scott knows this and the ship is appropriately aged, the crew is appropriately scruffy, and, we may assume, a mixture of two working-class lads who want more money and the crew and the officers who are quite satisfied with the pay scale as it is. The resulting realism, however unbelievable the dialogue, is certainly striking and illustrates producer Ivor Powell's comment that Scott could direct sci-fi "in the same way that he treated history." What is not believable is the almost ubiquitous cigarette smoking which Scott permits here and elsewhere in his films. The dangers of smoking were already well known when the film was made, and it is impossible to believe that the owners of even a ship as downscale as the *Nostromo* would allow it at any point in the future. Of course, *Blade Runner* is not exactly smokeless and it is, of course, possible that Scott, like his brother Tony "Shoot It in the Smoke" Scott, liked the visual effects produced by smoke spirals in an enclosed space.

Although it would hardly have been predicted when *Alien* appeared, Weaver's Ripley turned out to be what Keith Stuart has called "the most enduring female hero mainstream cinema has ever produced" (154). Although the statuesque and imposing Weaver has done outstanding work in films dramatic (*The Ice Storm*), comedic (*Ghostbusters*), and romantic (*Working Girl*), Ripley will always remain her signature role. Weaver was, as Stuart points out, "a stark, masculine shift away from the more glamorous screen goddesses of the day" (154). Her body is lanky and functional, a far cry from the traditional Hollywood actress, yet still feminine and attractive, sort of like a more appealing Katharine Hepburn who works out regularly. But masculine it ain't. It should be noted in passing that, whether or not the role of Ripley was originally written for a man, Weaver's casting was Scott's first salvo in his war to bring women more adventurous screen roles.

"Har." gave the film an enthusiastic review in *Variety* and predicted big summer box-office despite the film's R rating. According to the reviewer, the film was "an old-fashioned scary movie set in a highly realistic sci-fi future, made all the more believable by the expert technical craftsmanship that the industry just gets better and better at." The result is a somewhat inferior combination of *The Exorcist* and *Star Wars* which is high on thrills, but has little time for character development. Scott's direction is treated as simply one part of an ensemble project. This conclusion is certainly unfair since all the evidence clearly indicates that Scott's presence is the unifying ingredient in the film.

Reviewers generally regarded *Alien* as derivative, but well done. Vincent Canby, in the *New York Times*, called Scott "a very stylish director" with "a good deal of no nonsense verve." He called the film an "old-fashioned scare movie," but lamented that, with two exceptions, Weaver and Ian Holm, "the roles might have been written by a computer." A few reviewers, like *Newsweek*'s Jack Kroll, went into rhetorical overdrive. He warmed up by saying that the film has "no truck with metaphysics, eschatology, religiosity, philosophy or theosophy" and concluded that it was "a tone poem of panic in which the crew is pitted against a carnivorous creature whose 'structural perfection is matched only by its hostility.'"

Philip Strick, in *Sight and Sound*, called *Alien* "a gorgeous, leisurely horror film" exemplifying "a spectacularly British xenophobia, a parenthetical representation of invasion" represented by awakening at the beginning of the film and a return to sleep at the end. His conclusion is that the British are "better off with the strictest quarantine regulations in the world." He compares the infighting among the *Nostromo*'s crew with the fighting between the duelists of Scott's earlier film. Strick liked the film's visuals, particularly the scenes of planetary exploration, but criticized the film's "lack of variety" and its "closed construction" which "dutifully deals out the shocks." This is ironic, since the suspense engendered in the closed setting is the aspect of the film which he most praises. Strick's critique is a noteworthy but foolhardy attempt to see *Alien* in terms of its place in the history of British films. Fortunately or not, *Alien* was, with the exception of *Robin Hood*, the last of Scott's films which might be defended as particularly British. By any reasonable standard, Scott is among the least nationalistic of filmmakers. With the appearance of *Robin Hood*, however, Strick might be allowed another strike.

Alien was widely recognized as a genre film which showed Scott's ability to work with a disparate group of individuals to create "a believable futuristic world." The most discussed special effects were, of course, the chest-burster, which quickly became "a bloody classic," and the "face hugger," a less sensational but perhaps more interesting effect. Despite these wonders, the film, however, was "sadly lacking in characterization and emotion" (*Motion Picture Guide*).

Of course, the huge box-office success of *Alien* produced a certain amount of attention, and James Cameron (the young, newly successful director of *The Terminator*) and his producing partner Gale Anne Hurd eventually put together the 1986 sequel *Alien 2*, re-titled *Aliens* at Cameron's request. (For the making of the film, see Rebecca Keegan's *The Futurist*, 53–80.) The resulting film, which opened up the story, was much longer and more violent than the original. The released version was around 137 minutes, and the DVD version, which restored the story of Ripley's daughter and shows the LV-426 colony before the attack, runs to 154 minutes.

Cameron has said that, although making a sequel presents problems, it also presents opportunities. It is worth remembering that Scott himself is not afraid of sequels and that *Hannibal* is a sequel to one of the most successful films ever made. Glenn Hopp describes *Alien* as a "moderately paced" and "almost melancholy" film which derives much of its effectiveness from "the isolation and entrapment" of its characters. Cameron, by comparison, opens his film up and turns the cat-and-mouse hunt of the first film into a "full-scale war" (288). Weaver has said that she did not realize until shooting was underway that the Cameron film was essentially a war movie (Stuart, 155). Certainly, the scene in which Ripley in her fork lift challenges the

Sigourney Weaver as Ripley in *Alien* (1979): sexy, competent and tough as nails.

"bitch" is one of the great scenes in thriller movies. It is unlikely that Scott would have allowed so crass a scene. Subtle it ain't, thrilling it certainly is. The enormous popularity of Cameron's film led to a third and eventually to a fourth film.

Critics who prefer Cameron's film to Scott's original generally defend it as a feminist statement. Amy Taubin and Kent Jones argue that the entire series was "a response" to the rapidly changing status of women during the last years of the twentieth century. *Aliens* is, they write, neither so disturbing nor as complicated as the original (Andrew, 126). Nevertheless, it "brilliantly reflects" a shift in the political and cultural climate of the country from what they call "the relative liberalism" of the late 1970s to the "Cold War militarism of the Reagan era." Apparently, Cameron's film played on the fears of some feminists and gay activists by showing a cool female heroine and — the ultimate outrage — "an impregnated man."

Harlan Ellison called Cameron's film "a rather good action adventure" which gave Weaver her best role since *Alien*, "arguably the most terrifying film made in the last thirty years" (287). This is faint praise which takes away with one hand what it gives with the other. His chief complaint apparently is Cameron's fascination with "exotic armaments," a criticism fully justified by Cameron's later films.

It is generally agreed that *Aliens* "fetishized military hardware and the nuclear family," with Ripley reconfigured "as a mother, pure and simple." *Aliens*, it is fair to say, is bigger, longer and badder, but also looser and somehow less convincing. Although hardly scientific, a survey by the present writer among his friends shows a distinct preference for *Aliens* over Scott's original. For most people, bigger, longer and badder is better. The writer himself is clearly in Scott's camp.

The result was another box-office bonanza. Released on July 18, 1986, *Aliens* grossed $85,160,248 domestically. The foreign take added an additional $45,900,000. Although the website Box Office Mojo does not give the production budget, the film was extremely profitable, especially when augmented by the extended cut on DVD and Blu-ray alone, or in combination with others of the series.

Alien 3 (1992) was directed by David Fincher, who began his career in visual effects. His films include *Se7en* (1995), *Zodiac* (2007) and *The Curious Case of Benjamin Button* (2008). *Fight Club* (1999), a film about a group of bare knuckle pugilists, has a vocal contingent of supporters. Although *Alien 3* adds nothing new either in special effects or in drama, it efficiently moves the story forward, and Charles F. Dutton and Charles Dance do effective work. The worst sin of the film, no matter whose idea it was, is killing off Ripley at the end. Followers of the series, however, hardly seem to have been concerned. They knew that she could come back at any time.

And indeed she did — in *Alien: Resurrection* (1997). Based on the commercial and artistic success of *The City of Lost Children* (1975), French director Jean-Pierre Jeunet was chosen to direct. The film, set in a penal colony somewhere in the reaches of outer space, begins with the revival of Ripley 200 years after her death through some vague sort of DNA reconstruction. The story is more of the same, with Ripley warning all the men as they make sexist remarks and do not believe her until too late. The special effects are now old hat and Ron Perlman and Winona Ryder are lost in the din. At the end, Ripley is still alive, but the series is moribund for the foreseeable future. No matter. Karloff will always be the Frankenstein Monster and Weaver will always be Ripley.

Alien was an enormous hit. According to Paul M. Sammon, the shooting budget for *Alien* was approximately $8,500,000, but the actual production cost was approximately $11,000,000 (*Close-Up*, 53). According to Box Office Mojo the film domestically grossed a total of $80,931,801 (71.1 percent). The foreign total was an estimated $24,000,000 (22.9 percent). Revenues from television, VHS, DVD and three sequels continue to this day. While it is difficult to compare costs and revenues from different periods, *Alien* may be, in terms of percentage of profits to cost, Scott's most successful film.

5

Blade Runner (1982): At the Thanhauser Gate

Versions. The long non-fiction film *Dangerous Days: Making* Blade Runner, included on both collector's editions (DVD and Blu-ray) of *Blade Runner*, gives an interesting, but probably somewhat whitewashed, account of the turbulent making of the film, its moribund reception and its eventual resurrection. After testimonials by various people about the importance the film had for them, *Making* recounts its negative reception at the June 16, 1982, 70mm sneak preview at the Directors Guild Theatre on Sunset Boulevard, its poor reviews, its growing reputation both with the fans and the critics, and its eventual rebirth into five separate editions, all of which are included in the Blu-ray collection. The DVD "Collector's Edition" includes four, omitting the so-called "Workprint," which seems to have been added as an inducement to buy the Blu-ray.

Chronologically, the editions are:

1. The U.S. theatrical version (1982). The unpopularity of the U.S. theatrical version quickly caused it to develop what might be called "accelerated decrepitude," a description applied in the film to the rapid aging of both J.F. Sebastian and the replicants. Unlike them, however, it did not have a limited lifespan and, although much abused, continues to exist and even to flourish on DVD and Blu-ray. It contains Deckard's narration throughout with the alleged happy ending which shows Deckard and Rachael escaping through an improbably beautiful — but slightly sinister — mountain landscape courtesy of Stanley Kubrick's outtakes from the opening of *The Shining*. Scott says that this is not his preferred version, but that he hopes viewers will enjoy it.

2. The Workprint (1982). Apparently, the Workprint, which surfaced in some large-format theaters after the disappointing reception of the theatrical version, does not represent any proposed or even contemplated version of the film. It is simply "a work in progress." The Workprint — which was used in test screenings — was restored from the only extant copy, which had suffered serious deterioration over the years. It has been carefully restored for the Blu-ray edition, but does not equal the quality of the other versions. It features alternate footage and music and a commentary by author

43

Paul M. Sammon, author of *Future Noir: The Making of* Blade Runner. There is also a featurette with commentary by Charles de Lauzirika, the restoration editor.

3. The international theatrical version (1982). According to Scott, this cut is "very similar" to the American version with the exception of a few seconds of violence which were considered too strong for American audiences. This version was available on VHS for many years while, according to Scott, "the film found a new audience." In these days, when extreme violence is *de rigueur* for R-rated films, the discussion seems pointless.

4. The director's cut (1992). Although the term "director's cut" would seem to indicate a final version, such is not the case here, and the director's cut is only a way-station to the so-called final cut. Following the edition of the workprint in the 1990s, Scott says that he decided to issue something closer to his "original vision." This was the first cut to remove Deckard's narration and the happy ending as well as adding the dream sequences showing the unicorn and the suggestion that Deckard might be a replicant.

5. The final cut (2007). In 2001, Warner Home Video decided to do a complete restoration of *Blade Runner*. The question facing the restorers was: Are we going to do a restoration or a revision? Fortunately, all the original material, which nearly perished in 1998, had survived. For some reason, work on the restoration stopped in 2002 and did not resume until 2005. Although Scott was busy with *American Gangster*, he decided to deal with "tweaks and effects" issues, mostly small, but occasionally more important. In one shot, flowers were erased from the original until only "beloved flowers" — in other words, flowers with sentimental connotations — were left. There were more than seventy changes in sound reconstructions and additions. After more than two decades, Joanna Cassidy returned to help recreate digitally the spectacular fall originally done by a stunt woman. The original had been much criticized because of the incorrect hair coloring and general lack of verisimilitude. The head of the original was removed and Cassidy's head placed on the "headless replicant." In Deckard's talk to the Egyptian snake dealer, Deckard's lips, unfortunately, had not moved. Since Harrison Ford "was not available," his son Ben substituted for him, or at least his lips did. Measurements were made of Ben's face, and his lips now perfectly substitute for those of his father. Another "tweak" was the substitution of a more appropriate background when the dove, which has mysteriously appeared in Roy Batty's hand some time earlier and which presumably represents his soul, ascends into the heavens when he dies.

Scott now calls this his "preferred version" of the film, a description which allows him wiggle room to operate should another version become a commercial possibility in the future. It has been "completely restored from the original negative" and put through "a state of the art 4k digital intermediate process," presumably supervised by the director. Scott calls the result "an absolutely brilliant picture." The praise is completely justified, and it is difficult to imagine that the high-definition image could ever be improved. Scott personally supervised the new sound-mix from the original six-track elements of a film which is now more than a quarter of a century old.

The five versions of *Blade Runner* available on DVD and Blu-ray may surpass in number and certainly in quality the authorized versions of any other film. The question of quality is usually moot, since generally only one version has survived. However, an unknown number of silent films exist in two

Blade Runner (1982): replicants Roy Batty (Rutger Hauer) and Leon (Brion James).

distinct versions, as opposed to having one or two different scenes to please the censors. John Ford's *The Iron Horse* is currently available in three versions: the Brownlow-Gill Thames restoration, the Hollywood version and the European version. Among more recent films, the Godfather trilogy and the Star Wars films have circulated in various versions. Numerous films have "extended cuts," many of which are inferior to the theatrical release and do no credit either to the films or to their makers. For example, Michael Mann's slightly longer version of his great romantic film *The Last of the Mohicans* (1992), although billed as a director's cut, is, as Mann certainly recognized, inferior to the released version: It makes explicit what is clearly implied and much more artistically rendered in the released version.

After the commercial and artistic success of *Alien*, Scott chose a much more ambitious project, a film loosely based upon a 1968 science-fantasy novel by Philip K. Dick, *Do Androids Dream of Electric Sheep?* Although the novel was optioned at its publication, it was not filmed until 1981. Dick lived to see an early cut of *Blade Runner* before his death on March 2, 1982. The resulting film was greeted by mixed reviews and occasional bafflement, but its reputation, bolstered by differing critical analyses and seemingly endless tinkering by its director, has flowered into a critical consensus that it is one of the most important science fiction films ever made, perhaps even better than Fritz Lang's *Metropolis* and Stanley Kubrick's *2001: A Space Odyssey*, generally considered the gold standards of comparison. *Blade Runner* is directly in the line of the great science fiction films aimed directly at the popular taste. That this was not recognized seems to have been the result of the fact that the film was essentially a work in progress and, it might ultimately be argued, perhaps remains so to this day.

Dick was an American original, a pulp writer of genius who attempted, with an enormous outpouring of words and without any great success until near the end of his life, to support himself by writing fiction, most of which was published in mass market paperbacks. Strictly speaking, he was neither a pulp writer nor a science fiction writer. By the time he began to write, pulp magazines — cheap magazines printed on coarse acid paper with what looked like wood chunks embedded in the pages — were virtually things of the past, replaced by 25- or 35-cent paperbacks, but the phrase has been retained to refer to low-end writers who are paid by the word and must turn out thousands of words a week to make ends meet. Hard-line science-fiction, based on more or less informed speculation about the future, survived in *Analog: Science Fiction and Fact,* which had started as *Astounding Stories of Super Science* half a century earlier. *Do Androids Dream of Electric Sheep?* is neither science-fiction nor fantasy but, as its title clearly indicates, somewhere in between. Dick's imagination, fueled by the copious intake of a perfect storm of drugs and his native genius, produced in a relatively short lifetime a large, but uneven, body of work

Dick himself had a low opinion of Hollywood. "I have never seen any good news come out of Hollywood," he is reported to have said. Dick's now enormous reputation is almost totally posthumous and was fueled by *Blade Runner* and other films based on his novels and stories. In addition to *Blade Runner*, the more important films of Dick's constantly growing list of credits includes Paul Verhoeven's *Total Recall* (1990), Steven Spielberg's *Minority Report* (2002) and Richard Linklater's *A Scanner Darkly* (2006). The publication of three volumes of his novels in the august series The Library of America signals his arrival as a classic American writer. In the series, he takes his place on the shelf between Richard Henry Dana (*Two Years Before the Mast*) and John Dos Passos (*U.S.A.*). It is unlikely that anyone could have predicted such a fate while he was alive.

There is no doubt that the filming of *Blade Runner* was contentious. This should not necessarily be held against the film. Hundreds of happy sets have produced miserable films. Scott has said that he was used to having his own way and that he thought that the success of *Alien* showed that he knew what he was doing. The long documentary on the making of the film hints at the difficulties, but hardly analyzes them.

The story of the making, unmaking and remaking of *Blade Runner* is complex and contentious, and the interested reader may safely be referred to Paul M. Sammon's essential book *Future Noir: The Making of* Blade Runner. Although Scott initially turned down the film for complicated reasons, he eventually accepted. He worked on a screenplay of Frank Herbert's novel *Dune* for more than six months, but eventually passed on it because he thought that preparation and filming would take more than two years and he wanted to go back to work quickly after the death of his brother (*Future Noir*, 48). Scott has said that he had not previously been interested in science fiction and that the only two sci-fi films that had made any impression on him were *Star Wars* and *The Day the Earth Stood Still*. He does not mention the real competition: *Metropolis, Forbidden Planet* and *2001: A Space Odyssey*.

Filmways, a small company, was originally slated to finance *Dangerous Days*, as the film was then called, but eventually dropped out because of budget problems and what was considered a risky storyline. *Blade Runner* was eventually financed by the Ladd

Company, Sir Run-Run Shaw, an Asian producer primarily of action films, and Tandem Productions, then known primarily for its television work. The money was in place and the sets were being built, but the script was still a work in progress.

One of his chief problems during filming was an unhappy star. Scott notes that Harrison Ford was at the peak of success immediately following *Raiders of the Lost Ark* and *Star Wars: The Empire Strikes Back* and that when he first interviewed Ford late one day, he was still in his Indiana Jones costume. Scott obviously feels that Ford's complaint about the role, at least initially, was that Deckard was too dark a character. Scott has described Deckard as a man who is intelligent, drinks too much, has no relationships, and is violent and paranoid by nature. It might be noted that this could describe almost any noir protagonist either in novel or film. Ford's complaint that the director was more interested in the setting of the film than in the acting should also be filed away and, considering the greatness of the film, forgotten.

Scott spent most of his time building up the world of the film one accessory at a time. Unlike Scott's later epic films from *Gladiator* on, which profited from a generation or more of computer-generated imagery (CGI), *Blade Runner*'s imagery, done on the gad by Scott, was the work of an improvisational genius and, it can be argued, was all the better for it. The improvised surface of *Blade Runner* has all the surprising complexity of reality.

Blade Runner was a product of the inter-regnum, or rather of the beginning of the inter-regnum. The film business was turning from analog to digital almost as the film was being shot. Of course, the process was to continue for years before the transformation was complete. David L. Snyder, art director of the film, has said: "I look at *Blade Runner* as the last analog science-fiction movie made because we didn't have the advantages people have now. There [are] no computer generated images in the film." Except for the additional shooting, *Blade Runner* was filmed on a Hollywood sound stage during some three months of shooting (33 days and 55 nights). According to Scott, the budget was $20,000,000, then a middle-sized budget for a major film.

"Cart's" review in *Variety* was prophetic of the mixed reception the film had in the media. The heading described it as a "[b]rilliantly made, dramatically muddled look into the future which [w]ill divide critics and public." According to the reviewer, its dramatic core is the romance between the replicant who does not know that she is a replicant, played by Sean Young, and the "blade runner" whose job it is to kill replicants. Unfortunately, the film is taken over by "the top replicant," played by Rutger Hauer, while Rachael disappears for long periods of time and Harrison Ford mopes around his digs "staring at photographs." Like a number of other reviewers, "Cart." believes that the colorless blade runner is much less interesting than "the top replicant." His conclusion is that, while "the technical brilliance of the achievement is continually compelling, the film is dramatically weak."

Indeed, the reviewers generally praised the brilliance of the visuals while condemning the storyline, sometimes both in hyperbolic terms. Jeff Simon, in the *Buffalo News*

Blade Runner (1982) design: L.A. sky in 2019.

review visible in the background of a scene in *Dangerous Days: Making* Blade Runner, wrote that the plot was "so mechanical it could have been written by the Stepford wives" (a group of spineless, manipulated women from the movie of the same name) and "may be the season's biggest disappointment," but countered by calling the visuals "utterly mesmerizing" and "a truly spectacular film vision of the future."

David Denby, in *New York*, complained that it was "all visuals and no story," the summa of a "hundred naively bad experimental films." The most revered film reviewer of the time, Pauline Kael of *The New Yorker*, thought that the movie was a mess and did not think anything interesting was going on. She noted that the visuals were "musty" and nothing in comparison to their betters. She mentions *Metropolis, Chinatown* and *Fellini's Roma* and seems to think that Sebastian's "toy companions" ought to have come to his aid. In brief, the film "has nothing to give the audience," and everyone connected with it needs to have his "flue cleaned" (Kael, *Taking*, 365). Whatever we may think of the trio of classic films she mentioned, her attempted humor was off the mark and she was certainly wrong in her denigration of *Blade Runner*.

In an interesting essay, Gloria Pastorino compares William S. Burroughs' novel *Naked Lunch* with Dick's novel and Scott's film. In Dick's novel, set in "a recognizable San Francisco," people are addicted to what Dick calls a "mood organ" which they can set to fix their mood for the day. They can also dial into "Mercer," described by Pastorino as "a spiritual being, a god-like figure who controls human moods via cable." The difference between humans and robots, androids and cyborgs is slight and apparently getting slighter all the time. The essential question is, in Pastorino's words: "What is the real difference between an android and a human, if a human being can program his moods and enhance them through a mechanical medium?" (110).

Deckard meets an android that he is attracted to — in effect an inflated sex doll — and begins to have second thoughts, mostly sexual. Knowing of his problem, another bounty hunter suggests he have sex with her to prove that she is mechanical, then "retire"— that is, execute — her. There is, of course, an enormous paradox involved in the situation. While the sexual act is, in one sense, totally animalistic, it is also associated with love, family, and our deepest human needs.

As Pastorino points out, since replicants have no memories, they are given implants. Although these memories are only alluded to in the novel, they become essential to an understanding of the film. Rachael, the replicant with whom Deckard falls in love, has been given the memories of the niece of Tyrell, the genius who designed the replicants. The replicants are given photographs and memorabilia, all presumably falsely authentic — that is, they are real, but they are not theirs — to enforce the fake memories. Rachael presumably has a few authentic memories, that is, the ones that have developed since the time the fakes were implanted. The reason given later in the film for the "termination date"— the date when some of the replicants would "self-destruct"— is that the creatures could not be allowed to develop their own memories. As Pastorino succinctly notes: "Photographs in *Blade Runner* are an attempt to recreate a personal myth, to justify life (as in Rachael's case), and to create heroes" (114).

Pastorino correctly notes that, in the novel, Deckard "is more concerned with finding a real animal, than with caring about real people, such as his wife" (111). The film drops the novel's concern with real animals as opposed to artificial ones; indeed, it drops all other distinctions between man and the so-called lower animals in order to concentrate upon the essential question: What is it that makes us human?

When *Blade Runner* appeared, reviewers complained of the incoherence of its narrative. But the narrative, even in its earliest form, is simplicity itself. Scott's films typically have a simple narrative, a complex milieu and a large supporting cast.

Blade Runner is set in the near-future, said to be Los Angeles in 2019. Rick Deckard is a blade runner — a hunter licensed to kill humanoid robots (replicants). The film begins with the written definition of a replicant, followed by a series of episodes including the questioning of Leon, who is suspected of being a replicant, and Leon's shooting of his questioner; Deckard eating at a sushi bar, his being brought in by Gaff, a messenger, and, in effect being forced by his commander, Bryant, to "terminate" four "skinjobs walking the street." In his murderous quest, depicted in the long middle section of the film, Deckard kills three of the replicants and, in the process of tracking them down, falls in love with Rachael, an advanced female robot, a Nexus 7, a "sports and pleasure model" who is not part of the rebellion and does not know she is a replicant.

Since replicants have no memories of their own, Tyrell, the genius behind the enormous corporation who designed and programmed them, has given Rachael memories purloined from his niece. Tyrell, for some mysterious reason, has chosen to remain on Earth when everyone else who can afford it apparently lives off-world. Nearly blind, he works on the top floor of his enormous and rotting building and surveys his world through computer screens and thick glasses.

Because the replicants build up their own memories over a period of time, they are given a limited life span and a "termination date." Understandably unhappy with this state of affairs, a small group of replicants revolt and come to Los Angeles hoping to find a solution to their problem or, failing that, to kill anyone they can find who might be responsible. Of the remaining replicants, one has been killed along the way. It is the responsibility of blade runner Rick Deckard to "terminate" the other four. The story alternates between the replicants and Deckard's attempt to terminate them and their attempts to get to Tyrell. Their ultimate hope is that they can make him do something to help them. As the wary viewer might expect, the story is complicated by the fact that Deckard and the beautiful replicant Rachael fall in love along the way.

Zhora is the first replicant to die. After Deckard traces a bit of manufactured snake skin, he discovers her working in a cheap club as a snake dancer, and kills her in a spectacular scene that was reworked twenty-five years later. In his conversation with Zhora, Harrison Ford does an excellent imitation of Humphrey Bogart talking to an antiques dealer with an affected manner in Howard Hawks' *The Big Sleep* (1946). The scene and mannerisms would certainly have been interpreted at the time as a parody of gay speech.

The enormously strong replicant Leon, who has been shown near the beginning of the film killing the man who is giving him the so-called Vogt-Kampf test to determine if he is a replicant, is the next to die. When Deckard is involved in a losing physical struggle with Leon, Rachael shoots him to protect the man with whom she is now hopelessly in love.

The replicant Pris has been befriended by J. F. Sebastian, a genetic designer who suffers from "Methuselah's syndrome" (premature aging) and amuses himself by building automatons. She is dispatched by Deckard after she unsuccessfully attempts to hide in plain sight disguised as one of Sebastian's creations.

In Batty's showdown with Tyrell, his creator, Tyrell expresses admiration for his creature, but says that it is impossible for him to reverse the life-span limitation. He calls him "the prodigal son" and seems to accept his fate when Batty kills him. This leaves only Batty's desperate struggle with Deckard. The replicant, whose life-span is ending even as he fights, wins, but, knowing that his life is over, and that it is his "time to die," he allows his opponent to live. In the decayed and rotting detritus of a dying civilization, a dove, which we are helpfully told in the commentary represents Batty's soul, ascends into the heavens. (What Batty was doing holding the dove as he jumps from one building to another in a death struggle, we are *not* told.) In the different versions of the conclusion, Deckard and Rachael face the future together, but their fate is uncertain: As the voice-over says in the release version of the film: "It's too bad, she won't live, but then again, who does?"

Comparing the different versions of *Blade Runner* is somewhat like comparing the different versions of a novel as the novelist changes his mind about the sometimes shifting relationships and motivations among the characters. As we know, Scott customarily stands above the fray and says, well, this is my preferred version, but you are entitled to your opinion and may like another. Up to the final cut, *Blade Runner* was a work in progress, especially in the question of whether Deckard is a replicant. As Raw and other critics have pointed out, the ending of the original theatrical version emphasizes Rachael's mortality and the briefness of their escape from the polluted city to the green hills of Earth, if any still remain. The love between them, which she has recognized for some time, has finally been recognized in return.

In the so-called director's cut, "the unicorn clearly refers us back to the earlier dream-sequence one, suggesting that the memory has been implanted in Deckard's mind—and thus he (like Rachael) is a replicant" (Raw, 116). Except for the fact that the editing of the director's cut is smoother, the later ending is not an improvement. It is at least arguable that the director's cut weakens the film. It takes away Deckard's tragic humanity and makes Batty's death and Rachael's plight less — not more — tragic. Shakespeare, an authority on the tragic, would hardly have approved the revised ending, no matter how much more popular it turned out to be.

Not long after the appearance of *Blade Runner*, Phil Hardy (*The Encyclopedia of Science Fiction Movies*) emphasized the film noir quality of Scott's film with its "femme fatales and laconic violence on the rain-slicked mean streets of Chinatown, 2019 style." Hardy is scarcely alone in his belief that the slender narrative is overwhelmed by the film's "state of the art production design" and rightly notes that the voice-over indicates a loss of confidence in the film rather than generic homage, though his reference to "fragments" of Dick's original novel being introduced "without explanation" is mysterious. Like many other critics, Hardy seems to have revised his opinion of the film upwards as more criticism of the film appeared and as Scott continued to "tweak" his increasingly famous film. (See his different lists of science fiction films cited in *Variety Book of Movie Lists* and *The Overlook Film Encyclopedia: Science Fiction*.)

In the years since its appearance, the film has probably received more serious critical attention than any other film except perhaps Quentin Tarantino's *Pulp Fiction* (1994). It is probably fair to say that Tarantino's great film, for all its pop references, is essentially an art-house film some distance from the mainstream. Scott, however, has no interest in art-house movies, and his films have all been mainstream films intended for a mass audience.

Even by the standards of expensive Hollywood films, Scott is not a personal filmmaker. He does not have "a personal film" which identifies him with a certain religious or professional or ethnic group, in short a film which the viewer feels he wanted to make, whatever the financial or emotional cost. There is no film like John Ford's *The Informer* or *The Quiet Man*, or Sam Fuller's *The Big Red One*, or Wild Bill Wellman's *Wings* or *Lafayette Escadrille*, or Sally Potter's *Orlando*. While the legendary English past takes front and center in *Robin Hood*, present-day England hardly exists at all, except for *A Good Year* in which the protagonist's chief interest apparently is to make enough money to escape permanently to the Eden of Provence.

Sean Redmond has speculated that the representations of class in *Blade Runner* may be traced back to what he calls a particular type of representation of the British working class in social realist films. These films, which include *Kes* (1969), *Rita, Sue, and Bob Too* (1986), *Naked* (1993), and *Nil by Mouth* (1997), stereotyped working-class men as "misogynist, non-communicative, brutes," and their "working class spaces ... as pathological" (53). The deliberately drab photography and the dingy interiors are inhabited by men who lead drab lives, and fight and drink with each other and with their families. The literary influence here is almost certainly D.H. Lawrence, especially in the portrait of the father in *Sons and Lovers* and Jack Cardiff's excellent 1960 film version which contains superb performances by Trevor Howard as the father and Wendy Hillen as the mother.

Redmond hardly more than hints that working-class films were an influence on the plot or characters of *Blade Runner*, but he does suggest them as a visual influence. The idea is suggestive, but so many visual influences are floating around in Scott's mind at any moment that it can hardly be more than that. Certainly, the Hovis bread advertisement — and probably any number of his other advertisements show a firm grasp of working-class visuals, but that is scarcely a surprise.

Redmond's references to the British working-class films in *Blade Runner* deserve further study. Of all the international filmmakers of the first rank, Scott may be the most barren of what we might call biographical signifiers. All of his films after *The Duellists* appear, at least at first glance, to be totally international in scope — that is, lacking any references to a native hearth and home. His iconography is all over the lot, and references to marriage and family, perhaps most clearly expressed in *Someone to Watch Over Me*, seem generic rather than deeply and personally felt. If we compare (say) John Ford's treatment of the family in any number or films, we can see what has been left out. Scott deals frankly with the problems of love across the cultural and religious divide in *Body of Lies*, but the treatment seems scant and impersonal. Only *A Good Year* has the warmth and tenderness between lovers that we might reasonably expect from so great a director.

In addition to the real influence of both *Blade Runner* and *Pulp Fiction*, both films have come to express an idea of what a true artist can do operating even in the outer limits of the commercial cinema. In a review of William Gibson and pop-culture dystopian fiction, Christopher Tayler wrote in 2003 that *Blade Runner* "hammered out some sturdy templates for pop-cultural dystopianism." Scott supplied the look: "the ominous gadgetry, the endless neon and rain" (Tayler, 34). And, it might be added, Quentin Tarantino supplied the attitude.

It is difficult, although not beyond all conjecture, to speculate what the reputation of *Blade Runner* might be if only the original American theatrical version had survived. Although the film might have taken longer to achieve its enormous reputation, the present writer believes that it would have done so. Since science-fiction deals with possibilities, often about the future, it is, of course, an allegorical genre, and there is, as we might expect, a lot of free-floating religious symbolism in *Blade Runner*. Some of it is, or can be interpreted to be, organic, but some is not attached to any element in the film.

Questions of religion in Scott's films are often historical in nature, as in *Kingdom of Heaven* and *Robin Hood*. Such questions are grounded in a historical interpretation of a perceived reality. *Blade Runner* is different, dealing, as it does, with last things and ultimate reality. Sometimes the film's symbolism seems to have no connection to the story and to have been tossed in almost by chance in the hope that it has (or may develop) some meaning. The origami unicorn is a case in point. Although the reference in the Book of Job in the King James *Bible* to a unicorn may be a mistranslation, it developed through the centuries as a story of a horse (or horse-like creature) with a horn in the middle of its forehead, that could be captured only by a virgin. The story was a literary representation of the belief that the "virginity which arouses desire also destroys it" (Armand Steubel, in Brunel, 1147). Whatever the effectiveness of the story in *Legend*, it is clearly out of place in *Blade Runner*. By comparison, Batty's dove, wherever it came from at the moment of his death, has an excellent provenance. It goes back to the story of the flood in Genesis and is often used in Protestant churches as a symbol of the Holy Spirit. (See Robert Couffignal, in Brunel, 450–54.) The most obvious symbol at Batty's death is the spike driven through Batty's hand, which echoes the spikes driven through the hands and feet of Christ. It might be worth mentioning in passing that Batty's character has hardly been Christ-like. He has brutally murdered any number of people and has taken intense pleasure in so doing.

The story of the Golem and of his literary descendant, the Frankenstein Monster, is more relevant. Although the Jewish legend of the Golem dates to the Old Testament and the Cabbala, its literary embodiment, like that of Mary Shelley's creature, dates from the romantic writers of the early nineteenth century. (See Catherine Mathière, in Brunel, 468–87.) The German romantics popularized the story of the Golem, a giant figure made of clay brought to life by the learned Rabbi Low, and the story became a staple of German silent cinema. The creature animated into life from the remnants of corpses in Mary Shelley's novel *Frankenstein, or The Modern Prometheus* (1820) is somewhat more intelligent than the stupid Golem, but much worse tempered. Like Roy Batty, both creatures feel short-changed and want, with greater or lesser intelligence, to become fully human.

By the time the so-called "director's cut" of *Blade Runner* appeared in limited release in theaters in 1992, both reviewers and critics had begun to take the film seriously. Michael Wilmington carefully noted that the released film was Scott's new "final version" and "slightly different" from the "director's cut" that had broken house records at the Nuart Theater in Los Angeles. He also noted that the dropping of Deckard's narration had deepened the "mood and melancholy" of the film and interestingly compared *Blade Runner* to the recently released *Thelma & Louise*. He argued that the comparison makes the film more obviously "a poem of alienation, rebellion and its consequences: of exploitation and institutionalized brutality, of a world teetering on apocalypse," and concluded that the replicants are "finally sympathetic" and their pursuers "odious." And both killers and pursued are trapped in a world startling in its contrasts: vital yet decaying, nightmarish yet bewitching, sophisticated but brutal. The greatness of the movie has never been better expressed.

The last word may be left to Ridley Scott. According to Harlan Ellison, Scott told him in 1979: "The time is ripe for a John Ford of science-fiction films. I'm going to be that director" (203).

Whatever the cost of producing *Blade Runner* was, the initial public response was disappointing. According to Box Office Mojo, the $27,580,111 domestic revenue from the original release was boosted to $32,868,943 by rerelease. Of course, the film's growing popularity, its enormous critical reputation and its various versions, commentaries and extras on VHS, laser discs, DVD and Blu-Ray, combined with a variety of ancillary products, have returned the cost of the film many times over.

Approaches to Blade Runner

Like all great works of art, popular or elitist, *Blade Runner* is subject to a variety of often conflicting interpretations. A helpful beginning for the student is Sean Redmond's *Studying* Blade Runner, which offers a variety of critical approaches. Although these will, of course, be largely a matter of opinion, Redmond's introduction is aggressively titled "Reading [into] the Greatest Science Fiction Film Ever Made." (The brackets are Redmond's.) After all, Stanley Kubrick's *2001: A Space Odyssey* clocks in at number one of the American Film Institute's list of the greatest science-fiction films, while *Blade Runner* clocks in only at number six. Still, as an attempt to drum up business, Redmond's heading is fair enough. Historically, the amount of serious criticism written about a film is a much better guide to its critical and historical importance than its popularity. By that standard, *Blade Runner* and *Metropolis* top the list.

Redmond's headings include Genre, Narrative, Representation, Institutions and Authors, Audiences, and Textual Analysis.

Film Noir is a French appropriation used to describe a group of Hollywood city films of the post-war period characterized by expressionistic black-and-white photography, a professional detective (usually a private eye, occasionally a policeman), tough dialogue and an atmosphere of corruption. The genre, which originated in the tough-guy novels of the 1930s, fell on hard times after the coming of color and remains today mostly as an infrequent, but still potent, signifier from the past.

The released version of *Blade Runner* easily fits under the film noir umbrella. Scott's future city, although shot in color, is dirty and cluttered, Harrison Ford's tough detective with appropriate voice-over commentary is ersatz Dashiell Hammett, Tyrell is a corrupt profiteer, and Sean Young's Rachael is the epitome of film noir seductiveness. Wreathed in cigarette smoke, cigarette in hand (it could just as easily be a gun), 1940s hairdo framing a sexy, experienced but vulnerable look, she is as pure a film noir girl as Lizabeth Scott or Lauren Bacall. Scott himself has said that, since the film was set forty years into the future, it was appropriate to film it in the style of forty years in the past (Redmond, 25).

An ambiguous or mixed ending was allowed in film noir and even a happy ending often had a kick. In Fritz Lang's *The Big Heat*, the bad guys have been vanquished and detective Glenn Ford has returned to work, but the audience knows that the victory is only temporary and that the corruption will return, indeed probably already has. In *Blade Runner*, we are told that "some models" have no fixed termination date, and Deckard and Rachael fly off to outtakes from Stanley Kubrick's *The Shining*. The kicker here is that the outtakes, which come from the opening of Kubrick's film, possess in some way which is difficult to identify and which no one seems to have mentioned, a sinister undercurrent suggesting that even a happy honeymoon period is, at best, hypothetical.

Gloria Pastorino regards *Blade Runner* as "a horror film in the tradition of *Frankenstein*." In this reading, we have Roy Batty as "a monster more human than its creator, desperately trying to get more life out of him and rebelling against him when every hope of constructive life is abandoned" (112). Oedipal father and mother, Tyrell has no sympathy for any of his children, and Batty, his time running out, both kisses him and kills him in the same breath. This is not quite completely true. Tyrell expresses sympathy and understanding but says that, unfortunately, he can do nothing.

Of course, any generic formulation is likely to move around, especially when the various versions are as shifting and variable as those of *Blade Runner*, and it is fair to argue that the later versions of Scott's film, although they contain some characteristics of film noir, move the film away from film noir to some variety of science fiction.

Although none of the critics seems to have been concerned with the unities of time, place and action in *Blade Runner*, the question, although of some theoretical interest, is essentially moot. The city in the film seems to exist in some sort of permanent, polluted smog between night and day. As in *Black Hawk Down*, the entire film, except for the opening scenes — all with essentially the same setting — appears to take place in a concentrated blur of time with little regard for any unity except Scott's beautiful symmetry of movement from one shot to the next. Of course, a few films, most notably *High Noon*, represent themselves as occurring in real time. Strangely enough, the technique often seems ostentatiously to call attention to itself, as if every example were a warm-up for Andy Warhol's *Empire* (1964), which gives the viewer eight hours-plus of photography of the Empire State Building. In *Blade Runner*, however, the technique works precisely because it does not call attention to itself.

The debate over director of photography Jordan Cronenweth's contribution concerns both questions of authorship and genre. That Cronenweth, who was unfortunately forced to withdraw from the film before it was finished and who soon died, was a master of film lighting and technique is beyond question. Scott Bukatman, in his BFI Modern Classics volume, argues that Cronenweth's "characteristic method of lighting" was largely responsible for the look of the film. Although Scott has always praised Cronenweth in the highest terms, he was a meticulous craftsman whose slowness is said to have resulted in clashes with Scott. (Much earlier in his career, Cronenweth had been fired by Robert Altman from *Brewster McCloud* for the same reason.)

The issue, although academic, is not without interest, and a detailed comparison between the lighting and cinematography in Cronenweth's other films and in *Blade Runner* would be a worthwhile study in authorship comparable perhaps to the conflict between Ben Jonson and Inigo Jones, the designer of the costumes in Jonson's celebrated masques, a kind of early opera which flourished during the Jacobean period. The problem with such a study is that it would be time-consuming and difficult and would involve considerable expertise with little or no possible reward. The conclusion, based on the available evidence, would almost certainly be in favor of Scott.

The question of whether Deckard is a human or a replicant has been argued at length. In Dick's novel, he is a replicant, but this does not seem to have been considered when the film first appeared. Since the released version of the film was thought to be a film noir and Deckard to be a hard-boiled detective of the Sam Spade variety, the question seemed moot. As more versions of the film appeared, the narration disappeared and, lacking the film noir context, the question became relevant.

Scholars of the books of antiquity and of the plays of Shakespeare have long dreamed of a perfect text and have worked industriously for centuries to achieve it. Recently Shakespearean scholars have either, depending upon your point of view, given up the search in despair or perhaps continued it for crass monetary motives (selling books or perhaps even DVDs).

The issue is similar to the relationship between the three versions of Shakespeare's *Hamlet*. After spending decades attempting to establish a version of *Hamlet* which would be all-inclusive, scholars were reluctantly forced to concede that the animal they were hunting did not exist, or rather existed in three distinct variations of unequal authority. Scott, as usual, opines on this, as on other questions about interpretation, that it is strictly up to the viewer to decide. (Shakespeare would likely have done so as well, except in the case of the first quarto, which was clearly printed without his permission.)

Certainly, many viewers like the irony of having a blade runner track down and kill members of his own kind. Others are indignant and argue that a man like Deckard would not be so insensitive as to kill, apparently without remorse, humans like himself. (It might just as easily be argued that Deckard is exactly the type of man who would.) The argument is that such a man would not be human. Of course, as Stanley Kubrick knew, he would be precisely human. In Steven Spielberg's *A.I.* (2001), based upon an idea by Kubrick, it is the replicant child who possesses the moral virtues and the human child who is evil. Morality, it is argued, is not innate, but must be taught.

Even in our so-called enlightened era, human beings kill their own kind without remorse for a variety of reasons, often trivial. According to Robert Ardrey's *African Genesis* (1961), man was descended from territorial killer apes and, of course, had not appreciably changed during the process. Nobel laureate William Golding, who had a rat's view of human nature, also popularized the thesis in a more sophisticated form in his novel *The Inheritors* (1955). The idea, a popular one at the time, lacked scientific foundation and has since been discarded. The idea, however, did appeal to Sam Peckinpah and apparently influenced his film *The Wild Bunch* (1969), which appeared at the height of the Vietnam conflict.

Although most of the representations of the future in *Blade Runner* are outdated, at least one of them has assumed increasing validity. According to David Levy's book *Love + Sex With Robots* (2007), which does not mention *Blade Runner*, the growing sophistication of robots (read replicants) as sexual partners is likely to replace the use of sexual surrogates in therapy. Surrogate therapy is a complex, expensive, time-consuming process involving the client, the surrogate partner, and the sexual therapist. The entire process is controversial and raises complex legal, moral, professional, clinical and ethical implications. By comparison, the use of sexual robots is simplicity itself (Levy, 215). While none of the robots in the near future, at least, is likely to resemble Rachael, benighted men in the off-world colonies might find them attractive.

6

Legend (1985): I Only Wanted to Touch One. Where's the Harm in That?

Versions. *Legend* is available in two DVD versions: the original 1985 2.35:1 89-minute theatrical US release with a Tangerine Dream Score; and the so-called director's cut, produced in 2002, sixteen years after the film's original release. The original California previews were so savage that Scott believed that some of the audience members were under the influence of hard drugs. One could as easily have thought that the film's fantastic visuals might have enhanced rather than diminished the appreciation of the trippers. After the English opening, the film was reduced from 94 minutes to 89 for the American audience.

The 2002 version restored the originally jettisoned Jerry Goldsmith score and weighed in at 111 minutes. Since the term "director's cut" might seem to preclude his tweaking a film at some future date, Scott seems not to like the term and states merely that it is his "preferred version." This version, restored by Charles De Lauzirika, is said to follow as closely as possible the original version produced before the cuts forced on Scott by Universal Pictures. (For details, see Raw, 90.)

The eventual Blu-ray edition will probably also include a third version, the 94-minute international version which retains the Jerry Goldsmith score, or at least part of it, and perhaps even a fourth version prepared for television.

What producers do generally when they become unhappy with a film is to re-edit it for dramatic effect — that is, shorten it to speed up the action — and juice up and/or change the score. In this instance, Tangerine Dream was chosen to give *Legend* more energy. The group had done excellent work in heavy-duty drama, especially William Friedkin's *Sorcerer* (1977), an underrated version of Henri-Georges Clouzot's masterpiece *The Wages of Fear*. Tangerine Dream certainly supplied more energy. Whether it was appropriate for the film is another question.

Scott says that his original idea for *Legend,* inspired by Jean Cocteau's masterpiece *Beauty and the Beast* (1946), was to show "real characters in an imaginary environment." Cocteau, poet, junkie, artist and occasionally a master filmmaker, succeeds in blending together in full daylight realism and fantasy in the film, which Scott says that he saw in an excellent print. (Scott seems to be referring to a 16mm or 35mm print. It is worth remembering that Cocteau's film, available on DVD in the Criterion Collection, was not necessarily easy to find in those dark days, particularly in an excellent print.) Of its kind, it is certainly the masterpiece, sort of a *Wizard of Oz* for adults. Scott has also mentioned the 1935 Warner Brothers version of Shakespeare's *A Midsummer Night's Dream*, co-directed by master stage designer Max Reinhardt. Often referred to as "the genius," Reinhardt had come of age as an artist during the Weimar period in Berlin with theatrical productions which blended music, dance, set designs and acting into "complete" theater (see Willett, 33–52 *et passim*). On the available evidence, his four silent films, made with only limited resources, seem to have been duds, but his reputation was such that Warners put its enormous resources to work for *Dream*. The result, although lacking in drama and hindered by divergent acting styles, presaged new cinematic paths in commercial films. Reinhardt is credited as co-director with William Dieterle, another German refugee and experienced director who is best remembered today for *The Hunchback of Notre Dame* (1939) and *Portrait of Jennie* (1948).

While the comparison between *Legend* and the two earlier films is logical and valid, the black-and-white aesthetic clarity of the two classic films is markedly different from the colors of *Legend*, which mute the realism of Scott's film. In a perfect world, *Legend* might have been the great black-and-white film which Scott, who works with large budgets, will probably never be allowed to make.

Scott apparently looked at *Legend* as a substitute for *Tristan and Isolde,* a film which he has long contemplated, but has now apparently completely abandoned. The director was attracted to the fantasy world of William Hjortsberg and, under the instruction of the director, the novelist is said to have written some fifteen drafts of the script over a four-year period before one satisfied them both. Apparently, Scott rejected earlier versions which went too far toward the dark side; however, Scott's visuals at their brightest are hardly sweetness and light, and the film — which received a PG-13 rating from the MPAA — veers to within an image here and there of an R rating.

Scott cast the young Tom Cruise in the leading role. Scott showed Cruise the François Truffaut film *The Wild Child* (1970), the true story of a young boy found running wild in a French forest in the nineteenth century. He was unable to speak and moved on all fours like an animal. Scott wanted Cruise to grow his hair long and to imitate the boy's reportedly jerky gestures and apparently wolverine behavior. According to Cruise's biographer, "a childhood spent practicing backflips and Evel Knievel stunts did not go to waste" (Morton, 73).

The filming was beset with difficulties. *Legend* was shot at the world's largest soundstage, the so-called "Bond Stage" in London. Three weeks before the end of shooting, an enormous fire destroyed the entire set, including the artificial forest which had been built at enormous expense and which had to be replaced. Scott's DVD commentary contains a fascinating account of the difficulties of shooting the film.

The following summary is based on Scott's "preferred version," also called the "director's cut." Schwartz (52–55) gives a detailed summary of the American theatrical version.

The film begins with shots of what might be called a dark Victorian legendary landscape and a voice-over by the Lord of Darkness, a dictatorial figure who believes that the sun will set forever if he kills the last unicorn. Since he is confined to darkness, he sends his goblin, Blix, to do his evil work and to bring back the unicorn's horn.

According to the film, light was protected by the unicorns who were in turn protected by the purest of mortals, such as Jack (Tom Cruise) and the beautiful but wayward Lily (Mia Sara). The struggle between good and evil depends upon "an eternal balance" which produces "legends."

When Jack takes Lily out to see the unicorns, she touches one of the animals despite Jack's pleadings. "I only wanted to touch one," she says, "Where's the harm in that?" Attempting to play catch-up in Jack's affections, she takes what she calls her "wedding ring," throws it into the flood and vows to marry whoever finds it.

Tim Curry as Darkness in *Legend* (1985): horned evil incarnate.

Jack, of course, immediately dives in after it. Meanwhile, Lily runs through a world now frozen in winter to her home, where she finds her housekeeper-companion Nell now apparently dead. Blix and his evil companions invade the house, a place of baroque wonders which include a clock cribbed from Lang's *Metropolis*, but Lily hides from them.

The "forest child" Honeythorn Gump and his companions awaken Jack, who is sleeping in the snow. When Jack answers Gump's riddle, Gump agrees to help Jack, and they set out together. Jack asks forgiveness from the last unicorn and decides that the group needs a leader "to get the alicorn back" and — surprise — they decide that he is the chosen one. (In context, "alicorn" apparently means either the unicorn or his horn, or probably both.) Oona, a kind of fairy Tinkerbell, perhaps named after "Una," the heroine of Edmund Spenser's *The Faerie Queene*, offers her help. Brown Tom is wounded by the goblins, but recovers.

The stage — or rather the Bond Stage — is now set for the showdown between the forces of light and the forces of darkness. Hag Meg Mucklebones attacks Jack and finds him "a juicy morsel," but spares him when he cleverly praises her beauty.

Legend (1985)

Trapped in a dungeon somewhere in the middle of the Earth near what looks like a foundry in Hell for human sacrifice, Jack, Brown Tom, and Screwball escape with the help of Oona, but only after she attempts unsuccessfully to extract a kiss from Jack.

The Lord of Darkness, apparently the only character with a sense of humor, is unhappy and decides to make Lily one of his team. This leads to all sorts of complications when Lily gets lost in what looks like left-over sets from *Blade Runner*. "Darkness," as he is familiarly known to his companions, attempts to make Lily "one of us" by doing a bizarre dance of darkness. He is an aggressive and skilled dancer, and she responds favorably but is ultimately unhappy with his evil transformation and his cloven hooves, a sure sign of the Devil, and rejects him (see Shakespeare, *Othello*, 5.2.286–87). He even suggests that she is pregnant and brags, "Tonight, the sun sets forever."

Jack and his group set out to find "every shining object" in order to bring light to darkness. The plan is ultimately successful and, after a humongous fight, Lily frees the unicorn from what looks like Hades, light is restored to the world, Jack retrieves Lily's ring and awakens her, and the unicorns run free. Darkness is vanquished, but probably only temporarily. He is out there right now, probably in the Gulf working on a new oil spill and doing push-ups in his spare time.

Except possibly for *1492: Conquest of Paradise*, *Legend* received the worst reviews of any Scott film. Although not all the reviewers saw the same version of the film, none of them much liked the version they saw. The earliest review in *Variety* by "Strat." was more favorable than most. The heading reads: "Lavishly produced, but thin-scripted fantasy." The review proper begins by praising the visual skills of its director and a "spectacularly satisfying Satan." After some analysis of the plotting, the reviewer criticizes the archness of the dialogue and the insipidness of Cruise's hero. He exempts from the carnage Terry Rawlings, the film's editor, Jerry Goldsmith, who wrote the score, and Tim Curry's Darkness.

David Sterritt, in the *Christian Science Monitor*, wondered why a film which had "so much money" poured into it could come out "so stale and tedious." Or to put it another way, how could the man who made *Alien* and *Blade Runner* make such a bad film? His answer is that (1) the screenplay "traffics in boring elves," "pointless demons," and "trite heroics," and (2) Scott's cold approach to the material results in an "icy artifact, not a warm and living outgrowth of universally shared dreams." Sterritt believes that more mature subject matter might have helped.

Harlan Ellison (who admits that he has seen only the shorter version of *Legend*) first lauds it with superlatives only finally to condemn it. He writes that the film "steals our breath, captures our eyes, dazzles and sparkles and, like a 4th of July sparkler, comes to nothing but gray ash at the end." He attempts with only moderate success to describe the visuals, calling them "almost Dalí-esque, or perhaps reminiscent of the paintings of the school known as the Orientalist—Gérôme and Regnault and Debat-Ponsan." Whatever they are, he labels them "remarkable." But he also believes that Scott, "given the power to create any movie he desired, fled into a throwaway universe of childish irrelevance." The reason for the failure is that the film gives us "no touchstones for ethical behavior in the real world" (293).

In a sense, time has reeled in *Legend.* Modern fantasy films, even the R-rated ones, look more like *Legend* every year. The look of *Legend,* as Scott himself has admitted, derives from late-Victorian, early twentieth-century book illustration. Arthur Rackham seems to be the model. Of course, the movement and actions of most of the characters in the fantasy films of today, including Scott's, derive from comic books and so-called graphic novels. The variation is in the characters.

Scott's attempt to have real characters moving against an imaginary background is a failure. The chief problem is that the reverse seems to be true. The characters seem to be pure cardboard, if that. The environment, by contrast, is terrifying and there is little respite in the comedy and music that classical Disney films were so magical in supplying. A hit tune or two and a few laughs would have improved the mix. The whole enterprise seems overly realistic.

Young Tom Cruise looks like a hippie transferred to fairyland by mistake. He is not a plastic creature, but is always relentlessly himself. Imagine a young Johnny Depp in the role. Still, more realistic dialogue would have made Cruise more convincing in a difficult role. The other players are better, and Tim Curry received much praise for his performance as the Lord of Darkness. The story, however, is weak, slow-moving and lacking in drama. The dialogue is pseudo-folk, or stage Victorian: "Very good, just right ... there's something really special that I've been promising to tell you."

Of course, Scott did not give up on the film after its box-office failure and eventually restored the film to his original design. While the restoration unquestionably helped the film, it scarcely mended its faults. The best way to watch the film is to smoke pot and imagine it as an opera or a comic book or graphic novel in a language you do not understand.

According to Box Office Mojo, *Legend* was considerably less than a hit, grossing only $15,502,112 domestically. While neither the production costs nor the foreign box-office is given, *Legend* must be considered a failure. This, however, seems not to have hindered the careers of either its famous young star or its director. According to Paul Sammon writing in 1999, *Legend* was beginning to show signs of a "heightened audience interest after an initially disappointing release."

The film's renaissance began with the publication of the director's cut, with Scott's commentary, which became available in 2002. Although there is a website devoted to supporting the film, there is little evidence to support a re-evaluation which would significantly raise the reputation of what Sammon calls Scott's "most severely compromised work."

7

Someone to Watch Over Me (1987):
Is It Love, Mike?

Version. The 1987 American release version of *Someone to Watch Over Me* is the only available version. This is apparently the director's cut. It is shot in widescreen 1.85:1, runs approximately 105 minutes and is rated R. It is presumed to be definitive.

After the difficult shooting of two complex films, *Blade Runner* and *Legend,* one science-fiction and the other fantasy, Scott decided upon a less complicated film, a combination romance and gritty police saga. The screenplay was written by Howard Franklin, who had previously worked on the screenplays of the successful *Romancing the Stone* (1984), starring Danny DeVito and Kathleen Turner, and the prestigious *The Name of the Rose* (1986), starring Sean Connery. The film was shot in eleven weeks in Manhattan and Queens and in Los Angeles, with that city standing in for New York in some scenes. Scott has often spoken of the comfortable feeling of shooting in New York and later returned for the much more complex *American Gangster*.

Someone to Watch Over Me boasts one of the great opening shots in film, a pan over New York City described by James Sanders in *Celluloid Skyline* as "truly dreamlike." His wonderful description is too long to quote completely and readers interested in the film are strongly encouraged to look it up for themselves. The viewer sails "thrillingly" through the vivid skyline, past and over the famous buildings, "along glowing wells of light scooped out of the dark mass of the city and shooting northward like arrows," and so on. Sanders concludes his hyperbolic description by writing that we have clearly left the rude constraints of the everyday world behind and "entered a realm where earthly rules simply do not apply" (90). The good news is that the opening is as good as Sanders says it is. The bad news is that the rest of the film does not live up to the opening, but then it is difficult to imagine what film could.

Someone to Watch Over Me begins with a boisterous party in a working-class Queens, New York, neighborhood celebrating the promotion of Mike Keegan (Tom Berenger) to police detective. The plot kicks in when beautiful socialite Claire Gregory (Mimi Rogers) witnesses a violent killing at a nightclub in a dispute over ownership and a division of the spoils. Mike is assigned to "baby-sit," that is, to protect Claire until the killer can be apprehended. The culture shock is great on both sides: snobbish Claire and her boyfriend resent the intrusion of the police into their life, and Mike's wife Ellie (Lorraine Bracco) resents her husband's new job when she discovers that Claire has bought her husband a new tie: "You didn't tell me she's so beautiful." The film is built upon two interconnected stories: Mike's search to capture and convict killer Joey Venza (Andreas Katsulas) before he can kill Claire, and his internal emotional conflict which forces him to choose between his loyal, middle-class wife Ellie and the glamorous, beautiful and rich Claire.

Improbably not realizing the danger she is in, Claire insists on going to a party, where Venza accosts her in the rest room and threatens to kill her if she identifies him in a lineup. Mike chases Venza down, but Venza succeeds, against all probability, in turning himself in to the police. It is unclear whether Claire identifies Venza in the lineup, but Venza is released because the police did not read him his Miranda rights when he was arrested, if indeed he ever was. Mike's guilt for endangering Claire — "I set her up" — is aggravated by his falling in love with her. While Mike is on duty, Ellie reports a prowler to the police. While Ellie and Mike unsuccessfully attempt to repair their marriage, Venza is on the loose. After policeman T.J. (Tony DiBenedetto) has been sent to replace Mike as a guard for Claire, a henchman of Venza is sent to kill her. The would-be assassin shoots T.J. and heads to the bedroom to kill Claire. What he does not know is that Mike is sleeping with Claire. In a mirror sequence cribbed from Orson Welles' *The Lady from Shanghai*, Mike kills the intruder. Suspended and estranged from his wife, Mike moves into the "splash pad" of a friend. The pad is apparently a way-station between reconciliation or divorce.

While Mike is at an upscale dance attempting to explain to Claire why their relationship won't work out, he gets a call from Joey Venza, who has kidnapped Ellie and their son, Tommy. Venza says he has "two minutes" to come see him or he will "take his family out." Improbably, Venza wants to trade Ellie and Tommy for Claire. Venza is killed, the family is reunited, and the film ends happily. Or so we may presume to think.

Reviewers generally liked the film's visual style but were not always satisfied with the screenplay. They particularly praised the opening sequence of the New York skyline set to Roberta Flack's rendition of the Gershwins' title song. J. Hoberman, in *The Village Voice*, wrote that Scott's Manhattan "is as much a presence as the city in *Blade Runner*," but added as a caveat that "his characters are no less automatons." Most reviewers emphasized the plot in terms of the traditional Hollywood thriller, especially the then-new Michael Douglas-Glenn Close *Fatal Attraction,* or in terms of the real or potential conflict between the working-class policeman and the affluent and careless yuppie.

"Lor." in *Variety* praised *Someone* as "a stylish and romantic police thriller" which manages "through the sleek direction of Ridley Scott and persuasive ensemble performances" to overcome "hard-to-swallow plot developments." Comparing the film with

Fatal Attraction he wrote that both films have "lovable and supportive wives" whose husbands are led astray by chilly females. This resulting infidelity, "a key story element," is "difficult for the audience to believe." The reviewer also believed that the "hostage exchange ruse," although "suspenseful and well-staged," is "incredible and unconvincing." As compensation, "Lor." praised the strong performances of Berenger as the working-class cop, Rogers as the romantic interest, and Bracco as the long-suffering wife. "Lor." added that Scott's visuals changed "the otherwise gritty New York thriller" into "something out of *Blade Runner*" and cited the New York skyline, smoky backlit sets, foggy streets and other elements as supporting evidence.

Vincent Canby, in the *New York Times*, praised the film's "visual and aural decoration," but deplored its "commonplace drama." Roger Ebert, usually a Scott partisan, described the film's "high concept": Detective from working-class background falls in love with society beauty." He notes, however, that Bracco plays the wife "with great force and imagination." In the old days, the society woman would have been portrayed as a "brazen hussy," perhaps played by Joan Crawford. According to Ebert, the extra-marital romance between Berenger and Rogers "has all the excitement of an arranged marriage."

In an insightful review, Simon Cunliffe argued that the extravagant cultural affluence of Claire Gregory's lifestyle amplified "the spiritual poverty and moral vulnerability of the self interested." Oliver Stone's *Wall Street* and the age of "greed is good" was looming on the horizon, and is perhaps looming again some twenty-five years later. Claire's nerdy escort stupidly argues against involvement since, whether she likes it or not, she is already deeply involved. Cunliffe argues that the film's center is clearly located in the blue-collar, working-class world. The "flawed hero" is nurtured and protected within his own community and is "recuperated" into it at the end of the film. Indeed so, and would have been in the 1940s with Joan Crawford as the society woman and John Garfield as the policeman. The 1940s film, however, would not isolate "yuppies," or the Yale preppies of an earlier period, as the point at which "sexual and fiscal profligacy converge," unless, of course, the role was played by Cary Grant.

Julian Petley liked the treatment of the cross-class liaison, but noted that "it is perhaps necessary by now to look beneath such happy endings, focusing on the tensions and contradictions which they attempt to mediate and resolve." Richard Corliss was on target with his description of *Someone to Watch Over Me* as a combination of "tech-noir gloss" and "traditional thriller." Corliss's reading of the film's message: "Know your place, Manhattan or Queens ... and stay in it."

The film's main problem is that the plot is full of holes. The question of whether Claire identifies Venza in the lineup is fudged. Richard A. Schwartz writes in *The Films of Ridley Scott* that she does, but the film never explicitly says so. We are told only that Venza has been released because he was not properly given his Miranda rights. Leaving aside the questions of hot pursuit, illegal possession of firearms, and perhaps a half-dozen other reasons, Venza has presumably been identified as a cold-blooded murderer by the testimony of an eyewitness of impeccable character.

Schwartz's detailed summary of the plot makes the film seem more coherent than it actually is. Reviewers were quick to point out the lack of professionalism in the way the police respond to the crisis situations in the film, especially considering that a policeman's wife is at the center of the story. The hostage situation, which serves as the climax of the film, boggles the mind since there is no conceivable way that Venza could gain what he wants from the exchange. Even if the exchange works and he kills Claire, which may be what he intends to do, he would certainly be killed by the police.

We are told nothing that would explain Venza or the way he thinks. As Shakespeare knew, every villain has a point of view which explains his actions, or at least how he interprets his actions. Venza never has a chance to explain himself. He is simply a plot device, nothing more.

The coherence of the plot is not an absolute necessity for a great film. No one has ever been able to summarize Howard Hawks' *The Big Sleep* either, but that film, despite its tough-guy veneer, did not pretend to be realistic. It had Bogart and Bacall, crisp black-and-white photography, smart dialogue and was pure Hollywood all the way.

When I saw *Someone to Watch Over Me* during the week it played in Baton Rouge in 1987, I thought it the most beautiful film I had ever seen excepting only John Huston's *Moby Dick* and *Moulin Rouge*, and I recommended it enthusiastically to my friends. The film was so spottily released, however, that it is improbable any of them went to see it.

It is still perhaps an open question whether such beautiful color photography is appropriate for what most critics would regard as film noir. Crime stories are said to have begun with D.W. Griffith's *The Musketeers of Pig Alley* (1912), but did not come into their own until the Warner Brothers crime films of the 1930s. Film noir, however, is a term generally associated with the philosophically dark films of the McCarthy era of the late 1940s. The films were downbeat stories about criminal activity, often involving doomed lovers. The protagonists were generally city dwellers, although the occasional bank robber might be a country bumpkin. The protagonists were criminals because they needed the money, because they didn't have a chance, or just for the hell of it. Color photography was still very expensive and the world still seemed to be in black and white. Of course, *Someone to Watch Over Me* either is or is not film noir, depending upon your definition. Scott's careful attention to color need not disqualify the film, and bravura direction was almost a necessary ingredient (Hawks' *The Big Sleep*, Lang's *The Big Heat*).

Someone to Watch Over Me has the three-act structure that Scott customarily puts into his films: (1) the temptation or set-up, in which a committed family man is tempted, (2) the development, which puts the question and develops both the danger and the temptation, (3) and the conclusion, which resolves the situation in the way the audience knew it *would* be resolved. What does not work in the film is the construction of the plot. What does work is the carefully crafted psychology of the triangular relationship between the policeman, his wife and the rich socialite.

Scott's depiction of the contrasting lifestyles could hardly have been improved. No one has a better eye for sets, either found or created, and the two contrasting opening scenes are the work of a master. The boisterous policemen are certainly enjoying themselves much more than their decorous associates in Manhattan, but the viewer who gives any thought to the topic will certainly know where the trouble will start.

The leading players are actors who seemed to be on the rise at the time, but whose later careers did not quite attain the heights they probably wished for. After excellent performances in *The Dogs of War* and *The Big Chill*, rough-featured Tom Berenger reached prominence in Oliver Stone's much-lauded *Platoon*. Following hard on that film, *Someone* might reasonably have been

Someone to Watch Over Me (1982): The detective (Tom Berenger), his wife (Mimi Rogers) and the lowering gangster Joey Venza (Andreas Katsulas).

expected to make Berenger a major star, but alas that was not to be. He has, however, continued as an effective ensemble player and as the star of the money-making Sniper series.

The delicately featured Mimi Rogers is unfortunately probably best known for her early marriage to and subsequent divorce from Tom Cruise, but she has continued to do effective work in films and particularly in a variety of television roles without quite getting the roles she might have hoped for after *Someone to Watch Over Me*. Lorraine Bracco is a beautiful woman whose ethnic voice seems strangely at odds with some of the roles she plays. She is said to have turned down the Edie Falco role in the influential crime series *The Sopranos* in favor of the less important role of the psychiatrist. She has also written a tell-all book, *On the Couch*, about, among other topics, her tumultuous marriage to actor Harvey Keitel.

Described by *The Ridley Scott Encyclopedia* as "one of Scott's most audience-friendly films" (288), *Someone* was a failure at the box-office. According to Box Office Mojo, the film, which opened on October, 9, 1987, had a domestic gross of only $10,278,549. Although the foreign box-office is not given, all available information shows that the public, for whatever reason, did not like the film.

8

Black Rain (1989):
One Big Gray Area

Version. *Black Rain* is available on Blu-ray in the 125-minute 2.35:1 American R-rated theatrical version. As usual, Scott has contributed an illuminating commentary on an alternate track.

Although Scott usually develops his own material, *Black Rain* was brought to him fully formed. Producers Stanley R. Jaffe, Sherry Lansing and Michael Douglas asked Scott to consider directing the project. He liked the script and the idea of depicting an exotic world, as in *Blade Runner, Alien* and to some extent *Legend.* The difference, of course, is that those films were shot on sound stages and *Black Rain* would be filmed on location in the Far East.

Screenwriter-executive producer Craig Bolotin says that on a visit to Japan, he saw a group of large American cars and was told they belonged to the Yakuza, a group of Japanese gangsters similar to the Mafia; he developed a script from that beginning. The idea was for his protagonist to have to go to Japan for some reason and to team up with a Japanese cop. At the time, Bolotin was working on another project and had Warren Lewis take over writing the screenplay. The project sold to Michael Douglas immediately.

In 1990, after the success of *The Jewel of the Nile, Fatal Attraction* and *Wall Street,* Douglas was in a position to produce and star in nearly any movie of his choosing. At that time, Japan seemed on the verge of supplanting the United States as the world's greatest economic power. For Douglas, the film appeared to be a darker version of *Wall Street,* and he liked the idea of exploring a character darker than any he had previously played. Scott seemed the perfect director to depict "a strange new world" largely unknown to American audiences at that time. After Scott agreed to the project, he began, as usual, to work with the writers and to scout locations in New York and Japan.

Scott has said that, while New York has many excellent locations, Japan, by contrast, does not have much "old stuff." Indeed, the Japanese silent movies now available on DVD show a rural Japan of winding country roads and small towns far different from anything in *Black Rain* or current Japanese films. Scott said that, although the authorities were more helpful in Osaka than in Tokyo, the Japanese did not understand how an American film was made and put limitations on the shooting. Everything had "to be permitted," and "they would not let us change a thing." Even then, the Japanese would not let the Americans shoot all the scenes which had been agreed to. When working in Japan became increasingly difficult, he photographed the bloody climactic scene in California's Napa Valley wine country.

The writers agreed that the Douglas character was not "the most likable character in the world" for the first half of the film. This is an understatement; the character is frankly detestable. Douglas regarded the character as "a stretch" and saw the character Nick as attempting to regain his self-esteem. As a result, he had the costume and makeup people rough up his appearance and curl his hair. Andy Garcia became the neat anti-Douglas and Japanese actor Ken Takakura became "the silent warrior," whose calm, competent demeanor became a stark contrast to that of Douglas.

The romantic interest, Joyce (Kate Capshaw) is a beautiful Chicagoan who has made a name for herself in Japan as some sort of undefined, upscale hostess. She is blond, cold, distant, careful, and has been wrongly called the only pure noir character in *Black Rain*. She dresses like an Oriental femme fatale, but unfortunately has only a peripheral role. Laurence Raw writes, in the usually non-judgmental *Ridley Scott Encyclopedia*, that Scott does not seem "particularly interested" in her performance, and cites Joanna Cassidy's performance in *Blade Runner* as another example of the director's indifference (Raw, 66).

The other main characters are also carefully defined. Yusaku Matsuda, who played the villainous Sato superbly, was a well-known Japanese comic who was cast against type. Even if we disregard the Oriental stereotypes going back to Cecil B. DeMille's silent hit *The Cheat* (1915)—and even if we don't—Matsuda's Sato, as filtered through the crime fiction of the 1930s, is about as noir as it is possible to get. Although none of the Americans knew it as the time, Matsuda was dying of stomach cancer and did not long survive the shooting of the film. Producer Sherry Lansing now regards Matsuda's look as a warm up for that of Keanu Reeves in the *Matrix* films, what she calls "a modern approach to a traditional man."

Black Rain shooting began in Osaka on October 28, 1988, and continued there until December 8, 1988, continued in America in New York and L.A , and ended on March 14, 1989, with shooting in the California wine country standing in for the Japanese location Scott had abandoned. The film's biggest set, the nightclub location, was 150 feet long and three stories high (Clarke, 112). Because of the expense and procedural difficulties of filming in Japan, the studio decided to shoot in America whenever possible. This decision did not injure the film; since this is Scott directing and aiding in design, it might even have enhanced it. The concluding sequence, shot in the California vineyards, is memorable and totally convincing, even by Scott's high visual standards.

The story may be divided into three unequal parts.

1. **The Job**. Rogue cop Nick Conklin (Douglas) is a Dirty Harry clone who has

family problems, is behind in his house payments and is in constant trouble with his superiors. As the film opens, he is being investigated by internal affairs for stealing money. (This is a standard motif in crime films and in series such as *The Shield*, and will turn up again in Scott's *American Gangster,* where Richie Roberts, played by Russell Crowe, gets into trouble with his fellows because he is apparently the only policeman who refuses to steal.) Conklin and his straight-arrow partner Charlie Vincent (Andy Garcia) are involved in a shootout in which at least two people are killed. After they track down and capture the chief killer, Sato (Matsuda), they are delegated to take him back to Tokyo.

2. **The Death of Charlie**. Nothing goes well in Japan. When they arrive at the airport, the two American policemen, unable to read Japanese, are tricked out of their captive and told to go home. When they refuse, they are allowed to stay but are given a policeman named Masahiro (Ken Takakura) to look after them and are made to give up their guns. Unlike Nick, Charlie adjusts well to his new environment and shows himself to be a good sport and a reliable and amiable partner. In an unusual plot twist, Charlie is killed in a showdown with Sato. While it is not unusual for a partner to be killed, he is usually, as in John Huston's *The Maltese Falcon*, killed at or near the beginning of the film. Scott, however, justified the killing of an important character in the middle of the film as "the way things happen."

3. **The Reckoning**. Nick now has two interrelated problems: avenging Charlie and operating in a complex, largely unknowable new environment. As usual in a Scott film, the plot thickens, in this case into a complex interplay involving Yakuza wars and counterfeit money. The violent conclusion, or rather the several violent sequences that conclude the film, are predictable. We know that the dependable but stolid Japanese policeman will eventually team up with the wild man, throw aside the rules, and "go for it." At the end of the film, Nick redeems himself to Masahiro by showing that he is, at least in the matter of the counterfeit plates, an honorable man. (Richard A. Schwartz has a detailed summary.)

By the time *Black Rain* appeared, most mainstream critics would probably have agreed with *Variety*'s reviewer that Scott's films were "about 90% atmosphere and 10% story" ("Mac."). The reviewer's bark, however, turned out to be considerably stronger than his bite, and the review was more favorable than one might have expected. It praises *Black Rain*'s smooth and intelligent blending of American film noir with Japanese yakuza film and then, after due comparison, considers the film "much more effective" than Sydney Pollack's 1975 film *The Yakuza*, from a screenplay by Paul Schrader. This was, however, certainly a minority opinion. Pollack's film gave Robert Mitchum his last great role, his weathered face and deep, disillusioned humanity still memorable after a third of a century, and the price that Mitchum paid, the ritualistic cutting-off of a finger, reprised by Scott in *Black Rain*, is unforgettable. (It should be noted that in *Black Rain*, it is the villainous Sato and not the film's protagonist who is forced to slice off his digit.) Another reviewer, Edmond Grant in *Films in Review*, regarded *Black*

Rain as "an exciting tough cop thriller that rises over its own plot clichés through the sheer force of its dazzling imagery." Grant writes that the "big confrontation scene" near the end of the film bears more than a passing resemblance to the "stirring conclusion" of Sydney Pollack's "cross cultural cop drama." Pollack's film, which Scott had seen, also starred Ken Takakura, the leading Japanese actor in *Black Rain*.

Trouble in Tokyo: Yasaku Matsuda and Michael Douglas in deadly combat in *Black Rain* (1989).

"Mac.," the *Variety* reviewer, praised the film's moral complexity and "the omnipresent menace and descent into an amoral quagmire" summed up in the title. Eventually, Michael Douglas's cop comes to regard the entire world, not just the New York he is familiar with, as "one big gray area." After all, the postwar corruption that spawned the yakuza was begun by the American bombing of Hiroshima. According to the reviewer, the problem is that the film's generic formulations often seem at odds with the moral complexity represented. Indeed so. Although there is no evidence in the film that Douglas's Nick had ever previously considered the legacy of Hiroshima, it is hardly likely that any new knowledge so long after the fact would make him feel any responsibility, moral or otherwise, even if he had. Nick is not an abstract thinker. He regards the world as "one big gray area" to begin with, or at least Douglas's performance is so over-the-top from the beginning that it makes it seem so. Douglas himself regards the film as showing Nick's moral progression, but it is difficult to read that into the film as it exists.

Nearly all of the mainstream reviewers praised the film's mastery of the techniques of filmmaking while lamenting what they generally regarded as its hollow content, especially as compared to Japanese films such as *A Taxing Woman* (1987) and *The Funeral* (1984) which had received wide circulation in the U.S. While the comparison may be true, it is certainly unfair. *A Taxing Woman* is a comedy, albeit a wonderful one, and *The Funeral* more nearly resembles the American independent films of John Cassavetes than a big-budget American crime film.

David Denby, in *New York*, unfairly described Scott as "hollowly talented," compared him with his brother Tony and Adrian Lyne, Brits all, as "British advertising-world hotshots who are destroying what's left of American film aesthetics," and described *Black Rain* as "just another genre film about one cop who won't play by the rules and another who does." Denby, like some other reviewers, saw the film as the Dirty Harry triumph of Reaganism — then used as a catch-all scapegoat for the evils of the world — but now that Reaganism has failed "to do anything but increase urban crime," the rogue cop throwing away the rules and cleaning up the city "is an illusion that has pooped out." That conclusion is, or was, a heavy ideological burden to place upon a Hollywood film.

Jami Bernard, in the *New York Post*, fretted about Kate Capshaw's shifting perm style and the "rain of clichés" toward the end of the film before concluding that *Black Rain* was "a gorgeous-looking but disappointing washout." According to Bernard, the Japanese location shooting looks "really glorious," but can't stop the film from "springing those leaks." Similarly, Mike McGrady, in *Newsday*, called the film "pulp fiction" with enough "knock-your-socks-off visuals" to keep the viewer interested long after the screenplay "has settled into the predictable." Pulp magazines were cheap crime, westerns, science fiction and fantasy magazines of the '30s and '40s printed on thick, cheap pulp paper. They are generally forgotten now except for *Astounding Science Fiction* and *Black Mask*, both of which were pioneers in their fields. When *Black Rain* appeared, the phrase was not yet as common in critical jargon as it became after the appearance of Quentin Tarantino's canonical film, still some five years in the future. Like other critics, McGrady seemed mesmerized by what he interpreted as the contrast between the film's hi-tech filmic sophistication and its stereotyped violence and plot. He calls the script "routine formula swill" at best, as perhaps it is. Richard Corliss, in *Time*, cited the film as the work of "a gifted imagist between inspirations, biding his time without quite wasting ours."

"Black Rain" is a phrase used to describe a terrifying phenomenon occasioned by the two atomic bomb attacks on Japan during the concluding days of World War II. Scott's film is not to be confused with Shohei Imamura's Japanese film of the same name, which appeared on the screens of America the same year — or at least on the dozen or so of them that showed quality foreign films — and which deals directly and realistically with the aftermath of the attack on Hiroshima. Imamura's somber black-and-white film begins with a ten-minute segment showing the bombing of Hiroshima and jumps five years to show the continuing terrible price paid by its survivors. Watching Imamura's film shortly after watching Scott's furnishes an interesting contrast in film-making and its expectations.

More than twenty years after its appearance, what are we to make of *Black Rain*? Douglas, in his commentary, speaks of the film as being a product of its time, the 1980s, a period in which the Japanese ascendency was at its height and seemed at the point of relegating America to second place in world economic power. The downturn of the Japanese economy in the 1990s showed that was not to be, but the political ideology of the film, if we may call it that, has not weakened the film. It has merely made it recede into the historical past.

The question of the film's relevance to film noir is another dead end. Except for a certain emotional coldness, *Black Rain*'s relationship to classic black-and-white film noir, say John Huston's *The Maltese Falcon*, Howard Hawks' *The Big Sleep* or Fritz Lang's *The Big Heat*, was never very close. As Michael Wilmington, among others, pointed out in his interview, the plot is "standard '80s schtick" which resembles *Coogan's Bluff* "juiced up with a lot of Yakuza movie bits."

The plot and characters *are* standard stuff: the loyal, sympathetic buddy who gets killed, the dirty cop who follows his own rules (a character much more common today in series like *The Shield*, but a cliché even then), the bad dialogue, layers of seriousness (talk about "black rain" and evil Americans who are blamed both for corrupting the Japanese then and for furnishing them with a noble example for the present), trite foreshadowing (the early toreador cape business prior to the death of Charlie), and characters out of Central Casting. There are familiarities everywhere and surprises nowhere, although the producers believed (and, according to the commentary, still do) that the death of Charlie is a surprise. And perhaps to the majority of viewers, it is.

The Yakuza boss tells Nick that he remembers the American atomic bombing which occurred when he was a child and the black rain that fell following it. He says that the Americans created the villainous Sato and others like him. Anyone who has seen Masaki Kobayashi's nine-hour-plus film *The Human Condition* (1959) might reasonably think that Japan itself had some share of guilt in what happened. It is not clear how the Americans produced Sato and whether the boss considers himself and other gang leaders like him as being in the same class. Probably not, since his egotism is so great that he would consider himself one of a kind. Nick, of course, promises to help right the American wrong by killing Sato.

The problem is that references to the "black rain" seem to be dragged in from some other, less generic film. The present film is, as various critics pointed out, the type in which a bravura motorcycle race at the beginning signifies an even more bravura motorcycle race at the end, but they would not have expected references to America's use of the atomic bomb. Scott believes that it is possible to allow such commentary in big-budget Hollywood films. Indeed so, but it is a difficult task to make them seem relevant in such a generic film.

Strangely, the film has not aged at all and seems to get better every year. The question is *why*. Whatever ideology it may or not have possessed has gone, and has left only a mesmerizing surface. And what a surface! Many of the sequences have an indelible plastic beauty, including the death of Charlie in the mall, the three-story golf range, the shootout in the wine country and much more. Turn off your lights and your mind and watch on the best television set you have.

According to Box Office Mojo, *Black Rain* took in $46,212,055 domestically and an astonishing $88,000,000 overseas for a total of $134,212,055. Although the production budget is not given, the return was clearly sufficient to keep all the producers happy.

9

Thelma & Louise (1991):
On the Road: One Insult Too Far

Version. As of this writing, the only canonical text of *Thelma & Louise* is the 2.35:1 aspect ratio, 129-minute release version available with Scott's commentary on Blu-ray. It is not anticipated that any new version will contain significant changes or additions.

Thelma & Louise began as a screenplay by Callie Khouri which caught the eye of Scott in mid-1990, almost a year after the completion of *Black Rain* (Raw, 295). According to Khouri, Scott liked the screenplay, and the only notable alterations made to it were done to combine a few scenes in order to cut down the 136- page script to a reasonable length (Raw, 187). Principal photography was completed in a brisk two and a half months (June 11 to August 31) entirely on fifty-four locations in and around Los Angeles and two National Parks in Utah (Raw, 295–96).

Whatever may or may not be wrong with *Thelma & Louse*, it is certainly not the two leads. Susan Sarandon had done distinguished work in both film and television. She first appeared in the working-class drama *Joe* (1970) and then, more notably, in one of Billy Wilder's last films, *The Front Page* (1974), in the midnight cult classic *The Rocky Horror Picture Show* (1975), and in the moving *Dead Man Walking* (1995). She also played the lead, opposite French icon Catherine Deneuve, in Tony Scott's vampire film *The Hunger* (1983). Many critics believe that her best performance was as the amorous seasonal fan opposite Kevin Costner in Ron Shelton's baseball romance *Bull Durham* (1988), arguably the greatest American sports film.

Although hardly as popular as her co-star at the time *Thelma & Louise* appeared, Geena Davis was particularly known for her work in comedy, including the television sitcom *Buffalo Bill* and Tim Burton's first feature film, *Beetle Juice* (1988). She had also worked the dark side in David Cronenberg's *The Fly* (1988). Unfortunately, her career did not receive a boost from her appearance in Scott's film. Although she continues to work, perhaps most notably in the TV series *Commander in Chief*, she has not to date gotten the roles that one might have expected after her performance in *Thelma & Louise*.

Of the supporting players, Harvey Keitel had played one of the leading roles in Scott's *The Duellists* some fifteen years earlier. Although he had declined into generally unsympathetic supporting roles, *Thelma & Louise* gave him a chance to play an unusually sympathetic character. Michael Madsen, brother of the attractive and talented Virginia Madsen, has done his best work for Quentin Tarantino in *Reservoir Dogs* (1992) and the two parts of *Kill Bill* (2003 and 2004). His characters are usually grumpy and prone to outbreaks of violence. The person whose career was helped the most by *Thelma & Louise* was Brad Pitt, whose performance put him on the fast track to stardom, a position he reached a year later as the magnetic, tragic lead of Robert Redford's superb and underrated *A River Runs Through It*.

After the credits appear over a western landscape, the film opens in a busy restaurant with a waitress calling her friend about a proposed trip to find something new. The journey begins when the two friends, Louise (Susan Sarandon), a bored waitress with a troublesome lover, and her buddy Thelma (Geena Davis), a housewife with a husband named Daryl (variously described by critics as "preening," "cheating" and "a blockhead"), decide to take off on a vacation by themselves, apparently to fish, but actually to "scratch" some unspecified itch.

The women make an impetuous stop at a roadside country bar where Thelma gets drunk. When a local yokel attempts to rape her in the parking lot, Louise pulls her gun and urges the lad to leave. He is apparently ready to give up but, here as later in every crisis situation, he goes "one insult too far" and is dispatched to his reward, or whatever. "You watch your mouth, buddy," she instructs the dead body. Instead of waiting for the authorities and pleading justification, the two women take off in their convertible and spend the remainder of the movie running across the desert from the law.

A few hours after the shooting, Thelma has a motel room tryst with a cute rascal (Pitt) who tells her that he is a convenience store robber and demonstrates how he plies his trade. Quite unbelievably, she leaves what one writer calls this "moral mutant" alone in the motel room to steal Louise's getaway money.

Instead of turning themselves in to a sympathetic detective who wants to help them, they continue on the run. Thelma robs a convenience store. They punish "a foul-mouthed pervert" by spectacularly blowing up his gasoline-filled semi and lock a handsome young highway patrolman who has pulled them over into the trunk of his patrol car, where he surely would have perished quickly in the desert heat. In the end, the deadly feminine duo pull a Butch Cassidy and the Sundance Kid and send the T-bird convertible and themselves off into what looks like the Grand Canyon.

When it opened, *Thelma & Louise* was more widely reviewed than any earlier, or for that matter later, Ridley Scott film. It struck a nerve in the American psyche which, some twenty years later, seems difficult to understand and, some would claim, out of proportion to the film's merits. Except for the occasional grouch, the critics applauded the film's technique, but depending upon their political orientation either deplored or applauded what they perceived to be its political content. Readers going through the

Thelma and Louise on the road in John Ford Country.

criticism today may sometime wonder if they are looking at the same film the early critics and viewers saw.

The *Variety* reviewer called *Thelma & Louise* "a thumpingly adventurous road pic about two regular gals who shoot down a would-be rapist and wind up on the lam in their '66 T-Bird." According to the reviewer, even those few viewers who don't cotton to the film's "fed-up feminist outcry" will like its "comedy, momentum and dazzling visuals." Ultimately, the film is not about women versus men, but about freedom, and in that sense, "it's a classic."

Janet Maslin, in the *New York Times*, wrote that the film has "the thrilling, life-affirming energy for which the best road movies are remembered." The difference is that these "daring anti-heroes" are "beautiful, interesting women." Beautiful they certainly are; interesting may be another story. According to Maslin, Scott, despite his English roots, shows a hitherto untapped talent for American imagery and exuberant comedy. And more in the same vein.

Apparently, Maslin's outburst of praise agitated readers enough to evoke a response a month later entitled defiantly, "Lay off *Thelma & Louise*." Attackers of the film, according to Maslin, fall into various groups: toxic feminists who do not believe that the film deals with real problems (AIDS, using condoms, serial killers); critics concerned with violence in films, negative images of women in films, occasioned by sexist remarks by Thelma and Louise, and so on. Maslin argues that *Easy Rider* and *Bonnie and Clyde* were much worse in nearly every respect. While this may well be true, it is also beside the point. She does not mention a minority group who simply thought that *Thelma & Louise* was not a good movie.

David Sterritt, in the *Christian Science Monitor,* gave what is probably the best and fairest assessment of Scott's intention: "[The film is] aimed straight at the mass-market box office but also succeeds as a statement on feminist issues." Two unhappy women, Thelma, "a homemaker with a block-headed husband," and Louise, a diner waitress, light out for a few days to find something new. Sterritt's presumed objectivity quickly turns rancid when he writes that Scott's weakness for "flashy, shallow showmanship" turns what might have been "a slam-bang feminist manifesto" into "just another action picture with too many cheap thrills." Sterritt apparently believes that the women's shabby behavior cheapens the purity of its theme and complains that "a whole subplot" is developed for the sole purpose of blowing up a truck. Even if this is true, Sterritt's additional complaint that Scott has dumbed down the "densely textured cinematic style" of *Blade Runner* and *Black Rain*, is certainly unfair. Whatever feminist statement *Thelma & Louise* has, it is generically a western or a road movie, both of which require the open places of the American landscape which is, even today, relatively unspoiled, at least in comparison to the polluted spaces of the two films cited.

Manohla Dargis cites Jack Kerouac's 1957 novel *On the Road*, which was finally made into a movie in 2011, as a precursor of a distinguished line running from Nicolas Ray's *They Live by Night* and Robert Altman's *Thieves Like Us* to *Bonnie and Clyde* to *Badlands*, and beyond. This is quite a feat considering that Ray's classic film was made before *On the Road* was published. These films — and they are four of the greatest — removed romance from the "domestic sphere" to include "frenzied violence" provoked from sometimes obscure reasons. Scott's film explicitly separates itself from "the generic cliffhanger" by showing "the distinctive means by which the road to the self is travelled." Their crime is "self-defense" and their identities are forced upon them by their gender (86). The outer reaches of the subgenre, if that is what it is, includes *Wild at Heart*, *Gun Crazy*, and *Something Wild*. The appropriate place for the conclusion is Monument Valley and the appropriate conclusion illustrated in the film shows "women in nature … the liberated body in the absence of men."

Nothing in Scott's film is new; its tropes had been wandering around in the sub-basement of sexploitation films for decades. In Doris Wishman's *Bad Girls Go to Hell* (1965), a year before the term "women's liberation" appeared in Juliet Mitchell's article "The Longest Revolution" in the *New Left Review,* a young woman runs away to — where else? New York City — and begins working in the sexploitation industry after "accidentally killing her husband because he was trying to rape her" (McKendry, 59). In Wishman's later films, the betrayed women begin to fight back and emerge victorious in violent films described by one critic as "seedy grindhouse films with a weird 'feminist' feel" (cited, 59). In brief, killing bad men was not new, at least on the grindhouse circuit.

In a sense, all Scott films are generic, but few of them, and none of the best, fit into a convenient pigeonhole. *Thelma & Louise* is no exception. While it is almost always interpreted as at least in some sense a feminist film, any critical analysis, faced with the film's complexity, almost immediately shows the difficulty of a single interpretation. Complicated the film is, subtle it is not. The writer for girlswithguns.org correctly identifies the turning point as the scene in which Thelma is attacked by a rapist. When Louise sees what is happening, she puts a gun to the attacker's head, the man freezes, and Thelma pulls away. But when the man utters an obscenity, Thelma guns him down.

Is the film an empowering feminist statement? That, of course, depends upon your perspective. According to *girlswithguns*, Callie Khouri made a conscious decision for the "victim" to die when he is no longer a threat. The viewer is left with only two options: "lose empathy for a character capable of such a crime" or "somehow accept that it's okay to shoot someone for defense." "Rumblings of a previous incident" is not a defense, we are told, and would hardly win an Oscar for

Brad Pitt: blow-dried trouble in *Thelma & Louise* (1991).

Best Original Script and be described as "empowering" if the sexes were reversed. The writer concludes that the film is like having Andrea Dworkin (a well-known aggressive feminist of the period) "yelling in your face for two hours." The film's moral is that, if women empower themselves, death inevitably results. Or at least it will unless men shape up a bit.

Nearly all of the criticism of *Thelma & Louise* is concerned with the interplay between feminism and genre evoked by the movie. The difficulty of interpretation was clearly shown by the "Round Table" of written responses published by *Film Quarterly*. Harvey Greenberg began by noting, not very helpfully, that Scott's revisionism of genre dates back to what he calls the "ironic pacifism" of the "derring-do" of *The Duellists*. After naming the usual suspects (westerns, road movies, and buddy movies), he notes the "exceptionally polarized debate" aroused by the film. Extremes include a lesbian subtext, a profoundly feminist manifesto about women as "dangerous phallic caricatures of the very macho violence they're supposed to be protesting," and "a demeaning negation of feminine friendship" opposing patriarchal authority, and so on. Greenberg notes that large-scale popular entertainment often contains "both reactionary and progressive elements, more or less ajar."

The point is well made. One of the main differences between good and bad art is that good art always gives the bad guys a chance to explain themselves. Dostoevsky and Conrad were arch-conservatives, but their deep understanding of the great negative forces of man and society allowed them to treat their villains with absolute fairness. Little is known with certainty about Shakespeare's politics, but he was a public writer in a dark time who did not hesitate to tell his audience what the bad guys thought. Othello and Richard III are notable examples, among any number of others.

No matter what our final judgment on *Thelma & Louise*, it is important to remember that the film was beating against the masculine current, so to speak. Susan Jeffords writes that 1991 was "the year of the transformed U.S. man." There is, she writes, "hardly a mainstream Hollywood film" with a leading male figure who does not show that the macho male figure of the 1980s has been replaced by "the more sensitive, loving, nurturing, protective family" man (197). Jeffords may be right in arguing that the mad excesses of the earlier period had been replaced, but that does not necessarily mean that the women had decided to allow them in the door. Perhaps Harrison Ford and the new group of more sensitive men did not represent the average American male. At some level, the women in Scott's film may be echoing Billy's answer to Pat Garrett's comment about changing times in Sam Peckinpah's *Pat Garrett and Billy the Kid*: "Times, maybe, not me." In other words, *Thelma & Louise* may be saying that the Neanderthals are still out there and haven't changed at all, but if we shoot a few of them, they may. At least, we'll get rid of some of the really bad ones.

Still, it can be argued that Scott did not know enough about American society to make the great film that *Thelma & Louise* might have been. What would his take on Thelma and Louise have been if his two rebels had been English? While not doubting Scott's impeccable liberal credentials, Greenberg notes the director's matrix of narrative and visual references and the complications of what the script does and does not include, but concludes that Scott lacks the "subversive boldness, at its best," of Robert Altman or Blake Edwards.

This is fair. If we compare a viewer's response to the conclusion of *Thelma & Louise* with that of the viewer of Altman's *Nashville*, we can see where Scott's film comes up short. Certainly, the feminist subtext in Joan Tewkesbury's brilliant *Nashville* script has a multilayered complexity absent from Scott's film. Altman's film presents an empowered woman, Lady Pearl; a talented, exploited and ruined one, Barbara Jean; and a free one, or at least one who thinks that she is free, L.A. Joan — not to mention several others of similar complexity. All are presented in Altman's film as part of the fabric of American society. By omitting the context of Thelma and Louise's problems, Scott's film offers what can only be called special pleading. It can be argued that, given the same script, Altman's knowledge of the details of that society, present in every frame of *Nashville*, would have made their revolt plausible. The assassin in *Nashville*, omnipresent throughout, but nowhere explained, is made plausible by the richness of the context of the society depicted in the film. And Altman's *Three Women* may be an even better example. Ultimately, *Thelma & Louise*, like Michelangelo Antonioni's *Zabriskie Point* (1970), lacks an American sensibility. Howard Hawks, when asked what went wrong with his ambitious period film *Land of the Pharaohs*, is said to have replied that he didn't know how a pharaoh talked. Apparently, neither Scott nor Callie Khouri knows either.

Such comparisons are, of course, unfair. All artists are allowed what Henry James fancifully called their donnée, that is, their choice of subject matter. The real question is what they make of it. What Scott made of his is a thought-provoking film which, while very much a product of its time, continues to provoke controversy.

Carol J. Clover makes the point that many men liked the film. Even if this subjective evaluation is true, it makes little difference in how we should evaluate the film. Albert Johnson calls the film "a vivid portrait of contemporary America" and of contemporary American women's attempt "to run away from the boredom and sexual entrapment to which they are condemned." These two standard approaches are perhaps less interesting than Peter N. Chumo II's interpretation of the film as screwball comedy, which has the advantage of not hopelessly dating the film as a regressive product of the early 1990s. According to this interpretation, "liberation and growth through role-playing," an essential aspect of screwball comedy, gives the viewer an entry into the film. The problem, of course, as Chumo admits, is that that Thelma and Louise never achieve the clarity of vision required by the genre, unless, of course, the brief but passionate kiss and the clasping of hands before hurtling off into what the viewer interprets as the Grand Canyon may represent that vision ("Many Faces").

The idea of *Thelma & Louise* as film noir is pretty much a non-starter. There are no dark city streets, no femme fatale, no sinister crime bosses, no stool pigeons, and no bank robberies. Among Scott's films, only *Someone to Watch Over Me* fully qualifies, although *Black Rain* has some noir characteristics.

As might be expected from our best interpreter of the relationship between violence and pornography, Linda Williams offers genuine insight into the film in her comparison of *Thelma & Louise* to John Ford's masterpiece *The Searchers*. Williams argues that Scott's film shows in a way that so-called "serious films" about rape could never show how "victims of sexual crimes are unaccountably placed in the position of the guilty ones, positioned as fair game for further attack" ("Many Faces," 554).

Unlike *The Searchers'* Ethan Edwards, who was not molested or victimized — the two women set out to revenge themselves. The victims in *The Searchers* are innocent, but in his desire for revenge, Edwards comes to believe that Debbie has been so polluted by her relationship with Scar that she must be killed. Although Thelma and Louise show, at the very least, a substantial lack of good sense, the thrill of the film is presumed to come from watching the victims revenge themselves.

In *Film Quarterly*'s "Many Faces," Marsha Kinder compares *Thelma & Louise* to Alain Tanner's *Messidor* (1979). The similarities she cites are certainly striking, but it is unclear whether either Scott or screenwriter Khouri had seen the Swiss film. According to Kinder, in *Messidor*, the revolt is against the "respectable bourgeois institutions" ("Many Faces," 559). In Scott's film, it is the usual suspects. It may be that this is a difference between American and Swiss society, or it may simply be that the time had come for the usual parade of suspects, who vary in their degree of guilt, but are caught in the sexual politics of the period. In both films, rape is the triggering event.

While all narratives are characterized as much by what they leave our as by what they put in, classical Hollywood narratives were careful to explain all questions of motivation. The change seems to have occurred about the time of Arthur Penn's *Bonnie and Clyde* (1967) when Clyde is asked what he would change about his life if he had it to live over again, and he answers that he would not rob banks out of state. Earlier, this would have been his cue to talk about his unfortunate youth, his being led astray by "base company," or by some other ill. We may compare Clyde's pronouncement with what Brian Henderson calls Thelma's *ex post facto* analysis of the killing of Harlan, wishing only that she had done it herself, "My life would have been ruined much worse than it is now" ("Many Faces," 553). As self-analysis, this pronouncement is low on the Richter scale. Thelma and Louise have little insight into their own lives, and the film furnishes so little information about their past that the viewer is in much the same condition.

Henderson points out that the film's narrative strategies apply to the withholding of information about motivation, narrative time, police work and what is going on. The question then becomes: What, if anything, *is* going on? The film lacks the logic, real or ersatz, of a police procedural, and any real sense of motivated narration. The result is what Henderson calls the "divided temporality" of the two fugitives. To some extent at least, the withholding of information many directors would consider vital to their story is typical of Scott.

Of course, the punishment of a rapist by his victim is hardly new. Jane Wyman won an Academy Award for her magnificent performance as a deaf-mute rape victim in *Johnny Belinda* (1948). In that case, the woman who was raped was protecting her baby. Motivation was clear and unequivocal. Perhaps the answer in *Thelma & Louise* is that the motivation sometimes comes down to an existential choice, a mysterious tipping point that happens to be triggered by a bad boyfriend, a clod of a husband, an insult too far. The film's actual fault might not be too little motivation, but too much. The good old boys who worked for John Ford and Sam Peckinpah would understand that. When Pike Bishop in *The Wild Bunch* says, "Let's go," Lyle Gorch's response is a statement of an existential creed and not a question: "Why the hell not?"

Years after the release of *Thelma & Louise*, feminist critics defended the status of the film as a feminist statement. Sharon Willis noted that what she calls "a range of critics" accused it of "male bashing" and of "degrading men" and cited in support a number of quotes. These included describing the men as "pathetic stereotypes of testosterone crazed behavior," and calling the film "basically a recruiting film for the NRA [National Rifle Association]" and "a fascist version of feminism" (Willis, 120).

According to Willis, such critics overestimate the importance of "the film's few minutes of violence" and conclude that the film "should be read as a political tract."

The point is well taken, at least as far as the violence is concerned, since the violence against women by Freddy Krueger and his associates is both much more graphic and much more sustained than anything in *Thelma & Louise*.

Not all feminists liked the film or its message. Margaret Carlson thought that its women had become wildly self-destructive, "free to drive off the ends of the earth." Others complained that the filmmakers thought that feminist liberation, even if hurtling "into destructive excess," is "somehow glorious, which is surely the way benighted moviegoers are encouraged to view it" (cited Willis, 131). There is, of course, no way to predict how idiots will read any book or interpret any film. While the ending of Sam Peckinpah's *The Wild Bunch* certainly represents "destructive excess," it is unlikely that anyone has ever interpreted the ending of *Butch Cassidy and the Sundance Kid* as another example. And even if they had, why shouldn't women have as much right to such a glorious symbolic act, no matter how self-destructive, as men?

Willis rightly attacks the view that what she calls "anxious interpretation of spectator identification" by women "will translate directly into aggressive attitudes and behavior toward men in ordinary life." She does, however, cite several examples of women reacting to crude male behavior in symbolic fashion which may have been patterned after the film. According to Willis, the film "displaces its energy from narrative justification and explanation" to what she calls "less comfortable seductions—those of the road, the landscape, the traveling, the speed of motion, and those of the image" (123). This is fair. The imagery of films and of filmmaking used by Scott dominates the film. The visual references to the road film and the western are much closer to the film's center than images of violence against women or by them.

David Thomson in *Have You Seen...?* is clearly unfair when he writes that "two comely cows take it into their heads" that they are being wronged and set out, "bronzed arms interlocked on the bench seat," and seek revenge. To begin with, the 1966 T-Bird did not have a bench seat, although one could be added later, and neither Thelma nor Louise is bronzed. Toward the end of the film, their faces are shown as badly sunburned. Thomson decides that the film is "a very good-looking movie, catnip to the liberal blue states," but entertaining enough for the red ones as well. He concludes, generously enough, that the picture is "a real sleeper, making far more money than anyone had hoped for. And changing some minds." About what, he does not say.

Scott said rather strangely in the pressbook that "the emphasis — the driving force if you will — is almost totally on character rather than where a spaceship comes from ... Hopefully, after seeing the film, both male and female audience members will recognize something about themselves. If they like what they see, they'll keep it. If not, maybe they'll change it" (cited Raw, 295).

As Cathy Griggers points out, *Thelma & Louise* follows a number of "nightmare female" films which show terrifying women no man of even reasonable intelligence would dare to get involved with. Examples include *Black Widow* (1987), *Fatal Attraction*, a huge box-office hit (1987), and *The Grifters* (1990). In *Body Heat* (1981), arguably the best film of the group, Kathleen Turner tells William Hurt that he is "not very smart," a characteristic which she says she "likes" in a man. Unlike Thelma and Louise, however, none of these sluts has any difficulty achieving orgasm. In the film, "Aren't we going in the wrong direction?" is either a question or a statement. The answer,

Buddies: Louise (Susan Sarandon) and Thelma (Geena Davis).

in the case of the two women, is that you get "laid properly" and "at least … have some fun."

The reviewers generally ignored the men in the film, but they liked Brad Pitt, and *Variety* particularly praised his dancing in the rain scene. Unfortunately, Pitt's cowboy excepted, the men in the film are not particularly convincing. Peckinpah's cowboys and truckers are a crude enough lot and many of them are perfectly capable of any of the violence against women depicted in *Thelma & Louise*, but Scott's film lacks the dense particularity that would have made the violence convincing. A similar problem occurred in Englishman John Boorman's excellent 1972 film version of James Dickey's quintessentially American novel *Deliverance*. The hillbilly vulgarities are not quite properly enunciated and their rhythms are wrong.

Like the best movies, *Thelma & Louise* has been absorbed into popular culture. After Kathryn Bigelow's "two-fisted win" for Best Film and Best Director for her film *The Hurt Locker* in the 2009 Academy Award competition, Manohla Dargis defended Bigelow's choice to make "masculine films" in the tradition of Peckinpah and earlier directors of action films and cited *Thelma & Louise* as an honorable precursor. Dargis noted that, although the film was popular and cited the cover of *Time* magazine and T-shirts ("Thelma and Louise Live Forever"), it was attacked on ideological grounds. In *U.S. News and World Report,* "a male writer" accused the film of "an explicit fascist theme, wedded to the bleakest form of feminism." The reviewers seemed more interested in "policing women's behavior," including their heavy drinking and fast driving, than in their criminal actions. Dargis' conclusion was that Thelma and Louise did not have to tote around their copy of Simone de Beauvoir's *The Second Sex* to prove their "feminist credentials": the popularity of the film had already done that for them (Dargis, 17). As indeed it had.

Needless to say, not all women were happy with the film. Anecdotal evidence shows that highly educated women in their twenties and thirties were the devotees. The film was not a favorite with conservative women. Essayist and novelist Richard Stern writes that *Thelma & Louise* was the last film his dying sister went to see before her death. She did not like it. "It was," he writes, "a new territory, and Ruth lived in the old territory." Stern's oblique reference to Mark Twain's *Huckleberry Finn* is appropriate. Ruth was not a new American setting out, like Huckleberry Finn for the territory: She did not want to take revenge for the insults of a lifetime and did not "want to follow the almost satiric intrepidity, boldness, and, finally, suicidal drive of the two women" (Stern, 32). Whose idea was it to see *Thelma & Louise* instead of some other film? Was it Ruth's? She probably would not have liked the film if she had been in perfect health. Still, without knowing more about his sister than Stern's not necessarily totally objective account tells us, it is impossible to make any definitive judgments.

Two examples will show how deeply *Thelma & Louise* has penetrated into popular culture. On the excellent cable series *Friday Night Lights*, Becky, a high school girl, tells Tim Riggins when he arrives that she is about to watch *Thelma & Louise*. "What else you got?" he asks.

On March 5, 2010, President Obama said about health care, that this is not a "Harry and Louise" moment, this is a "Thelma and Louise" moment and we are headed off the cliff. Harry and Louise were the starring characters in a then-famous series of advertisements in the mid 1990s supporting health care reform. Although many Americans will surely have forgotten Harry and Louise, they are unlikely to forget Thelma and Louise, at least in the foreseeable future.

Thelma & Louise showed remarkable domestic box-office strength from the beginning. It was released on May 24, 1991, at the beginning of the summer season, a release date usually favored for films that are not regarded as contenders for Academy Awards, yet *Thelma & Louise* was nominated for six Academy Awards. (Only Callie Khouri won.) Both Davis and Sarandon were rewarded with Oscar nominations for Best Actress in a Leading Role, but since they were in competition with each other, neither won. Jodie Foster won for another strong feminist portrayal in *The Silence of the Lambs*. Perhaps the Academy members regarded Foster's Clarice Starling as a more suitable feminine role model than either Thelma or Louise. Other nominees included Adrian Biddle (Best Photography), Thom Noble (Best Film Editing) and Scott (Best Direction).

According to Box Office Mojo, *Thelma & Louise* had a production budget of approximately $16,500,000 and raked in $45,360,915 domestically. Although the foreign take is not given and is, considering the subject matter, unlikely to have been as robust as the domestic, the film was clearly a financial success and with ancillary rights must have kept everyone with money invested in it in a good mood.

10

1492: Conquest of Paradise (1992): I Think We Have Returned to Eden

Version To date, *1492* has been released in only one version, the 2.35:1, 155-minute theatrical release. Scott does not abandon his films, and a pre-release cut running more than three hours may eventually appear. The film was rated PG-13 by the MPAA.

Christopher Columbus has never been a popular subject for film; the only significant feature film before 1992 was the earnest *Christopher Columbus* (1949), starring Fredric March in the title role and his wife Florence Eldridge as Queen Isabella. But in 1992 two large-scale productions about the alleged discoverer of America appeared almost simultaneously. The occasion, of course, was the event's 500th anniversary. The first to appear was *Christopher Columbus: The Discovery*, directed by John Glen, best known for his direction of James Bond films, and with an overweight Marlon Brando as Torquemada upstaging Georges Corraface in the title role. The film did nothing to enhance the reputation of either actor. Brando, did not either believe or care that it would, and Corraface returned to the virtual obscurity from which he had briefly emerged.

The pre-production of *1492* was troubled from the beginning. Not only was the film expensive and its subject matter problematic, but haste was essential because of the competition. And while Scott was apparently enthusiastic about Gérard Depardieu, his overweight French star with a heavy French accent, the choice probably doomed the project from the beginning. Shooting began December 2, 1991, and continued for about eighty days. Exteriors were shot in Spain, the Dominican Republic and Costa Rica, the primary location for the New World sequences (Raw, 118).

As might be expected, *1492* is organized around the voyages of the famous sailor. Part One depicts Columbus's difficulties getting finances to support his theory, the dangers of the voyage, the discovery of the New World, the search for gold and the return. Part Two shows the raised expectations, the return to the New World, the establishment of a gold mine, the conflict with the natives and the eventual mutiny among the explorers themselves. After a hurricane destroys the settlement, Columbus is replaced as leader. Part Three shows Columbus's imprisonment, his ultimate return to the New World and his admission of failure amid the competing claims of Amerigo Vespucci. Of course, neither Columbus himself nor the viewers of the film are expected to believe the great explorer a failure.

1492 certainly received more unfavorable reviews than any other Scott film, with the possible exception of *Legend*. Roger Ebert, always a sympathetic viewer of Scott's films, saw this version of the character of Christopher Columbus as "more complex and humane" than his portrayal in previous films. Could he have seen the 1949 film? Scott's Columbus treated "Indians the same as Spanish noblemen" and seems content with the idea that nature, not the Catholic God, is their deity. Ebert's opinion of Scott's film was perhaps heightened by his remembrance of his recent viewing of Glen's film. Ebert complains that, of the three parts of the first voyage (the preparation for the voyage, the voyage, and the aftermath), the second is skimped. Of course, sea voyages are notoriously difficult to dramatize, particularly when the audience knows the outcome, and the film ran so long that cutting was considered necessary.

Ebert and other critics found it difficult to believe that Columbus was as enlightened as he is portrayed as being in the film. Ebert also believed that the film is "particularly handicapped" by the score by Vangelis, probably because the score's modern sound is out of keeping with the story. While this may well be true, the score was, ironically, much more popular than the film.

Historical errors are, of course, inevitable in such a large-scale film set in the distant past. Ebert cites the "touching moment" when Columbus hears Amerigo Vespucci described as "discoverer of the mainland," yet such distinctions could not have been made at the time and America was not named for Vespucci until after Columbus's death. Anyway, it is unclear why the film should be concerned with the issue.

Other reviews ranged from severe to tolerant, but the film seems to have had no real champions. Todd McCarthy, in *Variety*, was much less forgiving than Ebert and argued that not even Scott's famed visuals could turn *1492* from the lumbering, complex historical fresco it is to the "complex, ambiguous character study" the director apparently intended. Like other reviewers, McCarthy complained of its inability to hold the viewers' interest during the long running time. Unfortunately, Scott's "dazzling moralistic style" flattens out the unwieldy story, which takes place over many years, into what McCarthy calls the one-dimensional quality of "a medieval painting." McCarthy concludes rather obviously that the failure of the two large-scale films makes it unlikely that anyone else will tackle the story of Columbus any time soon.

David Denby, in *New York* magazine, had similar problems with the film, and believed that Scott "attempted desperately to fight off banality" by brewing up "a storm of imagery." Denby doesn't much like anything about the movie and muses over whether the film's gigantic paring away of the virtues of Columbus's character was inevitable.

Maria Garcia, in *Films in Review*, wrote that Scott's heroes are "too familiar and their struggles are so primeval that we recognize them only on a purely unconscious level." They chastise us for holding on "to ideas and beliefs that long ago proved self-destructive." While Garcia recognizes the difficulties faced by the makers of a film about Columbus, she believes that Scott's directorial style fails "to actualize the internal struggles" of its hero. Since we all know the outcome of the struggle, the tension must comes from within the character, and the film fails in this. It portrays Columbus as a man who is sensitive to "the plight of the Indians" and perceives in his discovery a new beginning for mankind. Since this is not supported by the script, the film ends up as "a history lesson."

According to Garcia, the film is "saved" by Scott's command of actors and of the medium. Unfortunately, Scott's heroes are ambiguous, his stories psychological, and his philosophy existential. In short, Scott "fails to connect the actual journey to the hero's internal quest." Although Garcia does not tell us how this might have been accomplished, she concludes generously that "even Scott's unsuccessful films" offer more interesting cinematic fare than most of the traditional fare "which cannot be remembered an hour after being seen."

Jami Bernard (*The New York Post*), an admirer of Scott, did not take the film seriously. Like other reviewers, she frets about its lack of definition of the character of Columbus. John Anderson, in *Newsday*, wrote that seeing the film "felt like seven weeks aboard the *Santa Maria*." Anderson continues by suggesting that we forget earlier discoverers who "probably got there first," and blame Columbus since "he is the one who brought along all those bad-natured Christians" and became "the whipping boy of western civ." This jovial reading has the advantage of absolving Scott of any responsibility for his film. Peter Aspden attempted to make the best of what he obviously considered a bad situation by comparing Columbus to "the obsessive swordsmen of *The Duellists*, the space-travelled replicants of *Blade Runner*" and "the fugitives of *Thelma & Louise*." However, except for the idea of the quest, either heroic or quixotic, the adventurers have little in common.

Kenneth Turan writes that the story was old hat and that the film was "dramatically inert," but that the recreations of the Old World and the New were ravishing. He writes that Scott's eye is "unmatched among directors of his generation," but that he is at the mercy of his writers. In spite of the years of research allegedly done by French journalist Roselyne Bosch, the film "sounds suspiciously" as if it were written after spending too much time watching old movies. Turan also complains about the inadequacies of Depardieu's diction and the variety of acting styles. He also does not like the script's notion of Columbus "as an egalitarian back-to-the-earth type" who wants "nothing but the best for the locals" while extracting "every last ounce of gold from them."

1492: Conquest of Paradise gave some reviewers opportunities to exercise their wit on an object of scorn. Jonathan Romney, in the *New Statesman*, cleverly said that Columbus was "second only to Woody [Allen] as American anti-hero of the year." The jibe was a reference to Allen's notorious relationship with Soon-Yi-Previn, then in the tabloids. Jack Kroll, of *Newsweek*, seems to represent the majority view in his conclusion that the $50,000,000 film "must be one of the least entertaining epics ever made."

In an essay in *Past Imperfect*, Carla Rahn Phillips and William D. Phillips, Jr., analyze the historicity of the two competing Columbus films. They note that Queen Isabella's off-the-shoulder gown worn in the dead of winter makes it difficult to accept her "as the pious warrior queen whom Columbus knew" and note that, in terms of geographical knowledge, the Spanish commission and the Portuguese possessed "the best geographical knowledge of the day" and that this knowledge "cast justifiable doubt upon Columbus's theories" (64). The Phillipses believe that the least accurate portrayal in the film is that of Martin Alonso Pinzon (Tcheky Karyo), "the case-hardened mariner who made Columbus's first voyage possible." However, the fact that the character fits neatly into a Hollywood stereotype is not in itself enough to discredit it. The essay concludes by stating that Fredric March's portrayal in the 1949 film is "the most believable film characterization to date of the historical Columbus — brilliant, pious, cranky, self-assured, single-minded, irascible, rigid, and thoroughly irritating" (65). Just so — but March was a better actor than Corraface or Depardieu and had a much less complicated script.

Patrick Sale, in *The Conquest of Paradise: Christopher Columbus and the Columbian Legacy* (1990), wrote that every age gets "the heroes it needs" and that, at least until the nineteenth century, Columbus survived "as a symbol more than a real person in history" and came in the mind of Europe to personify the Explorer, the Discoverer and the Hero, "three parts of the same being, but not necessarily the same thing at all" (235). Of course, the function of art is not to reconcile these three aspects, but to make them understandable. In film, this may be done in two ways: by the actors and by the screenplay.

Peter Wollen wrote that Scott attempts to "mellow the biographical record" by presenting Columbus "as something of an egalitarian" who appreciates the Indian ways but is undone by "reactionary churchmen and vicious hidalgos," whose violence "wrecks the idyll" and turns it into "a New World catastrophe." In an interesting comparison, Wollen cites Darryl F. Zanuck's authoritarian view of history in films as whatever he wanted it to be and compares it with Scott's more nuanced view (42). Wollen might just as well have cited Buffalo Bill's view in Robert Altman's *Buffalo Bill and the Indians, Or Sitting Bull's History Lesson*. But at least Buffalo Bill is funny and, as portrayed by Paul Newman, much more charismatic.

None of Scott's films is without interest; his mind is too far-ranging and comprehensive for that. All of them are, in one sense or another, meditations on history and/or genre. And if *1492* is a failure, it is an interesting and instructive one. It is easy enough to list its main shortcomings: Depardieu's English is grossly defective and he is not up to the task of portraying so complex and thoughtful a man as Columbus. The hypermasculinity of his earlier films has disappeared into an overweight body, and he has no interior life. The early Depardieu, whom Ginette Vincendeau characterized as representing an "aggressive French machismo" mitigated by a feminine side, had clearly morphed into a rotund hulk by the time he made *1492* (cf. Raw, 92). Even among the actors of the film, Armand Assante would have been a better choice, but he was not perceived as capable of carrying so large an international film. It would be interesting to know when Scott himself realized the impossibility of his choice.

And Sigourney Weaver, whose portrayal of the queen was generally reviled, could find no emotional or intellectual handle on her underwritten role and has complained of Scott's inability to assist her. Certainly, the script does not help. After the queen asks Columbus a question, he replies thoughtfully and then asks her how old she is. This is no more believable than the gown she is wearing. Such impertinence by a commoner to one of God's anointed would certainly have resulted in a thrashing or a stay in prison at the very least.

Scott has elsewhere shown a remarkable facility for pulling together disparate material, but does not manage it here. Too much is going on in too many places with too many divergent points of view and only Columbus to hold them together. Terrence Malick managed the Old World-New World conflict in *The New Land* (2005) by concentrating on the story of the celebrated liar and explorer John Smith and the beautiful Indian maiden Pocahontas. The story of the New World's first love story, part myth and part fact, moves easily between the Old World and the New and is culturally empowered (that is, it is not presented as entirely true). Malick's use of shifting points of view easily allows the objective (actually put on the screen) and sympathetic (felt by the viewers) presentation of different ideologies and perspectives which Scott, it is almost universally believed, conspicuously failed to do.

The historical importance of Columbus is beyond dispute, but the often contradictory reasons for that importance would be nearly impossible to deal with in a fictional film and are largely absent from *Conquest of Paradise*. Those reasons, as listed in the prologue to Patrick Sale's *The Conquest of Paradise*, could not have been known by the Admiral of the Ocean Sea himself and are hardly an unmixed blessing today (4–6). He would have approved of the expansion of the European subcontinent beyond its borders in an unprecedented manner, of the subjugation of the native people and of the riches it brought to Europe.

While those attitudes are hardly cherished today, they need not necessarily detract from the heroic nature of Columbus's enterprises. John Ford's silent epic *The Iron Horse*, about the building of the transcontinental railroad, confronted a similar problem much more effectively, but has recently been condemned on political and ethical grounds. And Ford did not even have the greater problem of sound to emphasize his chauvinism. Even if we put ideology aside — and the reviewers clearly were not willing to do so — the script of *1492* is a mess. It covers nearly a decade and moves rapidly from one crisis to the next. Taken as a whole, *1492: Conquest of Paradise* must be considered an honorable failure.

On a production budget of some $40,000,000, *Christopher Columbus: The Discovery*, released in the United States on August 21, 1992, grossed only $8,251,071 domestically. It was, in short, a failure both at the box office and with the critics. Scott's *1492:*

Conquest of Paradise, which opened on October 9, seven weeks later, fared no better. According to Box Office Mojo, it had a production budget of an estimated $47,000,000; in his commentary, Scott says $44,000,000. The film earned a miserable $7,191,399 domestically. Although Box Office Mojo does not give the foreign box office, Sammon lists it as a respectable $52,000,000 (*Ridley Scott*, 115). Although both films were box-office detonations, Scott probably escaped disaster by selling his film regionally. Scott's speculation that the film might have fared better in an early pre-release cut running over three hours seems unlikely. Neither the viewing public nor the critics liked either of the two Columbus films, and their later releases on VHS and DVD did nothing to enhance either their reputation or their popularity.

11

White Squall (1996): A Meteorological Phenomenon of the Imagination

Version. The 2.35:1 129-minute theatrical version is rated PG-13. The film was released by Hollywood Pictures, a Walt Disney subsidiary, and the only available version dates from the early days of DVD, is letterboxed and has no commentary.

Scott was pondering whether to direct *Mulholland Falls* (later turned into an excellent 1996 film directed by Lee Tamahori), when he saw the script for *White Squall* and decided immediately to direct the film (Raw, 317).

White Squall is, as they say, based upon a true story, a point which Scott notes in his interviews. The film begins in 1960 as thirteen preppies set sail with Ocean Academy Schoolmaster-Captain Christian Sheldon aboard a two-masted brig named the *Albatross* on a voyage from the Caribbean to the South Pacific and back. It turns into an eight-month trip of some 12,000 miles which contains all sorts of difficulties. The trip begins with an encounter with a Cuban gunboat on the eve of the Bay of Pigs and ends with the destruction of the ship by a white squall, a sudden storm at sea accompanied by black clouds, white-capped waves and broken or uneven waters. (Apparently, some authorities deny the existence of such a storm.) The *Albatross* sinks on May 21, 1961. Four young men and two crew members, including Sheldon's wife, perish. During the inquiry that follows, the captain is described as an disciplinarian whose severity almost caused a mutiny, a man who allowed the young men entirely too much freedom on shore, and a captain who did not properly instruct his immature crew. The young crew, however, stoutly defend him, following, perhaps foolishly, the Ocean Academy's musketeer slogan: "We go one, we go all." Captain Sheldon takes responsibility and offers to return his captain's "ticket," but his crew rallies around him.

Reviewers were substantially united: They loved the storm sequence and pretty much hated, to a greater or lesser degree, the rest of the film. *Newsweek's* Jack Kroll was in a grumpy mood. After trashing the film and its "visualholic director," he praised the storm's "lightning-cracking, wind-yowling, wave-heaving, human-flinging grandeur."

Mark Kermode, in *Sight and Sound* (a British film magazine usually sympathetic to Scott), called the film "a dramatically flawed generic hybrid" which contains all the "well worn staples of saleable big-screen blockbusters" and runs "the gamut of mainstream Hollywood reference points." The film is, however, so emotionally draining that it lacks the "feelgood factor" the studios consider necessary for a popular film. According to Kermode, the problem is that Scott cannot decide whether the film is "a rites-of-passage drama or a downbeat disaster movie." His conclusion is that the film is "a sporadically memorable hotch-potch, often enjoyable, intermittently amazing, yet ultimately unsatisfactory." Nonetheless, by virtue of the storm, it "finds a place" in film history.

Jack Mathews wrote that while all the events are probable, none of them rings true. Strangely, Mathews believes that it more closely follows *Dead Poets Society*— the movie — than Henry W. Longfellow's poem "The Wreck of the Hesperus." "It's a matter of genres," he writes rather mysteriously. Even Mathews, however, likes the storm, which he calls "both terrifying and weirdly exhilarating."

Michael Medved thought the images of the storm were as "breathtaking and terrifying as anything in *Blade Runner* or *Alien*," but the first three-fourths of the film was simply "wasting time." After praising the storm in hyperbolic terms, David Denby called the story "an old-fashioned fable that we know all too well."

Attacks upon the verisimilitude of the film have some justification. Scott, so acute in his attention to detail, can seem short-sighted. *White Squall* opens in Connecticut, but we see Spanish moss and palmetto plants in the shrubbery. And there are other errors as well. This is not quite the same thing as the reviewer who complained about the localized *American Gangster* being shot all around New York City. Only a person knowledgeable about New York would be likely to notice this and to believe that it might make any difference in our feeling about the artistry of the film. The juxtaposition of images of western America in *Thelma & Louise* occasionally seem inappropriate to a person familiar with the area, but it is hardly a flaw in the film. But the appearance of flora and fauna in inappropriate landscapes gives some viewers a sense of dislocation which enhances any suspicion that they might have of Scott's lack of knowledge of American landscape.

Harry Pearson, Jr., in *Films in Review*, made a valiant, if only partial, defense of the film. He began by noting that Scott's films are often poorly reviewed, but grow in esteem as time passes. He writes that he almost decided to avoid *White Squall* because a "professional critic" told him that he had seen the story a hundred times before. But when Pearson saw the film, he found much to praise.

Pearson writes that the boys are not carefully enough distinguished from each other and wants a "more diverse" group. Even if the actual boys were more similar than alike, this is fair criticism. The purpose of art is to express varied personalities, not to show how they are alike. Pearson praises the visual beauty of the film, likes the unusual rhythm of the sea scenes, and laments that much of the beauty of the film will be lost even on laserdisc, then the gold standard of home video. Pearson need not have worried. With Blu-ray and high definition television sets, *White Squall* will look just fine.

White Squall (1996)

Variety's reviewer Brian Lowry believed, wrongly as it turned out, that the appearance of young TV star Scott Wolf as the "movie's centerpiece and narrator" Chuck Gieg, might generate enough interest to make the film a commercial success. Lowry, like some other reviewers, compared *White Squall* unfavorably with what they perceived as the competition, *Dead Poets Society*, a recent hit. Like other critics, Lowry thought the structure of the film was flawed and that it took too long to get started.

It is always interesting to examine a work of art in terms of what the artist thought he was doing, or attempting to do. Of course, after the work is finished, his opinion, although privileged as that of the creator, is not necessarily better than that of anyone else. Scott regarded the film as an historical picture of an earlier generation:

> It's about a generation that's gone and lost.... And I don't think it's ever going to come back. In a way this film is really about the rite of passage from adolescence to manhood and I think the process has evaporated. The real values, family values, have collapsed.... Children have lost respect for their elders.... Now there is far too much toleration of bullshit.... If that had happened today everyone would have been sued.... [T]he most they would have done then would have been to have a hearing. In simple terms, the boys defended the honor of their captain. Consequently he was let off the hook [cited Raw, 317].

The first response to this of most Americans would be to wonder how Scott could think that the rich preppies of fifty years ago could possibly have been representative of American society as a whole. Certainly, the preppies are still around, but there is no proof that children of this generation have less respect for "their elders" than earlier generations did. Joel McCrea, the voice of the old order in Sam Peckinpah's *Ride the High Country* (1962), believed it to be true, as indeed do many conservatives of today. Here, as elsewhere, Scott's regard for a historical context, for depicting the actions of a group rather than those of individuals, has vitiated the power of his story. The classical method would have been to concentrate on two or three boys at most, and have them represent different social classes, or at least differences among the preppies — for example, *nouveau riche* versus old money.

White Squall, like all Scott movies, is a generic formulation designed to appeal to a large public. The film combines a teenage rite-of-passage story with a disaster at sea. Seagoing disaster films have been a Hollywood staple. The more memorable include Henry Hathaway's *Souls at Sea* (1937), which kept a youngster I knew from sleeping for a week, *The Caine Mutiny* (1954), and of course several *Titanic* films, including James Cameron's box-office monster *Titanic* (1997).

Tales of a youngster who comes of age at sea have a long tradition. Notable accounts include Richard Henry Dana's autobiographical *Two Years Before the Mast* (1840), filmed in 1946, and Rudyard Kipling's memorable *Captains Courageous* (1897), filmed in 1937. Usually, however, the stories concerned only one boy as compared to the gang of preppies in *White Squall*. *White Squall* was a box office failure. Box Office Mojo reports that the film took in a meager $10,292,300 domestically. Although *Mojo* gives neither the domestic gross nor the production costs, none of the producers of the film could possibly have been happy.

93

12

G. I. Jane (1997): Wild Thing

Version. The only available version is the 2.35:1 125-minute R-rated theatrical version. *The Ridley Scott Encyclopedia* describes a number of scenes which can either be integrated into the film or included as omitted scenes in a future DVD-Blu-ray release along with, of course, one of Scott's illuminating commentaries.

After the release of *White Squall* in 1995, Scott did not release another film until *G. I. Jane* two years later. In the meantime, he reorganized Scott Free, the production company he runs with his brother Tony, in order to privilege some lower-budget films, and worked on *I Am Legend*, which was to star Arnold Schwarzenegger. The aborted project was eventually filmed in 2007 with Will Smith in the starring role.

Danielle Alexandra had learned that actress Demi Moore was looking for a physically challenging role and thought that she had the "necessary personal and physical strength" to play the first woman SEAL in her screenplay. Apparently the producers wanted a more experienced writer and hired David Twohy (*Waterworld, Pitch Black*), who eventually shared screenplay credit with Alexandra.

Scott has said that he was attracted to the project because he wanted to work with Moore and had always wanted to make a film about the military. The provocative nature of the material was an additional lure. At the time, the service of women in the military was a hot-button issue. The ongoing Tailhook scandal, in which a group of female pilots in training had accused their male counterparts of sexual harassment, was in the news. Although a number of officers were disciplined or denied advancement in rank as a result of the investigation, the official response was generally considered inadequate. The incident and its repercussion had already been the subject of the 1995 TV movie *She Stood Alone: The Tailhook Scandal*, directed by Larry Shaw. The persecution of a prospective female cadet at the Citadel military academy was also in the news. It is hardly a surprise that the Pentagon refused any assistance in making the film, which was shot mostly in Washington DC and Florida.

As we might expect from the title, *G. I. Jane* is a classic military mission film (*The Dirty Dozen, The Wild Geese, Raid on Rommel*). Such a film is always divided into three parts: the necessity of the mission, the selection of the group, and the mission and its aftermath. *G. I. Jane* differs from the usual mission film because the main character is a woman who is not, at least initially, even recognized as a member of the group, much less its leader. The first and second parts of the film are told in great detail, and the mission itself gives the impression of having been added as an afterthought, even though it is so exciting that it seems to belong to another, and better, movie.

In mission films, the mission group is usually a gang of misfits molded together by a strong leader who is a master motivator. *G. I. Jane* is the first important big-budget Hollywood mission movie with a political agenda: in this case, to justify the role of women in combat. It did not succeed: The Navy, for whatever reasons, soon dropped women from the special operations (SEAL CRT) selection program.

The film opens with a Congressional inquiry concerning women's role in the military. After a contentious hearing in which the chair of the committee, Lillian DeHaven (Anne Bancroft in a testy mood), berates officials about the woeful lack of support for women in the military, the naval officials eventually agree that, if the women "measure up to the men, they get the job." The program chosen as a test case is the Navy SEALS in the firm belief that "no woman can last a week" in the program.

The woman chosen by the Senator and the brass is Jordan O'Neil (Moore), beautiful, intelligent, tough as nails and, some critics argue, totally unbelievable. One character who *is* believable is Master Chief John James Urgayle, superbly played by Viggo Mortensen, one of Hollywood's best actors and certainly its most underrated. The grueling and sadistic psychological and physical training is depicted in Scott's hyper-realistic and occasionally slow-motion visuals and classic editing. Of course, O'Neil has to fight prejudice from the other trainees, who actively sabotage her efforts, and from the politicians in Washington. When O'Neil complains that she is being treated differently and wants only to be treated the same as the others, "no better, no worse," the C.O. (Scott Wilson, thirty years along from Truman Capote's *In Cold Blood* killer) grants her wish and she is allowed to shave her head and sleep in the barracks. A scene showing O'Neil showering with the men was dropped from the film.

Meanwhile, back in DC, the military is unhappy with the publicity "G. I. Jane" is receiving and sends instructions to wash her out. The effort is unsuccessful. O'Neil sweats, strains, suffers, and deteriorates physically, but keeps on ticking.

She is accused of being a lesbian, but refuses to drop out of the program, has problems with her boyfriend, and generally goes through hell. She is dropped from the program when Senator DeHaven sells her out in exchange for keeping military bases open in Texas. DeHaven tells O'Neil that she has problems which would have "Solomon shitting golf-balls," but Jordan outfaces her and gets reinstated.

Of course, O'Neil proves herself in a difficult situation with her bravery and sound judgment and saves the day just as she had in her first training scene. While on a Sea Operational Readiness Exercise in the Mediterranean Sea, the SEALS are unexpectedly ordered to join the battle group Tango Chaser and to rescue a group which has been sent into Libya to retrieve a Ranger Recovery unit which has been unable to extract itself after a mission involving the retrieval of a downed satellite.

"Welcome aboard, ma'am," the chief tells O'Neil at the medal ceremony. This indicates recognition both that she is a member of the unit and that she is a woman. Later, he leaves her a medal in a copy of the Penguin edition of the poems of D.H. Lawrence in her locker. The book is open to a short poem called "Self-Pity" about a "wild thing, a bird" who falls to the ground and dies but never feels sorry for itself. In a moving coda over the credits, the master chief quotes the poem while introducing himself to a new group of trainees.

The contemporary reviews of *G.I. Jane* do not make pleasant reading. In general, reviewers savaged Moore, but were somewhat less harsh on Scott. The few who liked the film attempted to place it in the context of Scott's other films, especially *Thelma & Louise*. The attacks on Moore were often personal. John Anderson called her "a cultural symptom, a rabid careerist" and "a curiosity, a car wreck." This outburst is so extreme that it must surely have been occasioned by memory of Moore's earlier films, especially *The Scarlet Letter*.

Michael Medved, in the *New York Post*, compared *G. I. Jane* to *Top Gun*, a popular Tom Cruise film directed by Scott's brother Tony. Medved wrote that *G. I. Jane* is "positively Tolstoyan in its dramatic complexity" and suggested that it should have been called "*G.I. Junk* or *G.I. Joke*." The criticism could be, and has been, applied to nearly all of Scott's films, which customarily take a generic form and complicate it nearly out of existence.

Among the favorable reviews, Amy Taubin's is perhaps the most interesting. She believes that Brit Scott "reenvisions classic American movie landscapes through alienated eyes," calls *G. I. Jane* "a gender fuck film" with "surprisingly subtle dialogue" and compares it to *Thelma & Louise* which she describes as "a women-driven road movie, a western adventure into the uncharted territory of feminist existential freedom."

Reviewer Peter Travers called the film "a surprisingly scrappy workout that is bound to disappoint those who are drooling to see the star in Top Gun Barbie." Travers argues that the beating that Moore takes from Mortensen is only slightly harsher than those the critics gave this most vilified of actresses, but believes that Moore "finds the heartbeat of her character and a career beyond vanity and hype." Unfortunately, as it turned out, the performance did nothing to support her career and, it may be argued, was her last important starring role.

Kenneth Turan called the story a traditional female star vehicle "joined to an old-fashioned combat movie." Moore's heroine, "Joan Crawford in combat boots," projects "an intensity that is strong enough to touch." The politics of the film is only "window dressing," and everything that happens is only "a well-thumbed cliché." Turan concludes that a more interesting story would be how the actress in *Ghost* morphed into "someone who is most interesting doing push-ups." Turan believes, perhaps rightly, that Scott is "most comfortable in the physical aspects of the film, the panorama of purposeful chaos."

David Denby, in *New York*, noted that the film was "explicitly conceived" for

Moore, but calls the result "very bizarre" and believes that Scott's "rousing visuals" work against the grain of the film and add "precisely zero" to it. Consequently, the film ends up as merely "a charged-up commercial for military service."

Paul M. Sammon describes *G. I. Jane* as a "film which, while ultimately relegated to the lower tier of Scott's catalog, nonetheless also reveals this perpetually underrated director's ongoing (and canny) method of fusing personalized art with mainstream artifice" (Knapp, *Interviews*, 133).

Todd McCarthy nailed both *G. I. Jane* and its reception by the public when he opened his *Variety* review by calling it a "bracingly gung-ho film for a nonmilitary-minded time ... a very entertaining get-tough fantasy with political and feminist under-pinnings." He writes that both the star and the director have returned to top form after a series of missteps. As it turned out, McCarthy's belief that the film would appeal both to men who liked military movies and to women as a success story of women in the military was essentially wrong. Neither audience liked the film.

Perhaps Richard Schickel's review was the fairest. He praises the "often astonishing beauty" of "the brutal, frantic (and generally drenched) scramble of training exercises." And in general disagreement with most mainstream critics, Schickel argues that the film does not "eroticize" the movie's violence and praises its "sardonic objectivity" in the portrayal of Mortensen's master chief. His conclusion is that the film makes the viewer "feel authentic pain, isolation and courage — shocking stuff to find in an action movie these days."

The influence of *G. I. Jane*, if there was any, faded rapidly and the argument about women in the military settled into the type of compromise typical of American democracy. Although women were to be allowed on equal terms in the military, their role in combat was limited, and the SEALS training was considered too physically demanding. The film quickly became what all works of art become sooner or later: a period piece to be judged by the same historical and critical standards as other films of the same period.

As always, Scott is careful to place his film in a historical context. O'Neil's conversation with the African-American soldier carefully, if unnecessarily, compares the struggle for the rights of black soldiers in World War II to Jordan's attempt to do the same for women. While the analogy is hardly complete, it is near enough to be cited. Whether it adds to the film or is merely a distraction, is, however, an open question.

Much of the film is indigestible. Anne Bancroft's character is over-the-top and her mannerisms and accents grating; it is impossible to believe that she could ever have been elected in Texas or anywhere else. All of the politicians and most of the military are so scummy that it comes as a surprise, although it ought not, to see them standing at attention at the awards ceremony at the film's end. The horrors and rigors of Jordan's training, although photographed in Scott's wonderful hues, are brutally realistic and sometimes painful to watch.

Bancroft's role is so large and her performance so unsympathetic that the decision to portray her thusly must have been Scott's. While Bancroft had often played unsympathetic roles (her classic role as the aging seductress of Dustin Hoffman in *The Graduate* is hardly sympathetic), the harsh voice, deliberately ugly photography, weird accent, and crudely explicit language are not necessary either for the character or for the movie. If the audience had been made to feel that at least one important person were rooting for O'Neil instead of her just saying so, her suffering might have seemed more bearable. After all, the audience is never in doubt that Viggo Mortensen's master chief is secretly, if impartially, wanting O'Neil to succeed and is hardly surprised when she does. He is, however, astonished at her bravery and coolness under fire, and profoundly grateful when she saves his life.

Is *G. I. Jane* a feminist movie? A better question would be: Is O'Neil a feminist? The answer to that question is certainly no. Raw puts the question nicely: The answer turns on the question of "whether one believes that women have to behave like men in order to be accepted on equal terms" (Raw, 109). The answer to that would be another question: What men? Certainly, O'Neil comes to accept the shedding of her femininity as necessary for becoming a warrior. Unfortunately, the concluding section showing her reading the poem of D.H. Lawrence may indicate that she has shed not only her femininity, but her humanity at well, and has become a "wild thing." This is not, of course, the same thing as saying that the struggle was not worthwhile.

Critics have compared Moore's O'Neil to the portrayals of Jodie Foster and Julianne Moore as Clarice Starling in *The Silence of the Lambs* and *Hannibal*. The characters of Clarice in the two films are hardly comparable since they are filtered through very different lenses, that of the original novelist and those of the two successive directors. Raw cites Linda Mizejewski's observation that the character of Starling is "more acceptable if read through Jodie Foster, whose persona makes some of these contradictions or unanswered questions acceptable" (Raw, 109). This apparently means "more acceptable" to certain feminist critics, but it has nothing to do with Scott's films or their interpretation. The perhaps subconscious images projected by the two actresses are indeed different, but the image of Moore is perhaps more generally sympathetic. Foster's image is, at least in the mind of the present writer, clearly sexually ambiguous, while that of Moore is clearly heterosexual. While that has nothing to do with the evaluation of the films, it makes the comparison between them somewhat more problematic.

The concluding two sections of *G. I. Jane,* the rescue or "extraction" and the medal ceremony, run some twenty minutes, not counting the credits, and bring the film to blazing life. The rescue gives the film a heart and the coda gives it a soul. Unfortunately, by that time, most of the original audience seems to have lost interest.

The rescue is a model of narrative action, impeccably shot and edited with flair. The intensity of combat has seldom been so successfully communicated and O'Neil's "grace under pressure" could hardly have been illustrated with greater effectiveness. The editing is brisk and unhurried, and the battle sequences occur in something like real time. The desert landscape and the hovering helicopters may be seen, if only in retrospect, as a warm-up for *Black Hawk Down*. The rescue is one of the great sequences in a Ridley Scott film, right up there with the Gothic Florence section in *Hannibal* and the pursuit of Roy Batty and his death in *Blade Runner*.

G. I. Jane seems to have outlived its detractors. If the film has not survived as evidence of empowerment, it has certainly survived as a

Wild Thing: Demi Moore and Viggo Mortensen in *G.I. Jane* (1997).

kick-ass female fantasy which chronicles the deeds of a more realistic Wonder Woman. It seems to be playing on television somewhere every time I turn on the set. There are worse dreams of empowerment.

According to Box Office Mojo, *G. I. Jane* had a domestic gross of $48,169,156. According to reports, this just about covered its cost. After a series of box-office failures, the film essentially ended Demi Moore's career as a film star. Both Moore and the film deserved better.

13

Gladiator (2000): There Was
Once a Dream That Was Rome

Versions. The 2.35:1 theatrical version of *Gladiator* runs 155 minutes. The 2005 extended version runs 164 minutes and includes 17 minutes of material which was previously available only as DVD extras. The Blu-ray edition includes both versions. The added material is generally redundant and, it might be argued, retards the narrative.

The genesis and filming of *Gladiator* have been well documented in Gladiator: *The Making of the Ridley Scott Epic*. *Gladiator* was a successful attempt to reestablish the large-scale sword-and-sandal epic after more than a third of a century. Four separate crews were coordinated in the shooting of *Gladiator*: one in London, one in Malta, one in Morocco and one which moved from location to location. Scott, ever concerned with giving his films a realistic but striking look, is said to have had four hundred acres of Surrey woodland burned for the opening battle in Germania, two thousand sets of armor constructed and twenty-six thousand arrows prepared. Numidian scenes were shot in Morocco, and Roman scenes were shot in Malta. (See the *Gladiator* book for details and illustrations.)

As usual with Scott's epic films, the basic conflict is elemental, but the working-out of the plot is complex and involves a large supporting cast. *Gladiator* has a basic three-act structure. The first act begins with the battle in Germania in the winter of 180 AD and the murder of the Emperor Marcus Aurelius by his son Commodus, who learned that his dying father wished to disinherit him in favor of General Maximus, whom he has charged with the reestablishment of the republic. Maximus returns home to discover that his estate has been ravaged and his wife and son murdered. He is captured and sold into slavery as a gladiator. The second act tells of Maximus' training as a gladiator, his growing fame in the hinterlands, and his eventual return to Rome as a gladiator slated to perform in the Coliseum. (The chief influence here seems to have been similar scenes in Stanley Kubrick's *Spartacus* [1960].) Meanwhile, the new emperor, Commodus, has decided that the way to win the love of the people is by presenting elaborate gladiatorial games and by occasionally appearing himself as a gladiator.

The long third act narrates the growing fame of Maximus and the growing political opposition to Commodus, who decides that the way to gain popularity would be to kill Maximus in the arena. Commodus wounds Maximus the day before he is to fight him. In one of the best touches in the film, Commodus, in dire straits during the fight to the death, begs Quintus, who is apparently a kind of umpire, for his sword. Quintus is an old officer of Maximus whom we met at the beginning of the film where he asked the general why the Germans they are fighting do not know when they are beaten. Quintus has survived in uncertain times, but he feels a certain loyalty to Maximus, or to fair play, or to both, and he ignores the request, tells the guards to sheathe their swords, and allows Maximus to kill Commodus.

The crowd is silent. There is a shot of what is presumably a pagan tomb. In a vision of his life after death, Maximus pushes open the gate which leads to his home. Dying, he tells Quintus to free his team of gladiators and for the Senate to reinstate Gracchus as leader of the Roman republic. The dream that was the wish of Marcus Aurelius shall be realized. (The cynic might respond, "Good luck to that.") Maximus runs his hand through the ripe grain, tells Lucilla goodbye and goes down the path to greet his son and wife. The body of Maximus is borne from the Coliseum in triumph, and Lucilla says: "You're home." The African says that he is free and will see him again, "But not yet." And the film concludes with a memorable shot of the sun setting over the now empty Coliseum. All in all, despite a variety of trite elements, the conclusion is the most memorable ending of any sword-and-sandal epic. The exterior of the pagan tomb is a particularly striking image, a vision of a cold, rather remote, but still hospitable other world as imagined by a non–Christian.

Although *Gladiator* was the first large-scale film on Roman history in more than a generation, it trod a well-worn path and borrowed heavily from earlier films, particularly in the sets and in the relationship between the characters. As might be expected for such a huge film, the screenplay (by David Franzoni) blended many familiar elements with a few themes which, if not absolutely new, were at least unusual. The presumed audience for the film, if not more sophisticated, was generally more knowledgeable than earlier audiences had been about Roman history, and many of the references to earlier films cited by various critics would have been spotted by viewers familiar with VHS and DVD versions of classic Hollywood and foreign films.

Ideologically, the two chief differences between *Gladiator* and, say, the two versions of *Ben-Hur*, silent and sound, are the greater level of violence and the fact that the hero is a pagan who does not convert to Christianity. Although the improvement in digital effects in the closing years of the last century had once again made such an film financially possible, *Gladiator* is clearly as much a product of its times as earlier sword-and-sandal epics were of theirs. From the earliest days of the silents more than a hundred years ago, Roman epics were predominantly stories of Christian heroics ending in conversion and martyrdom. Italian films of the teens regularly showed the Christians being fed to the lions. A few Italian films of the period, such as *The Last Days of Pompeii* (1913) and *Cabiria* (1914), showed the full decadent splendor of paganism, but Christianity held sway at the end.

General Lew Wallace's *Ben-Hur* (1880) was one of the most popular American novels of the 19th century, probably second only to *Uncle Tom's Cabin*, and like Harriet Beecher Stowe's novel, it became the basis for a popular stage production which debuted

in 1899 and ran for twenty-one years. The chariot race featured eight horses on a treadmill with a moving cyclorama as a background. The first filmed version, done by Kalem in 1907, was the subject of a famous Supreme Court decision giving an artist the exclusive rights to possession of his subject in a new medium.

The spectacular 1925 MGM version of *Ben-Hur* does not include Christians being fed to the lions, but it features almost all of the other standard ingredients. Judah Ben-Hur might have been born a Jew, but he ended as a

Defiance: Russell Crowe as Maximus in *Gladiator* (2000).

Christian after, of course, achieving his revenge against the evil Messala. Although the 1959 version, directed by William Wyler, has several memorable scenes, it is not a notable advance over the silent version, and in at least one sequence, the sea battle, is clearly inferior.

Films of today, however, especially big-budget epics, must appeal to a world-wide audience which has little interest is seeing films about Christian martyrs being fed to the lions. Scott filmed scenes of persecuted Christians, which are included as extras, but did not include them in the released version, presumably because they would distract attention from the main story. In *Gladiator*, Maximus, our heroic protagonist, is a pagan, but his vision of life after death will hardly offend anyone. Paganism is, of course, a catch-all term for a large number of religious beliefs. Since all the varieties of paganism are now dead, or underground, *Gladiator* is perhaps both historically and politically correct and can play anywhere throughout the world without controversy.

A second difference between *Gladiator* and earlier sword-and-sandal films is the level of violence. Earlier epics, up to and including Anthony Mann's *The Fall of the Roman Empire* (1964)— usually considered the last of the great sword-and-scandal epics before *Gladiator*— contained much action, but none of the hacking-off of limbs, splitting of skulls, beheadings, etc., which have become the cinematic coin of world-wide cinema today. Mann's *Fall* had been advertised as "launching a new epoch in motion pictures," but in actuality its financial debacle ushered in a forty-year hiatus in the making of epic films.

The gladiatorial arena was a staple of the Italian epics of the teens, but the emphasis seems never to have been on the gladiator himself, but on his journey toward Christianity. Kubrick's *Spartacus* was different. It centered on a slave revolt led by a gladiator and was widely and reasonably interpreted as an allegory attacking the anti-communist repression of the Cold War period led by Senator Joseph McCarthy. The script was the first screen credit in some ten years for Dalton Trumbo, a blacklisted novelist and once highly paid screenwriter.

Gladiators were professional fighters who battled to the death in the arenas. Although *gladius* means "sword," the contests involved a variety of weapons. They are said to have originated in Roman funeral rites. It was apparently believed that the losers would serve the dead man as armed attendants in the afterlife. The first known competition was in Rome in 264 BC. The contests became popular and lasted for some six hundred years before eventually being abolished by Emperor Constantine in 325 AD, only to be revived before being permanently abolished by Honorius a century later (Carnes, 41). Although the famous revolt by Spartacus and seventy other slave gladiators lasted nearly two years (73–71 BC), it was eventually a failure and the games continued.

One of the reasons that *Gladiator* is successful is that it allows the villain Commodus a chance to speak for himself. In his conversation with his sister and in his last conversation with Maximus, he tells how he yearned for the love of his father, but that it was denied him. Maximus loved Aurelius and the love was returned, but Commodus, his own son, could do nothing to please him. They both loved him: "That makes us brothers."

Films, like all works of art, are clearly products of the age which produces them. *Gladiator* is particularly so, and not just because it is a film set in a determinate historical past. Jon Solomon notes that the film "enjoys the economic and visual advantages not just of computer-generated special effects but of an entire generation's worth of developments in film technique" (93). These include the entire four tiers of the Roman Coliseum, aerial shots and sweeping eye-level views. Strangely, however, the development of digital effects was moving at warp speed, and the special effects, in spite of a reputed budget of over $100,000,000, were antiquated almost as soon as the film appeared. There is presently no reason to believe that the released version of *Gladiator*, unlike that of *Blade Runner*, is not Scott's preferred text; however, considering the way that the versatility and popularity of DVDs and Blu-ray has destabilized the idea of a definitive text and considering Scott's tendency to reshoot, revise, and "tweak," it is probable that the film addict will eventually see a new and "improved" version of *Gladiator*. Indeed, there is a suspicion that one or two of the shots of the Coliseum may already have been tweaked.

The reviews for *Gladiator* were generally enthusiastic, with only the occasional naysayer among them, most notably an unusually grumpy J. Hoberman. From his perch in *The Village Voice*, the generally affable Hoberman laid waste not only to *Gladiator*, but collaterally to James Cameron's *Titanic*, which had appeared recently. Hoberman called *Gladiator* "a fearfully expressive high tech revival of deeply retro material … complete with sentimental love story and otherworldly palaver" and sarcastically lamented that the concluding fight was not staged "in old Pompeii the day Vesuvius blew its stack."

David Sterritt called the film "150 minutes of non-stop spectacle and violence … a movie to rush out and see." Like others, he considered it a satisfying return to a type of film not seen for forty years. Peter Rainer liked the film but puzzled over exactly what Scott was selling, claimed quite rightly that it was not "the Roman-epic revisionism" it had generally been taken to be, and ticked off its similarities to earlier sword-and-sandal epics: the loyal Roman soldier who wants only to serve Caesar and to return to his wife, the son Great Caesar always wished he had; the evil, scheming heir eager to send the old fellow on his way; the gladiator ringmaster, and the noble African yearning for freedom (Dijimon Hounsou standing in for Woody Strode of *Spartacus*). Although Rainer's review is somewhat marred by his addiction to low tropes ("Joaquin Phoenix's Commodus—think commode"), he is correct in believing that *Gladiator* is not "terribly revisionist." His only criticism of the film is its "terrible percussiveness," and he skirts around the idea that Scott has somehow sold out. Scott "treats his audience alternately like epicures and like a vulgar, bloodthirsty mob not dissimilar to the one that crowded the Coliseum."

Jonathan Foreman, in the *New York Post*, hailed the film's set scenes as "equal in excitement to the classic arena contests in *Ben-Hur* and *Spartacus*." Foreman, like other reviewers, praised Russell Crowe's performance extravagantly and writes that unlike its ancestors, the film contains "no Christian message and, more surprisingly, no sex." (Actually, there is perhaps a hint — it is no more than that — that Commodus and Lucilla have had a relationship at some time in the past. He also once speaks of marrying his sister so that there could be no possible doubt that the resulting heir would be the unquestioned legitimate heir to the empire.)

Among the reviewers, only Foreman seems to have complained much about the film's historical anachronisms, specifically the use of artillery in a siege, the use of heavy broadswords for slashing, and the cavalry charge (impossible due to the lack of stirrups, which are first recorded only in the 4th century AD). Quite apart from the difficulties of having a cavalry charge over the uneven, forested terrain in the snow, Hans Delbrück's masterful history of ancient warfare discusses no example of a cavalry charge until hundreds of years later. The fireballs also come from a later period, and in any case would have been impossible in mud and snow. The enormous number of arrows unleashed here — and a decade later in *Robin Hood*— is quite impossible. Both the long bow and the arrows it required were difficult to manufacture, and skill with them required constant practice (Santosuosso, 135).

Gladiator (2000)

Even a cursory examination of the complex popular antecedents of *Gladiator*—especially the sword-and-sandal and biblical antecedents, the space operas and science fiction films, including the *Star Wars* films — should give the critic pause before making any large claims to historical accuracy. And yet the popularity of the film guaranteed that the subject would be examined in detail, as indeed it was. An entire collection of essays entitled *Gladiator: Film and History*, edited by Martin M. Winkler, a professor of classics, and written by historians and classicists (not a film critic among them), examined the historicity of the film in fascinating detail, and the viewer of the film interested in the topic should seek out a copy. Professor Kathleen Coleman of Harvard University served as historical consultant on *Gladiator,* but was so unhappy with the results of her labor that she asked that her name not appear in the credits.

In the commentary upon the film and the extra features included on the DVD and Blu-ray editions, the multitude of people who worked upon the film laud the search for historical accuracy in the artifacts — costumes, architecture, paintings, indeed anything having to do with the look of the film — and generally ignore the known historical happenings and the details of the battle with the barbarians at the beginning of the film.

Scott is said to have gotten his initial inspiration from Jean-Léon Gérôme's famous 1872 painting *Thumbs Down*, depicting a helmeted Roman gladiator standing over a conquered foe and receiving a "thumbs down" verdict from the crowd on the fate of a conquered foe. Although Gérôme is said to have done extensive research, we must remember that all the visual representations of warfare in the period come from a much later age, and the covers on the paperback volumes of Delbrück's *History,* among many other visual representations, are hardly models of historical accuracy. And when CGI is added into the equation, there is always an additional loss.

It is, however, fair to say that, by the standards of sword-and- sandal films, *Gladiator* is generally accurate in visual details, but much less so in historical facts. During the period of the Roman Republic, gladiators were always slaves, but during the Empire period, free men and even some aristocrats participated. Frank McLynn calls the participation of Commodus the "ultimate absurdity." Clearly, the enormous number of contests in which Commodus is said to have competed and emerged victorious is impossible, even with the "advantages" of superior weaponry and perfidy of the type depicted in the film which shows him wounding Maximus the day before the contest.

There is a nearly universal belief that the so-called trinity of gladiatorial combats, chariot racing and animal fights were regarded as "compensation" to please the populace and to make up for the curtailment of political rights during the Empire. One need not be cynical to believe there is a certain amount of truth in this belief. According to all accounts and to Clint Eastwood's film *Invictus* (2009), Nelson Mandela used rugby to unite the peoples of South Africa. Whether modern audiences to such contests are more sensitive than the audiences of earlier times is a delicate question, but not beyond all conjecture.

Russell Crowe received nearly universal praise and an Academy Award for Best Actor for his portrayal of Maximus. At the time *Gladiator* was filmed, however, his casting was hardly obvious and must have seemed a risk. The young Australian was clearly a talented actor on the rise who had done excellent work in *L.A. Confidential* and *The Insider*, but he lacked the chiseled features and noble mien thought appropriate for such a role. He also seemed plebeian. What he did have, and the reason he was chosen was the intensity he could project on the screen. It was a quality that no one could have predicted from his performance only five years earlier in the western *The Quick and the Dead*, and although he had matured rapidly and had shown evidence of it in *The Insider* (1999), Crowe's casting as Maximus must surely have required a great deal of faith by the producers of *Gladiator*. Joaquin Phoenix was also highly praised for his role as the evil Commodus and duly rewarded with an Academy Award nomination for Best Supporting Actor.

In his masterful biographical and critical study of Marcus Aurelius, Frank McLynn furnishes a photograph of Richard Harris, describes him as an "Irish hellraiser with a roistering 'feedback image,'" thinks him an unfortunate choice to play the emperor, and insultingly omits his name. Perhaps, but in his old age Harris had a decayed physical presence and a gravitas far removed from his testosterone-laden youth in Sam Peckinpah's *Major Dundee* (1965) and other films. Of course, no one knows what the Emperor, who spent most his adult life as a soldier, actually looked like, but the highly stylized sculptural representations show an impressive figure, and McLynn's "feedback image" would hardly bother most reviewers, even if they had read Marcus Aurelius. Hollywood knows what a warrior looks like, but nobody has a representative visual image of a philosopher or sage. Who knows? He may even have looked like the aging Richard Harris and have written philosophical essays in a tent in Germania.

While McLynn admires the "dignity and gravitas" of Alec Guinness, who played Marcus in Anthony Mann's *The Fall of the Roman Empire* (1964), he has only scorn for the differing ways in which the emperor is dispatched in the two films, smothered to death by his son in *Gladiator* and assassinated by a poisoned apple in *Fall*.

Gladiator is a wonderful film which easily surpasses its considerable competition with its visual splendor. Scott's original inspiration was Gérôme's famous Victorian painting and any number of the scene-paintings of the film are nearly, if not actually, its equal. The closing shot of the twilight of the Coliseum is particularly memorable, as is Maximus's screed when he unmasks before Commodus and promises his revenge "in this world or in the next."

Scott's main interest, here as elsewhere, is in advancing the story visually rather than dramatically. He does not slow down enough to develop complex relationships of sex, race, and ethnicity. In both the silent and the sound versions of *Ben-Hur*, there is a wonderful scene in which an Arab, "a coarse gambling man," played by Hugh Griffith in the sound version, goes into a Roman bath house to wager a large amount of money on his "own poor horses." He has helpfully brought along a bushel of money to show his sincerity, and he taunts the Romans into giving him highly favorable odds. The tension of the scene is almost visceral and clearly presents both the basic conflict of the film — the revenge story — and the competing ideologies involved in a dramatic fashion that *Gladiator* never manages.

Gladiator was a box office monster. According to Box Office Mojo, it earned $187,705,427 domestically and $269,935,000 around the world for a total of $457,640,427, and continues to earn residuals from television, DVD and Blu-ray receipts.

14

Black Hawk Down (2001):
Bird Down in the City

Versions. There are two editions of *Black Hawk Down*, the 144-minute 2.35:1 theatrical version included on the Blu-ray edition and the 151-minute "extended cut" originally included as "Deleted and Alternate Scenes" on the 2004 DVD release and later on DVD as the "Extended Cut." Although Scott never uses the term "Director's Cut," the theatrical version on the 1080 Blu-ray is clearly his "Preferred Cut," and lacking any evidence to the contrary must be presumed to be definitive. The film is rated R for language and graphic violence.

Black Hawk Down originated as 1997 article by Mark Bowden written for *The Philadelphia Inquirer* and later expanded into book form as *Black Hawk Down: A Story of Modern War* (1999, with new afterword in 2000). Bowden is also the author of *Killing Pablo: The Hunt for the World's Greatest Outlaw* (2000*), D-Day, June 6, 1944* (2002) and *Guests of the Ayatollah: The Iran Hostage Crisis, The First Battle in America's War with Militant Islam* (2006). None of his other works have achieved nearly the success or fame of *Black Hawk Down*.

Bowden's *Black Hawk Down* is a mesmerizing account of America's attempt to bring order into the chaos of Mogadishu, a seaport on the Indian Ocean in Somalia, on the east coast of Africa. A raid was carried out by a select, specially trained force of U.S. Army Rangers and Delta Force Operations. It began on the afternoon of October 2, 1993, and was designed to last an hour, but went terribly wrong and lasted through the night. The raid is said to have involved 19 aircraft, 12 vehicles and 160 men. Four teams of U.S. Rangers dropped by helicopter secured the building as Delta Force commando units apprehended the two "targets" of the raid. The "initiative"—Major General William F. Garrison's word—was lost when, after the two "targets" had been captured and within minutes of departure, Black Hawk helicopter Super Six One was shot down. Later, Super Six Four was also destroyed.

Bowden's book, certainly the most famous account of combat since the Vietnam conflict, is, as the author himself admits, hardly the account that the military might have wished. It has, however, been highly praised by the military even though it reveals miscalculations, inter-unit squabbling, and simple blunders such as failures to take sufficient water, night-vision devices, and other necessary equipment, including heavy Kevlar helmets and armored plates for their bullet-proof vests (Bowden, 355). These mistakes were either toned down or eliminated from the film. For example, a soldier who is filling a canteen is told by another that he will not need it for the short duration of the mission.

The raid was a failure by any reasonable standard. It was alarmingly ill-conceived by the United Nations and U. S. activists. Of course, they were not the ones who had to carry it out after President Clinton ordered it. Even if the raid had been successful, it probably would only have substituted one warlord for another. Afterwards, the United States, which had begun ambitious pacification and humanitarian efforts, reconsidered and President Clinton scaled down U.S. peace-keeping efforts.

Although the raid accomplished its mission, "to surprise and arrest" two top lieutenants of warlord Mohamed Farrah Aidid, it was, as Bowden writes, "a Pyrrhic victory." A raid which was supposed to last twenty minutes stretched into two days. The expensive, hi-tech Black Hawk helicopters proved more susceptible to SAM (Surface to Air) missiles than had been believed. Two helicopters were lost during the battle and two more were forced to crash-land back at the base, By the time the force was extracted the next day by a multinational rescue force, nineteen American soldiers had been killed and dozens more seriously injured. (Michael Durant, a helicopter pilot, was held captive for eleven days.) The Somali toll is unknown, but catastrophic. Conservative estimates numbered some 500 dead and more than 1000 wounded (Bowden, 333). The political fallout, although hardly more than hinted at in the film, was enormous. The raid was a propaganda disaster. Images of joyous Somalis abusing American corpses were shown around the world, the White House was embarrassed, Congress complained, the campaign against Aidid was canceled; he lived until 1996 without, however, achieving his objective of becoming dictator of Somalia. A day after the death of Aidid was reported, General Garrison resigned his commission in the Army.

In *Guts & Glory: The Making of the American Military Image in Film*, an authoritative history of the sometimes troubled relationship between the Pentagon and Hollywood, Lawrence H. Said calls *Black Hawk Down* "a movie of unrelenting, uninterrupted combat for almost its entire 144 minutes, a synthesis of *Zulu*, *Starship Troopers*, and the first twenty-four minutes of *Saving Private Ryan*" (Said, 670).

Of course, any cooperation between a producer and the Pentagon is certain to be a matter of considerable negotiation; fortunately, Jerry Bruckheimer, the successful producer of many big-budget films, including the later *Pirates of the Caribbean* series, was a savvy veteran of such negotiations, and arrangements were worked out. Such negotiations are, of course, time-consuming, and eight Black Hawk helicopters were assigned to the film company only at the last minute before filming was slated to begin in Morocco. According to Said (670), the cost for the use of the helicopters and one hundred soldiers used for military instruction for the actors was $3,000,000.

The Pentagon certainly had legitimate concerns. The raid was by many standards a defeat, but the Pentagon saw it as "a tactical victory" and "an important opportunity to help depict both the distinctive valor of our soldiers during the Somalia operation, as well as the challenges of conducting operations in ambiguous situations that our forces may encounter in today's uncertain security environment worldwide" (Said, 670). Whatever the Pentagon may have thought of the resulting movie, Said regards Somalia as a defeat. His caption on the still from *Black Hawk Down* notes that Americans will pay to see war movies "regardless of whether the United States wins or loses" (672).

Bruckheimer had bought the rights to the story in galley form before the book was published. The screenplay was written by Ken Nolan, who also wrote the screenplay for the miniseries *The Company* (2007), which chronicles the adventures — and misadventures — of the CIA over some forty years.

Black Hawk Down was filmed on location in Morocco in the working-class district of a small town on the Atlantic Ocean. Although Scott is a genius in the use of CGI, he argues that it likely degrades the reality a film presents and believes in using it sparingly. In the words of Josh Hartnett, star of the film, actual filming is a lot more real "than running away from a monster on a green screen." In *Black Hawk Down*, CGI was used only for sequences that were too dangerous or too impractical to shoot live. Viewers will know that scenes showing people being killed or mutilated will be faked in a variety of sophisticated ways. Nonetheless, it is fair to say that, frame by frame, *Black Hawk Down* achieves an astonishing degree of realism from the opening shot of an African closing a body bag to the closing shot of the body of an American soldier being loaded into an aircraft in an image that strangely anticipates another film of American guilt, *American Gangster* with its dope-laden coffins.

Although *Black Hawk Down* runs for some two hours and a half, it gains an intense concentration by dealing only with the raid. Motivation and character development have been almost totally abandoned for the depiction of action. True, the raid continues through the night and into the following day, but the rush of events is so overwhelming that time, at least for the viewer, passes rapidly. The three-act structure largely favored by Scott has gone by the boards. The film consists of a relatively short first act showing the soldiers waiting for the go-code; a very long second act, sometimes almost minute by minute, of the raid and the extraction; and a brief coda which shows children playing around a downed Black Hawk, bodies being loaded into an airplane and a list of the dead on the screen.

The reviews of *Black Hawk Down* were not as favorable as one might have expected. Elvis Mitchell, in the *New York Times*, praised Scott's "eye" with a poisoned pen by linking it with producer Jerry Bruckheimer's "bluntness" "to turn the material into an empty, muddled piece of high-content jingoism that leaves the Africans and the Americans so undifferentiated that it verges on racism." Whatever else this statement might be, it is unfair to Bruckheimer since there is no evidence that he interfered with Scott's "vision" of the film in any way. The fear that the film might be attacked because of the scarcity of African-Americans in Delta Force — only one has any prominence in the film — seems to have been largely unfounded, and although mentioned by several reviewers, the mainstream reviewers hardly noticed it.

Bob Graham in the *San Francisco Chronicle* praised the film generously, but offered little analysis. He pronounced it an "excruciating" and "sobering" account of battle and believed that the only proper response to its "brutal and heartbreaking experience" is "thoughtful silence." Although Graham also expresses some surprise that Bruckheimer should produce such a film, he believes that the film still "hits at gut level but transcends exploitation." The story is told almost purely in visual terms and the dialogue is "sparse but telling." His final verdict is that, in the film, "rescue becomes a heroic substitute for victory."

Neither Bowden nor the "great variety" of reviewers considered the film anti-military. For example, Mike Clark in *USA Today* wrote that the appearance of the film was "ironic screen timing" that reminded the public of a battle that turned the U.S. against American troop commitment. The film extols "the sheer professionalism of America's elite troops Delta Force — even in the unforeseen disaster of Mogadishu."

Liberal reviewers of the film fretted at what they regarded as its lack of context. Philip Strick, in *Sight and Sound*, wrote that the book author's involvement in the project appeared "as the guarantor of a horrendous authenticity," but worried that the characters were not differentiated. The amalgamation of several characters into an imaginary "Grimes," which he observes quite rightly sounds like a name out of Charles Dickens, serves little purpose since the characters, in uniform and soiled by the grime of battle, quickly become indistinguishable anyway. Strick concedes the characters "minor touches of individualism." Strick's main complaint is that the film does not explain the ferocity of the Somali response. They are ready, in overwhelming numbers, fully armed, as the hated Rangers begin to "terrorize" the center of Mogodishu. The reason, explained in Bowden's book, was that the city's main warlord, Mohamed Farrah Aidid, believed that the U.N. was planning to restore a deposed rival clan to power. Precision attacks by copter pilots had killed people only a few weeks previously. According to Strick, Scott has "created, with immense technical skill and spectacular photography ... a biased historical reconstruction" which includes "a string of clichés." Adding injury to insult, Strick concludes triumphantly that *Black Hawk Down* reads as if *Band of Brothers*, the celebrated HBO miniseries, had been made by Scott's brother Tony.

Strick sets up a standard of historical consciousness that no fictional recreation could meet, and certainly not one which takes place over a period of some 18 or so hours. The film, even more than the book on which it is based, is, as it must be, intensely concentrated. Scott believes in hitting the ground running, so to speak, and includes nothing which might impede the narrative. Within this limitation, the filmmaker of necessity can include only a limited amount of context. Certainly, Scott includes context, particularly in the beginning in graphic scenes showing the warlord's men terrorizing the natives and taking the U.N. food supplies that have been brought in to feed the starving multitude. Food is graphically shown as an instrument of war.

He might, of course, have included a conversation similar to that included in *Body of Lies* between the protagonist and a similar warlord. The conversation might then have suggested that Garrison's point of view must be heard — after all, he has force on his side — but it also might have suggested that he is not the only sophisticated thinker on the Ponderosa. The film clearly shows that, while the natives lack the hi-tech equipment of the U.S. military, they are not without resources. The youngsters hold up cell phones to the sky to pass on the sound of the Black Hawk helicopters on their way. Perhaps their cell phones worked better than those of the Americans.

J. Hoberman, in *The Village Voice*, regarded the film as a great man biopic — General Garrison? — which treated "history as immersion, or maybe assault." His review saw the film as — perhaps paradoxically — both too bloody and too fussy and notes that it raises all sorts of questions about American military intelligence and army procedures, and suspects that "these white American soldiers," minus African-Americans, are part of the film's "design element."

Thoughtful reviewers pondered the film's political significance. David Denby noted that Osama bin Laden cited the failure of the mission as an example of American weakness and that President Clinton soon pulled the Special Forces out of Somalia. Denby believed, however, that the film was "fundamentally pro-war" and showed that the soldiers were willing to die for each other. Overall, the film demonstrated not weakness but strength and characterized the mission as an "exceptionally noble failure" of which the country should be proud. Denby's criticism, although fair, burdens the film with an ideology it does not possess. Scott, as usual, whatever other faults he may have, is even-handed. The best verdict is probably Roger Ebert's description of the film as "single-minded in its purpose ... to record as accurately as possible what it is like to be one of the soldiers under fire on that mission."

The terrors of war have never been more graphically portrayed in a Hollywood film. Indeed, the thoughtful viewer might be reminded of Goya's *Disasters of War*. The violence is extreme and often harrowing. A young teenager shooting at an American kills his father by mistake and, appalled, falls upon him weeping. The American soldier involved spares the youngster and moves away. A soldier picks up a severed hand and puts it in his tote bag. The hand's owner, whose body has been messily and totally severed below the waist, says, "Tell my girls I'll be okay." The top half of his body, presumably the only part left in one piece is shown being loaded on a Black Hawk. Sam Peckinpah's *Cross of Iron*, a much underrated film, is one of the few war films with a comparable level of violence. The language of *Black Hawk Down*, is, however, relatively restrained considering the violence of the action.

Long after the film's release, critics continued to fret over its political attitudes, or lack of them. In a 2008 essay entitled "Arts and Culture in the Bush Era," Evan Thomas argued that although *Black Hawk Down* "may have been antiwar on the surface" and "depicted a shameful defeat, the soldiers were heroes willing to die for their brothers."

Black Hawk Down is not an actor's film. There were no stars in the large cast; there were, however, a group of talented actors on the way up. Top-lined Josh Hartnett (Eversmann/Everyman?) had starred in Bruckheimer's *Pearl Harbor* and was in the process of becoming famous. Ewan McGregor (Grimes) had appeared as the young Obi-Wan Kenobi in *Star Wars: The Phantom Menace*. Eric Bana (Hoot) and Orlando Bloom (Blackburn) were beginning their careers. Bloom hardly appears in the film. He shows up in the base sequence and then promptly kills himself when he misses the rope on his helicopter drop. More importantly, Bloom

The Go Code: Josh Hartnett in *Black Hawk Down* (2001). Note the dramatic composition.

got to know Scott and when he tested for the leading role in *Kingdom of Heaven*, Scott was already acquainted with him and with his star-making turns in *The Lord of the Rings* and *Pirates of the Caribbean*. Tom Sizemore (McKnight) had appeared as the titular hero of Spielberg's *Saving Private Ryan,* a role which is hardly as important as the title might make it sound. Bana's earlier appearance in *Chopper* (2000) may have helped him land his choice role in Scott's film.

Reviewers generally complained that the soldiers all looked more or less alike. They were all young, dressed identically, and had short haircuts, and the viewer never got to know them as individuals before they were rushed off to war. Presumably most viewers recognized Hartnett and Bana's distinctive looks, but the others were difficult to sort out. The problem of recognition has become a recurrent one, especially in war films, and the reviewers of the 2010 miniseries *The Pacific* complained that they could not tell the soldiers apart.

Classic Hollywood would have solved the problem by a variety of methods: by concentrating on only four or five characters, by using a flashback which would make the actor memorable, by using well-known character actors with distinctive styles, and by giving the actors distinctive patterns of speech. Of course, Scott is aware of all of these methods — Bruckheimer says that they considered flashbacks — but he discarded them in the interests of realism, of the compression of time, of immediacy, of the moment. Whether Scott gained more than he lost by that decision is a nice question, but it certainly separates *Black Hawk Down* from other Hollywood war films

The only actor who received any praise from the reviewers was Sam Shepard as General Garrison, who oversaw the mission from his hi-tech command headquarters. Shepard is, along with David Mamet, among the best-known active American play-wrights, but unlike Mamet, he occasionally appears in films. Often compared to Gary Cooper, Shepard has generally disdained movie stardom in favor of his work for the stage, but he has done notable work for the screen and has never been better than in *Black Hawk Down*. Shepard is the glue that holds the film together. He superbly portrays tension at ease, a superb and alert command of the situation at hand combined with an intense concern for his men. Within minutes of the successful completion of the mission, when a Black Hawk helicopter is shot down by a hand-held surface-to-air missile, Garrison's *sotto voce* comment about losing the "initiative" is the most memorable line in the film. Unlike Scott, he is a student of acting and, in his comments on the DVD, he says that he was not interested in portraying the real Garrison, but in showing a military man under the stress of a particular situation. Shepard's performance is the still center that holds the huge film together.

The complexity of *Black Hawk Down* has generated some strange responses. Finke and Shichtman believe that Scott celebrates retreat and that the film presents "a new paradigm explaining the successes of postcolonial upstarts to an American audience overwhelmed by the politics of defeat" (230). The film demonstrates "the failure of hard-boiled masculinity to transform the politics of Africa — or of the Middle East" (231). The blame here is placed solely on the Americans, but the raid was undertaken by President Clinton at the request of the United Nations. Causes and effects are men-tioned, but are clearly outside the range of the film. Scott's purpose was to show in detail the complexity and costs of modern warfare. The result is a great film — arguably Scott's greatest — and it is also a fair-and-balanced film. *Black Hawk Down* has no agenda. It merely says: This is the way modern warfare is. Deal with it.

Black Hawk Down opened in limited release on December 28, 2001, in order to qualify for 2001 Academy Awards. It won a number of prestigious awards, including two Academy Awards (Best Film Editing and Sound). A wide opening followed at the beginning of 2002. According to Box Office Mojo, *Black Hawk Down* had a production budget of approximately $92,000,000. The domestic box office was $108,638,745, but the foreign box office was a relatively disappointing $64,350,906. Perhaps not all foreign countries were happy with a film showing heroic Americans. Still, the film's stout showing on DVD and Blu-ray must have provided solace for its backers. The popularity of the film also spawned an Internet boon to the makers of model helicopters, especially Black Hawk models and kits.

15

Hannibal (2001):
Hannibal the Cannibal

Version. The only currently available text of *Hannibal* is the 131-minute R-rated theatrical version. The DVD and Blu-ray also include over 35 minutes of deleted and alternate scenes and an alternate ending.

Dr. Hannibal Lecter, aka Hannibal the Cannibal, began life as a minor character in Thomas Harris's 1981 novel *Red Dragon*. Deft of mind but slow of pen, the estimable Harris has published only four other relatively short novels during the course of his forty-year professional career: *Black Sunday* (1975), *The Silence of the Lambs* (1988), *Hannibal* (1999) and *Hannibal Rising* (2006). All the novels, except *Black Sunday*, deal with the horrific deeds of Hannibal Lecter. The novels are carefully researched, intensely dramatic and full of convincing procedural details. Harris is a favorite of Hollywood, and his five novels have been turned into six films — *Red Dragon* has been filmed twice — with almost certainly more to come.

Although publicity-shy, Harris is not a fanatical recluse of the J.D. Salinger or Cormac McCarthy type. He is said to have been born in 1940 and to have grown up in Rich, Mississippi. He attended Clarksdale High School, where his mother taught biology. He received a BA in English from Baylor in 1964, spent time in Europe, was married and divorced, worked as a reporter in New York, and eventually began writing what Benjamin Szumskyj calls "grisly crime stories"(2). He apparently likes good company and fine food; Dino DeLaurentiis reportedly flew his pasta chef across the country in an attempt to speed up his pen, but does not seem to have had any appreciable success. *Hannibal* is said to have appeared six years after its original deadline.

Harris's first novel, *Black Sunday*, already showed the author's characteristic attention to authentic details and psychological precision. The novel almost seems — and perhaps was — written with the movies in mind. The film of the same name (1977), about the planning and executing of a terrorist attack on the Super Bowl, was ably helmed by John Frankenheimer and successfully mixed authentic Super Bowl footage with scenes shot for the movie. The film was A-list all the way. Produced by Robert Evans, scripted by Ernest Lehman, who wrote Hitchcock's *North by Northwest*, and starring Robert Shaw, Bruce Dern and Marthe Keller, it was sold as a blockbuster disaster movie of the type then popular. It was only a moderate commercial success, perhaps because of script problems. Unlike the other Harris films, *Black Sunday* has a huge cast and "multiple plotlines." Stephen B. Armstrong, in his study of Frankenheimer's films *Pictures About Extremes*, believes that the film's depictions of the characters' states of mind retarded the narrative and perhaps harmed the box office (96, 98).

At some point, Harris's second novel, *Red Dragon,* caught the attention of Michael Mann, who was at the time best known as the producer of the successful television series *Crime Story* (1986–88) and the wildly successful *Miami Vice* (1984–90). Both series were famous for their hard-driving musical scores and bright colors. Mann, who had no interest in making a horror film, changed the title to *Manhunter* and made it into a police procedural centered upon a detective who develops psychological problems when he enters too deeply into the mind of a serial killer. The 1986 film was superbly shot by Dante Spinotti in the bright colors Mann favored, well-written, and well-acted, especially by William Petersen, whose performance in the leading role reminds us of how much big-screen audiences lost when Petersen decided to spend a decade peering at crime scenes in *CSI: Crime Scene Investigation.*

In *Manhunter,* Hannibal Lecter was not the major serial killer, but shared screen time with another of his perverted kind, the so-called "Tooth Fairy," played by Tom Noonan. The spelling of Lecter's name was changed to Lecktor, presumably to make it sound more sinister. Immaculately clean and neatly attired in prison garb, Lecktor, played by Brian Cox, was brightly photographed in his cell, presumably to contrast his digs with those of the hideout of the other serial killer. Cox is a burly English actor who has done excellent work in a wide variety of roles on stage and screen. Although capable of playing sympathetic roles, he has more often worked the dark side.

Manhunter was a failure. According to Box Office Mojo, it had a domestic gross of $8,620,929. The film, whatever its production cost, which is not given, was certainly not cheap, and the foreign box office and ancillary rights could hardly have compensated. Clearly, producer DeLaurentiis was disappointed with the returns and passed on its sequel, *The Silence of the Lambs.* This turned out to be a mistake.

The film version of *The Silence of the Lambs* was a monster which earned $130,742,922 domestically and an estimated $142,000,000 from the foreign market. In short, it grossed nearly a quarter of a billion dollars on a production budget of some $19,000,000 and became one of the most honored films of all time. It became only the third picture, following *It Happened One Night* (1934) and *One Flew Over the Cuckoo's Nest* (1975), to win all five major Academy Awards: Best Picture, Best Actor (Anthony Hopkins), Best Actress (Jodie Foster), Best Director (Jonathan Demme), and Best Screenplay adapted from another medium (Ted Tally). It was also nominated for Best Score and Best Editing, but did not win. No police procedural or horror film had ever come close to such acclaim. Ironically, the competition included Ridley Scott, who was nominated for what the AMC website calls the "stridently feminist buddy-road picture" *Thelma & Louise.*

Silence fully deserved the awards it received. Writing, acting, direction and production values were all top-of-the-line. It was the breakthrough film of director Ted
Demme (1969–2002), who never managed to approach its quality again throughout
the remainder of his relatively short life. Foster gave her finest performance as Special
Agent Clarice Starling. Hopkins, although recognized as a fine actor, achieved a new
level of stardom with an iconic performance. He is particularly effective at portraying
what one writer has called "power and its perversions" (Johnson, 25). His many excellent
earlier performances include the insane ventriloquist and his dummy in *Magic* (1978),
Dr. Frederick Treves, who treated the Elephant Man in the 1980 film of the same name,
and Adolf Hitler in *The Bunker* (1980). Among the supporting players, veteran character
actors Scott Glenn and Frankie Faison approached career highs; Faison reprised his role
as Barney Matthews in *Hannibal* ten years later.

Although *Silence* was smartly directed and included a classic portrayal of evil from
an actor of enormous talent, it was primarily hailed as a parable of female empowerment,
especially by the feminist critics, and clearly required a follow-up. The first problem
was that Thomas Harris was very slow in providing a sequel. Then, a success of such
magnitude creates problems of all sorts, including unhappy actors wanting more money,
directors wanting changes in the script, and so forth. And producer DeLaurentiis, for
whatever reason, brought in his own crew to create his new film. Foster did not approve
of the portrayal of Starling in the novel and refused to portray the character "with negative attitudes she's never had." Undoubtedly, her main objection was to the conclusion
of the novel, which portrays the triumph of Hannibal Lecter, who has turned Starling
into a kind of zombie and is traveling around South America with her in tow, showing
her off at the opera and other cultural events. Barney Matthews, who had been Dr.
Lecter's jailer and who later had sold souvenirs of the famous killer's captivity for large
sums, is traveling with his wife and identifies Lecter, but is in turn recognized. Knowing
Lecter's powers, Barney immediately strikes out for home. The ending, as Foster recognized, can hardly be read as a statement of female empowerment. Quite the reverse,
in fact. Lacking script approval, she opted out, and DeLaurentiis hired Julianne Moore
to play Starling and Scott to direct.

After the success of *Hannibal*, DeLaurentiis produced two more Hannibal Lecter
movies. Recognizing that *Manhunter* was a police procedural, that Will Graham was
the main character, and that Hannibal was not even the main killer, DeLaurentiis
decided to make Dr. Lecter the main character and to remake *Manhunter* under the
original title of the Harris novel, *Red Dragon*. Brett Ratner directed and the film earned
$209,451,898 worldwide. By comparison, the failure of *Hannibal Rising* (2007), directed
by Peter Webber, based on Harris's novel of the same name depicting the youth of the
famous psychopath, earned only $82,169,884 worldwide and must be considered both
an artistic and commercial failure. The film suffers from the absence of Anthony Hopkins
and from the lack of a unified visual style. Webber must have seemed a reasonable
choice to direct since his well-received film *The Girl with a Pearl Earring* had depicted

the artistic milieu surrounding the creation of Vermeer's famous painting. The integration of the Japanese aesthetic regarding the way of the sword into the crazed world of the young Lecter would have been food and drink for any number of Oriental directors — including Ang Lee — but was beyond Webber's ability, even with the formidable Gong Li on board. Additionally, the inexperienced Gaspard Ulliel was out of his depths as the young Hannibal. With *Hannibal Rising*, Lecter's filmic career came to an end. Since he is, however, one of our favorite monsters — right up there with Frankenstein's monster and Norman Bates — he is certain to return.

The development of *Hannibal* seems to have been rancorous, with people shouting at each other and threatening to sue. The competing screenplays of *Hannibal* by Steven Zaillian and David Mamet became a matter of considerable discussion. Eventually, the credit was shared. Significantly, Zaillian appears with Scott on the DVD commentary and discusses their collaboration in detail, but neither mentions Mamet. Zaillian, a talented writer of screenplays, wrote Steven Spielberg's *Schindler's List* (1993) and Martin Scorsese's *Gangs of New York* (2002). He also wrote and directed *Searching for Bobby Fischer* (1993) and *A Civil Action* (1998). His ambitious *All the King's Men* (2006), based on the famous novel by Robert Penn Warren, was almost universally panned, especially when compared with Robert Rossen's Academy Award–winning 1949 film version.

"Stax," in *Screenwriter's Utopia*, which offers on-line analyses of screenplays, is very hard on Mamet's rejected screenplay. He calls it "horrible" and condemns its "convoluted plotting, under-developed characters and an overall sloppiness." This version was replaced by Zaillian's screenplay, described as "intelligent, well-structured, full of rich descriptions and elegant characterizations … a whole new interpretation of Harris' novel" with "far better dialogue." In rebuttal, Mamet took the unusual step of placing his script on-line where it may be consulted so that readers may make up their own minds.

Whatever the verdict on Mamet's work may be, the jibe about "far better dialogue" is a totally unfair judgment of the man who is almost universally regarded as having the finest ear of any American writer of his generation. Mamet is one of America's most highly regarded playwrights, an occasional television writer and director (*The Unit*), and a distinguished film director. His stature is shown by the fact that two films which he both wrote and directed, *House of Games* (1987) and *Homicide* (1991), have been included in the prestigious Criterion DVD collection. His generally right-wing politics are a refreshing change from the almost universal conformity of politically correct left-wing writers.

Hannibal was filmed in Florence, Italy; Washington DC; Richmond and Montepelier, Virginia; and Asheville, North Carolina, with America's largest private house, some 150,000 square feet, standing in for Mason Verger's mansion.

Like *Gladiator*, *Hannibal* has a classic three-act structure. The first act takes place largely at Mason Verger's castle-like residence somewhere outside Washington, the second takes place in Florence, and the third returns to the United States and, except for a brief epilogue, ends where it began. The structure is somewhat obscured by the shifting around occasioned by the plotting, especially in the second act.

The film begins with a voice-over by Barney Matthews, who had spent six years as Dr. Lecter's guard and had gotten to know him well. (Frankie Faison had had a small role as Lt. Fisk in Michael Mann's *Manhunter*, before playing nurse Barney in *The Silence of the Lambs* and *Hannibal*.) Barney is interrogated by Verger, or what is left of him. Verger, the only one of Lecter's victims to have survived, had been horribly mutilated in their nearly fatal encounter years earlier, and his sole mission is life is to revenge himself, a process facilitated by his wealth. Barney has a large collection of Lecter's memorabilia, or "cookies" as Verger calls them, and sells them to him for large sums. This time, he has a mask of the fiend which he sells to Verger for $250,000 before the credits roll to surveillance video scenes of Venice.

Gary Oldman is reported to have wanted his name removed from the credits, but considering the greatness of his performance, it is difficult to understand why. He disappears behind the five hours of makeup and emerges looking like the sole survivor of a cannibal bakeout. Although the makeup is horrifying, Scott has said that he wanted to make Verger look "more touching than monstrous," and the talented Oldman certainly does that, but he also does more — much more. His off-the-wall religious references and his cavalier treatment of his doubtlessly well-paid, but verbally much-abused factotum Cordell strike the proper tone between horror and shrill humor.

Meanwhile, FBI Special Agent Clarice Starling is leading a combined force to arrest Evelda Drumgo, an HIV-positive criminal packing both an automatic handgun and a baby in a sling. Assessing the crowded market where the arrest is to be made, Starling tells the group to stand down, but is ignored by a headline-hunting local policeman. The newspapers blame Starling for the ensuing carnage — she is said to have killed five people — and cite her earlier use of deadly force.

In the ensuing investigation, the loathsome Paul Krendler (Ray Liotta) of the Justice Department firmly fixes the blame on Starling, but Verger uses his influence to have the charges dismissed, or as he puts it ironically when Starling visits him in his palatial country residence, "to cleanse the stigma of your recent dishonor." In a terrifying flashback, Verger tells of his encounter with Lecter, their game of temporary asphyxiation and his subsequent mutilation. Starling talks to Barney, who gives her clues to renew her hunt for Lecter.

In Florence, Dr. Lecter has arranged the "disappearance" of an art historian and applied for his job. Police Inspector Renaldo Pazzi discovers Lecter's identity and plans to collect the reward that Verger has placed on his head. Pazzi overreaches by attempting both to collect Verger's reward and to take credit for his capture to impress his beautiful and cultivated wife and to support her in expensive style. Lecter discovers the plot and kills Pazzi in high historical fashion by eviscerating him and hanging him out on the same building and in the same manner — entrails out — in which an ancestor of Pazzi had died centuries ago.

Verger, apparently plotting the most terrible end for Lecter he can imagine, has had killer hogs imported from Sardinia for the purpose. Back in the United States, Lecter is menaced by the killer hogs, but escapes. Verger is not so fortunate. He is fed to the hogs by his physician-caretaker Cordell, who is apparently seeking revenge for being bossed around for years by a madman. Of course, Cordell himself does not escape. Lecter scalps Paul Krendler and feeds him parts of his own brain. The climax occurs when Starling, fighting off a drugged stupor, handcuffs herself to Lecter, who chops off his own hand to escape. Apparently, his affection for Starling is so great that he would rather mutilate himself than her. The cleverness of this climax, whoever thought it up, is that it depends upon Starling's acute analysis of Lecter's character. In an epilogue on an airplane, Lecter, his arm in a sling, feeds an appreciative young boy some brains, presumably those of Krendler, from a tray.

The ending was the cause of considerable concern. It is one thing to reject the ending of the novel in which Lecter is shown touring the world's great culture spots with a zombie-like Starling in tow. It is quite another to decide upon a better ending. With the new ending, Lecter is still out there somewhere, perhaps in Bogota, plotting his return. He is minus a hand, but he is still in love with Starling, or in what passes for love in his mind. The ending of the novel would have been a more appropriate ending for the pure horror film that Scott made, but the present one will do nicely.

The casting is strong throughout. Hopkins moves effortlessly back into form after a ten-year absence, and Julianne Moore, although lacking the ambiguous sexuality and cornpone mannerisms of Jodie Foster in the earlier film, is effective as Starling. Giancarlo Giannini, as Pazzi, reminds us how much we have missed him since his classic performance in Lina Wertmüller's *Swept Away* twenty-five years earlier. Pazzi's wife, played by Francesca Neri, is a beautiful and cultivated woman in love with her husband. She is a pearl of great price and makes the viewer understand how easily Pazzi might overreach to impress her.

The good-natured interchanges between Starling and Nurse Barney (Frankie Faison) are particularly effective. Starling knows that Barney is profiting from selling Hannibal memorabilia, but she also knows that he is a kind-hearted man who tends injured birds. Barney knows that she knows exactly what he is doing, but that she will not betray him. Their exchanges give the often dark film a humanity it would otherwise lack.

Strangely, at least from the viewpoint of a decade later, the reviews of *Hannibal* were largely unfavorable. Kenneth Turan in the *Los Angeles Times* called the film "a disappointment" with "something missing from the first film." It treats the material with "too much respect," does not allow itself "to get down and dirty," and its portrayal of a more assured Clarice Starling takes away from the film. Like many other critics, Turan did not like the ending. None of Turan's criticisms seems to make any sense today.

Jonathan Foreman called *Hannibal* the weakest of the three Hannibal Lecter movies calling it "deliberately campy." He writes that Mason Verger "bears a disturbing resemblance" to Montgomery Burns in *The Simpsons* and, like Burns, even has an "effeminate factotum." Foreman's belief that some of the scenes might be "too repulsive for many viewers" clearly turned out to be incorrect.

J. Hoberman's review was perhaps the grumpiest, certainly the cleverest and arguably the most unfair. The film was "less monster than monstrosity—albeit as superfluous sequels go, not on a par with the memorably idiotic *Godfather 3*." There

is, he asserted, "no redemption here, just the quest for a paycheck." Moore's performance "projects little of the solitude or vulnerability Foster brought to the role." The film is "showy filmmaking" and Hopkins "a sinister Truman Capote—portly and soigné, peeking coyly from beneath his trademark Panama hat." Hoberman has here, perhaps unfairly, identified the difference between *Silence* and *Hannibal*. Scott makes no attempt to equal *Silence*

Hannibal Lecter (Anthony Hopkins) on the move, Clarice Starling (Julianne Moore) in tow.

on its own grounds as a horrifying police procedural of female empowerment. Instead he attempts to film a gothic horror story.

Peter Rainer, in *New York* magazine, wrote jocosely that *Hannibal* was about the "difficulties of staying retired" and complained that the film takes much too long for the two "kindred spirits" to get together. While *Hannibal* has a classic three-act structure, Hannibal and Starling meet only at the end. They do, however, talk on the telephone. Rainer admits that the now-portly Hannibal perks up after he learns that Starling is again on the trail and looks less like a "loggy moray eel." Unable to accept the gothic premise, Rainer accuses the film of "dogged loopiness and icky bloodletting."

In the *Christian Science Monitor*, David Sterritt wrote that the new adventures of Dr. Lecter "lack the sense of audacity and surprise that mark his previous incarnation." Sterritt believes that Dr. Lecter is "one of today's most vivid pop-culture icons," speculates about the nature of his appeal, and concludes that his personality and charisma may be the secret. His cannibalism is a metaphor for his ability to get inside people's minds and, citing Professor Mita Brottman in support, concludes that Hannibal is a perfect villain for a postmodern age which operates in a fairy tale atmosphere of dungeons, cells, people being fed to hogs, and other horrors. The characters do not change. Such an analysis is, of course, hardly news.

Newsday's John Anderson correctly called *Silence* "a police procedural, augmented by a madman." Scott, however, is "the definitive head-on director," and *Hannibal* is "predictably stylish, visually elegant and entertaining," and the action and imagery are "sharply defined." He believes, however, that the purity of Lecter's evil has become "boring." While Anderson has identified the film's strengths, "boring" is an unlikely word to apply either to the movie or to the character of Dr. Lecter. At any rate, "boring" is a subjective concept which could be applied to much of the great literature and films of the past and present. Michelangelo Antonioni's *L'avventura* (1960), for example, has been called one of the greatest films ever made and the most boring.

Reviewers as a group usually fight the last battle instead of the present one. They knew that the last battle was about the heroism of Clarice Starling, but they were clueless as to what the present one was about. They suspected that the battlefield had been moved and they attempted with little success to figure out where. *The Silence of the Lambs* was a police procedural with a noble heroine, and they assumed that Scott was attempting to do the same thing and was not succeeding.

Composer Hans Zimmer has said that the film may be read in several ways: as an archetype of Freudian beauty and the heart; as a treatise on corruption in the American police force and in the Congress; as a nostalgic yearning for the beauty of the Renaissance and its corruption; and as a dark love story, passion in its truest sense, what Scott has called "kind of romantic." Zimmer is generally correct in his manifold interpretations, but Scott is right on the money. Above all else, *Hannibal* is a gothic exercise in style comparable to Charles Robert Maturin's *Melmoth the Wanderer,* the tales of Edgar Allan Poe and *The Phantom of the Opera*. Perhaps the most precise reading of *Hannibal* is as a perverse version of Victor Hugo's *The Hunchback of Notre Dame.*

The opera in Florence is, of course, a fraud, but a beautiful one. It exists only as Patrick Cassidy's haunting aria "Vide Cor Meum" ("See My Heart"), based upon the first sonnet in Dante's *La Vita Nuova* (*The New Life*). The poem describes Dante's vision of Beatrice and his falling in love with the beautiful nine-year-old girl. In the poem, the God of Love appears, holding Dante's heart in his hand and with Beatrice, his beloved, sleeping in his arms. He wakens the girl and feeds her the poet's bleeding heart.

The imagery of a bleeding heart, which survives today only as an archaic image in Catholic iconography, still exercises a residual power. Early Christians were sometimes accused of being cannibals because they maintained that the Eucharist contained the body and blood of Christ. Although the bleeding heart imagery maintained its force at least through the Middle Ages, Christian iconography probably never included any imagery showing the eating of the heart. Obviously, the bleeding heart imagery would have a particularly strong appeal to Hannibal Lecter, although, being an intellectual, he seems to have preferred brains to hearts.

According to Scott, the beautiful music of the opera becomes "a metaphor for corruption." The irony of the situation in the film is that Hannibal and Allegra recite Dante's first sonnet together while her husband is plotting to sell out Hannibal for a motive which Hannibal might even have approved of, at least, in theory: to give his beautiful wife a higher standard of living. Hannibal would have given the elegant Allegra the luxuries which she deserves and which her husband cannot supply. (Admittedly, he might have turned her into a zombie in the process.) The staging of the opera resembles the studied elegance of Luchino Visconti, who in addition to directing films also staged operas and included scenes from an opera in *Senso* (1954). The scene in which Lecter loads Pazzi on a dolly, strangles him, eviscerates him and shoves him out the window either honors or debases the memory of Pazzi's ancestor who had been murdered in similar high style centuries earlier. The bravura sequence is a classic of Grand Guignol staging which will have a permanent place in the history of cinema.

Hannibal is a gothic masterpiece which rewards repeated viewings and has never received the recognition it deserves. Reviewers caught in the moiling and churning of the movies they saw last week and the week before lose the ability to discriminate which time provides. Following a film as famous as *The Silence of the Lambs*, widely interpreted as a tale of female empowerment, *Hannibal* never had a chance with the critics. In its coldness, the film resembles a combination of Fritz Lang's *Dr. Mabuse* and Joe May's *The Indian Tomb*, courtesy of Lang's screenplay. Time will treat it more fairly. It will brush off a few cobwebs and set it beside the great gothic film masterpieces —*Frankenstein, The Golem, Nosferatu*, and the silent version of *The Phantom of the Opera*—as a classic film.

Hannibal was budgeted at $87,000,000 (Raw, 153). Although the publicity surrounding Foster's public rejection of the role, the ten-year wait between films and the controversy over the screenplay credits could hardly have helped either the box office or the reviews, the interest in Dr. Lecter was so great and Scott's film so satisfying that the take was $165,092,268 and the worldwide total an enormous $351,692,268 (Box Office Mojo).

16

Matchstick Men (2003):
Mean Street Men in Bright Colors

Version. The 116-minute theatrical cut shot in anamorphic widescreen 2.35:1 is the only available version. Considering the popularity and critical standing of the film, it may or may not be supplemented or changed in the future.

According to the commentary on the DVD, *Matchstick Men* began as a novel by Eric Garcia, which was read in galley proofs by brothers Nicholas and Ted Griffin in the early spring of 2003. They liked the novel as a film project, but thought that the ending, which left the protagonist "daughterless, partner-less and moneyless," was a "downer." They rewrote the ending and cut out the fake daughter and the big con. Producer Robert Zemeckis liked the project, but wanted the original ending to be restructured and restored in some way. The big con (an elaborate confidence trick designed to trick the victim or victims out of a large sum of money) was restored and the ending was softened.

The project came together rapidly and was completed in a remarkably short time. The pre-production, which included some rehearsal with the actors, was followed by fifty days of principal shooting. The post-production took fourteen weeks and seems to have caused some stress. According to Scott, it took that long "to really find the movie." Doubts arose about the nature of the film, particularly about "the trick" and the type of score which would be appropriate. These questions should, of course, have been settled during pre-production. Scott says that he had always considered the film a comedy rather than a drama.

Since the film had a variety of different themes, the charm was intended to come from the interaction of the players with each other. The film tested well but the sheets were hardly enthusiastic. Eventually, the role of the cashier was augmented, and the film ended — or was supposed to be interpreted — as a fairy tale about a man who lost a daughter and gained a child. Such, at least, was the theory. The poster showed the appropriate emphasis, with a wary Nicolas Cage, briefcase in hand, on the left, a somewhat smaller Sam Rockwell, also wary and tense on the right, and between them Alison Lohman, skateboard in hand.

The story is deliberately deceptive. Of course, the viewer has no right to complain about this since any movie named *Matchstick Men*, by its very title, announces itself as a game involving the filmmakers and the audience. The game is a delicate one. If the puzzle is too easy, viewers will complain that they "saw it coming" a mile away. Indeed, they may say that even if it is not true. After all, they paid for the tickets.

Any effective con involves the art of misdirection. The con artist(s) must first gain the trust of the mark so that he, she or they will not notice when the real con arrives. The film begins by showing us two con men at work. The elder and the leader is Roy Walter (Cage) and the younger, Frank Mercer (Rockwell), to whom he has apparently taught the tricks of the trade some years back. The team has been successful. They have specialized in the small con and have avoided the big, or long, con which would be certain to get them serious attention from the mob or the law or both. There is no indication that they have ever been in trouble with the law and they have made a great deal of money which Sam has apparently spent. Roy keeps his share in a stone dog at home before stashing it in a safe deposit box at a bank.

The kicker, which causes difficulty when they are working, is that Roy suffers from a perfect storm of obsessive-compulsive disorders and when he is off his meds, he is a helpless prisoner of repetitive routine in his expensive, well-lighted and well-cared-for house in the valley. When he nervously dumps his meds down the drain, he goes to a psychiatrist, Harris Klein, superbly played by Bruce Altman, who attempts to aid him in returning to what is, at least for him, a normal life.

Roy has an ex-wife who separated from him fourteen years ago when three months pregnant. Mysteriously, or perhaps not so mysteriously in this movie, Roy has never looked up his wife and does not know what happened to the child or even, for that matter, if there had *been* a child. Back on his meds and back at the game, Roy is surprised to meet a teenager who announces herself as his daughter. He takes her into his house and begins to accept the mixed joys of fatherhood. When she discovers that Roy is a crook, albeit a very successful one, she tells him that, if he makes a career of being a criminal, "it's just a bunch of something strung together."

When the complex plot reaches its conclusion, Roy is shown to have been the victim of a big con and his partner, his fake daughter, the fake psychiatrist and their fake cohorts have conned Roy out of the $1,000,000 or so which he has accumulated over the years. The good news is that, although he has never recovered his money, he has found happiness working in a carpet store selling remnants and returning home to his pregnant wife, who turns out to be the comely cashier in the convenience store he has been seen eyeing from time to time earlier in the story.

Reviewers generally praised the film, but were perplexed and thought something was wrong. Uncertain what it was, they generally decided to give the film a pass. Rob White called the film "a strange hybrid: a comic con-trick thriller with elements of a moralistic fable," and compared it to *About a Boy* and *Three Men and a Baby*, which he described as stories about a child's ability to feminize father figures "and so redeem them." James Berardinelli compared *Matchstick Men* with other con films and praised it as the first Oscar-worthy movie of the fall season, but somehow seemed unenthusiastic. The anonymous reviewer on moviegazette.com praised it for breathing new life into a tired subgenre of the crime film — the confidence film — and compared it to *Paper Moon, The Grifters* and *The Zero Effect*. The comparisons are fair. Cage is a risk-taking actor, but he falls considerably short of the charm of Ryan O'Neal, or for that matter even of Bruce Altman, the ersatz doctor in *Matchstick Men* who turns out also to be a con man, and Scott's film has neither the toughness nor the sophistication of Stephen Frears' adaptation of Jim Thompson's original tough-guy novel *The Grifters*.

Roger Ebert courageously championed the film. In a thoughtful and analytical review, he divides its complex narrative into three strands: (1) a man crippled by neurotic obsessions faces a crisis, (2) two con men, the matchstick men of the title, happen upon a big score and (3) a man meets a teenage daughter he never knew he had. Ebert admits that the stories add up "to more, or perhaps less," than the sum of their parts.

David Sterritt, in the *Christian Science Monitor,* damned *Matchstick Men* with faint praise. He called Scott "reigning king of the Hollywood epic," but welcomed *Matchstick Men* as "a humble addition" to the "small corner of his career" devoted to "character-driven films." Renee Graham (the *Boston Globe*) wrote that Scott went "all gooey" in this "off key adaptation" of Garcia's novel, and criticized the epilogue which is as "improbable as it is unsatisfying." In the DVD commentary, Ted and Nicholas Griffin, the brothers who wrote the screenplay, stoutly defend their ending saying that neither they nor the moviegoing public could allow the downbeat ending of the novel.

The best confidence films work when the marks are less sympathetic and more venal than the con artists. Con men and women, usually but not always sophisticated, have been a film staple since at least 1932 when Ernst Lubitsch's *Trouble in Paradise* appeared. Big or long con films are, however, comparatively rare, and George Roy Hill's popular film *The Sting* (1973), starring Robert Redford and Paul Newman, is easily the most famous. The reigning master of the con film is David Mamet, whose sharp dialogue and clever construction in *House of Games* (1987) and *The Spanish Prisoner* (1997) set new standards for the con man film. It would have been interesting to see how Mamet would have handled the screenplay of *Matchstick Men*. Mamet had worked on the screenplay of *Hannibal* and received co-credit, with Steven Zaillian, who shares commentary time with — and praise from — Scott on the DVD, while Mamet is never mentioned. Mamet's expertise was sorely needed on *Matchstick Men*'s screenplay.

The plot of *Matchstick Men* is impossible to believe and full of absurdities, but is carefully enough worked out for the viewers to suspend disbelief. The film's problem is in the casting and in the treatment of the material. Mamet knows that con men are congenital liars and, no matter how much money they have stowed away, live from hand to mouth. They are also clever and witty talkers. It could be argued that Scott's bright Southern California visuals are inappropriate for such a dark story.

Nicolas Cage, the nephew of celebrated director Francis Ford Coppola, began his career with small parts in two excellent movies, *Fast Times at Ridgemont High* (1982) and *Valley Girl* (1983), before his breakthrough performance in his uncle's memorable ensemble film *Rumble Fish* (1983) He gradually moved into more ambitious and larger roles, including David Lynch's *Wild at Heart* (1990) and *Red Rock West* (1993), and won an Academy Award as Best Actor for his performance in *Leaving Las Vegas* (1995) as an alcoholic screenwriter who goes to Las Vegas to drink himself to death. Though overweight for an alcoholic, he gave a magnificent performance opposite the underappreciated Elisabeth Shue.

His later films have varied from large commercial projects such as *National Treasure: Book of Secrets* (2007) and smaller but still expensive films such as *Matchstick Men*. It has been argued that the brutally realistic actor is miscast in Scott's film. Cage is a heavy presence at best, and being afflicted in the film with a variety of obsessive-compulsive tics robs him of the sympathy the character should command. Certainly, if the tics had been dropped, the character would have been more appealing.

Sam Rockwell is more convincing as Cage's confederate, but Bruce Altman as the ersatz psychiatrist Dr. Klein steals the acting credits. He is totally convincing as a laid-back '60s leftover who must have been at Woodstock in a prior incarnation. On first viewing, at least to the present writer, Alison Lohman's Angela projected an indefinable sense of dislocation which fostered a growing sense of uneasiness. She is supposedly fourteen in the film but is, like the actress who portrayed her, actually twenty-two. The performance is wonderful for what it is, but if we imagine the Tatum O'Neal of *Paper Moon* in the role, we quickly realize that an actual fourteen-year-old would have been better. The viewer needs to like the con men and to identify with them, but unfortunately, except for the fake psychiatrist, there *is* no one to like.

Although *Matchstick Men* has never been a public favorite, it is reassuring to see that it has received Leonard Maltin's seal of approval in *151 Movies You've Never Seen*.

Matchstick Men was a financial failure. According to Box Office Mojo, it grossed $36,906,460 domestically and $28,565,672 elsewhere, for a total of $65,565,672 worldwide.

17

All the Invisible Children (2005): "Jonathan": The Rediscovery of Life Through Childhood

All the Invisible Children is an omnibus film containing seven segments, each of which has a different director and tells a story about a different child. In addition to Scott and his daughter Jordan, the directors are Mendi Charef, Spike Lee, Emir Kusturica, Katia Lund, Stefano Veneruso, and John Woo. The film was made for UNICEF, a United Nations relief organization, undoubtedly to raise money to assist the millions of starving children around the world. "Jonathan," which runs about 17 minutes, was written by Jordan Scott, and likely designed as an opportunity for her to gain experience in filmmaking. The DVD of the film is difficult to obtain and was apparently not released in the U.S. In the "making of" featurette, she is prominently shown, but her father appears only briefly. The supposition is that Jordan wrote the film and directed it with her father watching over her shoulder.

The seven films vary widely in quality. Spike Lee's heart-wrenching entry, "Jesus Children of America," is about the difficulties of a young HIV positive girl who goes through hell at school and greater hell at home from her dying AIDS-ridden parents. Hong Kong master John Woo has a wonderfully written and directed story about a rich girl and a poor girl linked together by a doll. In many ways, the most satisfying entry is Emir Kusturica's gypsy story, originally planned as a feature, of a young boy trapped in a lifestyle which can lead only to his destruction. "Blue Gypsy" serves as an interesting pendant to Kusturica's Johnny Depp film *Arizona Dream* (1993), and the two films gain by being shown together.

Except for "Jonathan," the other six films deal in some way with the victimization of children. Jordan's film, however, begins with a quotation from Wordsworth — in German in the version I saw — and shows a regression to childhood as a solution for the problems of Jonathan, a shell-shocked photojournalist (played by David Thewlis, the Hospitaler of *Kingdom of Heaven*).

Profoundly damaged by what he has seen and heard, Jonathan somehow regresses to a series of apparently imaginary incidents from his childhood which presumably restores his faith in himself. He jumps into a lake and becomes a child again, or imagines he does. He is shown in a boat with two other boys (he is the one with a camera), moves across a war-torn landscape, meets many cheerful and "generally fine" children of all ages who apparently live communally in a kind of gypsy camp, until he is "ready to go back." According to Jordan's commentary, children have an "enormous capacity for survival and a contract to take care of one another."

All the Invisible Children received little circulation in the United States.

18

Kingdom of Heaven (2005):
Jerusalem: The Center
of the World for Forgiveness

Versions. The theatrical cut of *Kingdom of Heaven,* shot in an aspect ratio of 2.35:1, runs 144 minutes. The so-called "road-show version" or Director's Cut runs 194 minutes and was briefly shown in theaters before being released on DVD and later on Blu-ray.

Considering the dramatic possibilities inherent in the material, the Crusades received remarkably little attention during the first century of filmmaking. In 1923, Wallace Beery played what must have been an improbable Richard to Charles Gerrard's Saladin in *Richard the Lion-Hearted.* In 1954, Sir Walter Scott's Crusades novel *The Talisman* (1825) was the basis of a UK miniseries and the movie *King Richard and the Crusaders,* directed by David Butler, starred Rex Harrison as Saladin. Egyptian director Youssef Chahines's *Saladin and the Great Crusades* (1963), although lacking in production values, is said to be the plea "of an Arab nation whose experience of nationality extends back nine hundred years to the medieval Crusades" (Finke, 208). A comparison of the novel by the great Nobel Prize–winning novelist Naquib Mafouz and the film said to be based on it would be interesting. By any standard, however, the most important film about the Crusades before *Kingdom of Heaven* remains Cecil B. DeMille's *The Crusades* (1935).

Made in the depths of the Depression with what seems to have been an unlimited budget, the film is even today a wonder to behold. The film stars DeMille stalwart Henry Wilcoxon as Richard the Lionheart, and a radiant twenty-three-year-old Loretta Young as his eventual queen. Supporting players include Alan Hale, as Blondel the Minstrel (doing his best Little John imitation from Douglas Fairbanks' *Robin Hood*), the sneering Joseph Schildkraut as Conrad of Montferrat, and a host of players from the silent period.

The talented writers included Dudley Nichols, who wrote John Ford's *The Informer* and *Young Mr. Lincoln,* Harold Lamb, author of a popular book on the Crusades, and Waldemar Young, who had worked with DeMille on several earlier films. The result was a historical mishmash which only a Scrooge — or a Muslim — could dislike. Many of the characters are given historical names, or as in the case of the man called "The Hermit," a name presumably intended to remind the viewer of Peter the Hermit, a charismatic monk instrumental in rousing pilgrims for the First Crusade, who had actually lived a century or so earlier.

The Crusades, which takes place roughly in the same period as *Kingdom of Heaven*, begins with the persecution of Christians and their expulsion from Jerusalem and ends when Saladin (Ian Keith) opens the gates of Jerusalem to everyone who comes in peace. Since the film for nearly two hours reads as if the only good guys are Christians, it comes as a shock when Saladin makes his noble gesture. Nonetheless, Queen Berengaria ends up by pleading what Simon Louvich calls "a very modern cause," a plea for toleration for men who travel different roads to God, whether they "call him Allah or God" (Louvich, 336).

The Crusades begins with the complicated conspiracy by Henry's younger brother and Philip of France to control the throne of England by marrying Richard the Lionheart (Henry Wilcoxon) to Alice of France (well-played by Katherine DeMille, C. B. DeMille's adopted daughter). Although the marriage had been sanctioned by Richard's father, Richard escapes from it by pledging himself as a Crusader, a pledge which supersedes all others, and eventually marries the Princess Berengaria. Of course, Richard, although initially a reluctant warrior, eventually confronts his destiny, and the film ends with the Crusaders' conquest of Jerusalem.

After reading Scott Eyman's account of the making of *The Crusades* in his biography of DeMille, it is impossible to watch *Kingdom of Heaven* without recognizing the similarities between the two films and the two directors who made them. While the personalities of DeMille and Scott, and certainly their politics, were wholly dissimilar, they both possessed a fanatical attention to the details of history, while at the same time respecting the demands of the audience (Eyman, *Empire*, 315–20). Eyman writes, "DeMille's dramatic tastes and his imposing visual sense were far more suited to silence than sound" (5). A critic might argue the same for Scott.

DeMille's attention to what might be called "the look" of the period equaled or surpassed that of Scott some seventy years later. The research and reconstructions included "thousands of wash-drawings of the Crusades and six feet of piled-up Byzantine armor, chain-mail, cuirasses, and visors" copied from the Metropolitan, mountains of books both well-known and obscure, trained falcons, massive catapults and mangonels (a kind of catapult), and more — much more (Higham, 239–42; cf. Louvish, 333–34). Unfortunately, the expensive film does not seem to have been a success, at least by the standard set by DeMille's preceding historical epics of the 1930s, *The Sign of the Cross* and *Cleopatra*.

Certainly, critics of today would judge *Kingdom of Heaven* to be more accurate than *The Crusades*, and future generations might judge that it is so, but standards change. As far as how the Middle Ages looked, DeMille may well have fought Scott to a draw. Few things change faster than the art of illustration, and there is a loss of realism in any complex computer-generated image, and a film which contains as many of them as *Kingdom of Heaven* may not age well. The more interesting question is how fair and accurate *Kingdom of Heaven* will seem after another seventy-five years. The question of realism, at least in the visual sense, is not the same as the question of ideological fairness, and here Scott's film sets a new standard. His film is aimed directly at a world-wide audience of different religious backgrounds and beliefs and it has apparently succeeded (or so the present writer believes) on the basis of both objective and anecdotal evidence.

We live in a multicultural world with many voices competing for supremacy. From all directions, extreme voices clamor for violence in the name of God, whatever that name may happen to be. Robert Fisk, who has lived in Lebanon for some three decades, emerged from a Lebanese cinema with tears running down his face after watching *Kingdom of Heaven*. Fisk is hardly a fan of Scott's films; he characterizes *Black Hawk Down* as showing the Arabs of Somalia as "generically violent animals" and *Gladiator* as having a screenplay that might have come from *Boy's Own Paper*, presumably an English version of a Tom Swift story of some kind.

The Beirut audience was watching a story which may have been set hundreds of years in the past, but which had occurred only hundreds of miles away and which was as familiar to the film's audience as the signing of the Declaration of Independence would be to an American audience. Fisk wondered with some apprehension how the predominately young Muslim audience would react when the moderate Crusaders were overtaken by "crazed neo-conservative barons while Saladin is taunted by a dangerously al-Qaeda–like warrior." He need not have worried. During a parley, Saladin sends his own doctor to assist in the treatment of the leprous Christian king of Jerusalem. At this point, a round of what Fisk calls "spontaneous applause" broke out in the audience at the act of mercy by their warrior hero.

Fisk notes that Scott's film has been denigrated in the west because of Orlando Bloom's improbable turn from "blacksmith to crusader to hydraulic engineer." The "hydraulic engineer" refers to Balian finding water in the desert in a short time when everyone else has failed, apparently for centuries, but he might have added jeweler as well since Scott also gives him expertise in that art. Fisk speculates that the critics' real objection may have been to the term "crusader."

Scott Alan Metzger, in an essay in *Social Education*, calls *Kingdom of Heaven* the first Hollywood movie to seriously address the Crusades and their present-day implications and recommends the use of the film in schools despite its R-rating. The film focuses on what Metzger calls "one of the most fascinating episodes of the Crusades — the last few years of the Kingdom of Jerusalem" which ended with the disastrous battle of Hattin in 1187 and the return of the Holy City to Muslim control. Most of the major characters are historical, but, although a Balian of Ibelin actually existed, the character is a composite, and his actions in the film are fictional.

Metzger's conclusion is that, although the events of the film are simplified, it paints a surprisingly fair picture of the political and religious conflicts of the period. The Muslims are presented as "reasonable, sympathetic figures," and the portrayal of Saladin as "merciful and honorable" is supported by the historical record. The crosscurrents of the past are simplified or omitted: The Muslims are presented as more unified than they, in fact, were; the Byzantine empire has vanished; the religious intolerance of the "good guys" on both sides is omitted; and the *de rigueur* Hollywood ending is phony. Metzger is clearly wrong about the religious issue, at least as far as Christianity is concerned; the opening sequence, although comparatively brief, is one of the most horrifying depictions of Christianity ever put on film. As usual, Scott prefers not to use the term "director's cut," but speaks always of his "preferred cut." According to Scott, the additions include "organic organizations" put back into the movie which should not have been taken out. New material includes additional information about the child of Sybilla, the young regent Baldwin V, who also has leprosy. There is also a fight between Balian and Guy of Lusignan after the surrender of Jerusalem and the release of Guy.

The so-called road-show cut clarifies the general murkiness, but the viewer is likely to conclude that DeMille would have insisted upon a clearer and simpler identification of both the players, who are many, and the situations, which are complex. In most instances, material added to a film for DVD is done for commercial rather than for artistic purposes. In the case of *Kingdom of Heaven*, however, it distinctly improves our understanding of the events of the film, particularly in the opening sequences.

Kingdom of Heaven begins in France and ends there three years later. Half a world away, Christian armies have occupied Jerusalem for nearly a hundred years. The opening sequence is difficult to follow. In the extended cut, it is less perplexing, but no more convincing. As the film opens, the wife of Balian, a gifted blacksmith, has killed herself in grief over the death of their stillborn child, and in accordance with the church's doctrine, has been buried at a crossroads (cf. Shakespeare, *Richard II,* Act 3, Scene 2). We are told that Godfrey of Balian has returned home in search of his son. The photography is dark, and it is difficult to piece out that Balian's brother is a priest and to figure out a reason for his malice, which seems unmotivated.

The explanation does not, however, make the sequence any more palatable. The real question is: How could Balian, a man of substance who is shown throughout as capable of handling any crisis, have allowed the situation to become so desperate? Did he not understand that his brother, a priest called "almost crazed by his own poverty," envied him and wanted to drive him away to the Crusades in order to take over his land and possessions in the name of the Church? Why had Balian's father, the Baron of Ibelin, failed to contact his illegitimate son? Why did they not know about each other? It is understandable that Balian might have been unable to console his wife and to prevent her suicide, but he surely would have been able to keep his brother, a scumbag priest, from having her decapitated body buried at a crossroads in unconsecrated ground after he has stolen the crucifix from her neck. When the brother, who must surely have known that he was taking the whole business several steps too far, jeeringly tells Balian that his wife's head has been cut off and flaunts his stolen crucifix, Balian kills him on the spot. Taken in context, the sequence seems to have been included to show that the Christians could be more barbaric than the Muslims and to give Balian an excuse for setting out for the Holy Lands. The anticlerical novels of the eighteenth century hardly treated Christianity worse than this. Artistically, it would have been simpler to present Balian as a man with some sort of unexplained scandal in his past. Scott himself admits that perhaps the whole sequence should have been omitted.

The Leper King in *Kingdom of Heaven* (2005), with Edward Norton behind the mask.

The rest of the long film deals with the events leading up to the Crusaders' loss of Jerusalem to Saladin. Having murdered his brother, a priest, and fleeing from the wrath of the Church, Balian meets Godfrey of Ibelin, who has returned home as Baron of Jerusalem after twenty-six years as a Crusader. After Godfrey reveals himself as Balian's father, he dies a lingering death from wounds he receives in a ferocious battle against the pursuers of his son. Balian survives and heads for Jerusalem, where "Italian is no longer spoken." He has his father's sword and his own determination to win his title.

The battle sequence in which Godfrey is killed, the depiction of his death, and Balian's journey to the Holy City are brilliantly filmed. Washed up on a Syrian beach, Balian has a violent encounter in which he kills a man and spares his companion and finally arrives at Jerusalem, "the center of the world for asking forgiveness." Balian shows his father's sword as a sign of his identity and is accepted as Godfrey's heir.

In Jerusalem, Balian falls in love with the beautiful wife of an evil Crusader, eventually becomes king and, after a series of bloody battles for control of Jerusalem, is forced to surrender the city. At the finale, he has returned to France with his sweetie and taken up his old trade. Richard the Lion Heart, on his way to Jerusalem, passes by and asks directions. The Crusades go on.

In an unusually thoughtful review, Roger Ebert wrote that he admired Scott's bravery and even-handedness in dealing with such a difficult subject and cited in evidence the fact that both his Christian and Muslim friends had invited him to see the movie with them "to point out its shortcomings." Ebert is convinced by Hamid Dabashi's assertion in *Sight and Sound* that the film is about Balian's search for faith: "All religious affiliations fade in the light of his melancholic quest to find a noble purpose in life." The film shows the peacemakers on both sides who are attempting to navigate between their extremists. For Ebert, the film is "above all about the personal codes of its heroes." Both Muslims and Christians are men of honor who have seen too much bloodshed and want it to stop. While Ebert appreciated Scott's skill at big-budget spectacle, he "admired the dialogue and the plot more than the action." This is a strange conclusion considering the convolutions of the plot and Scott's perhaps unequaled mastery of action sequences.

Kingdom of Heaven deals with the fall of Jerusalem (after almost ninety years of Crusader rule) to the army of Saladin in 1187. Nick Jones, in his review, wrote that, at its core, the film is a glum account of a Christian defeat brought about by the "military aggression of Christians who overreach." The film is a romance told in "grand tableaux and conscientiously recreated details of furniture, clothing and weaponry." Jones, however, is less certain of the political analysis.

Although it is difficult to agree with Finke and Shichtman's relentless emphasis on "American exceptionalism," "hegemonic masculinity," and so on, their concluding analysis of *Kingdom of Heaven* deserves some respect, although as usual they overstate the case. They see the film as focused "not on the outcome of the conflict between the Crusader Kingdom and Saladin but on the way it was fought, on means rather than ends, performance rather than goals." How Balian "performs is more important than that he lost the battle and surrendered the city" (231). All of his "American ingenuity" are "little more than preparation for him to strike a truce with Saladin and lead Christians to retreat from Jerusalem after its fall" (232). The business about "American ingenuity" is a bit strong for a film made by a British citizen who has his own studio and does pretty much what he wants to.

According to Finke and Shichtman, the film's main interest seems to be "rehabilitating masculinity in the face of defeat." They support this thesis with analysis of the contrasting close-ups among various characters in the decisive battle sequences, focusing especially on the close-up of the beautiful Sibylla as her face morphs into the leprous face of Baldwin, her dead brother (234). Here, as elsewhere, *Kingdom* is, we are told, "a deeply reactionary film in almost every way" (236). This conclusion is supported by the casting of the relatively unknown Eva Green as Sibylla instead of a more famous actress and the absence of any "women warriors" (236). Unfortunately, for Scott, "the weight of history is too unbearable to allow for the sort of hard-bodied masculinity that might reside in the realm of nostalgia" (239). Although the meaning here is unclear, it is apparent that a director who deals with the Crusades will have to check his gonads at the door.

The film is well cast, although Orlando Bloom, like Heath Ledger in *A Knight's Tale*, is underdeveloped for a blacksmith. The blacksmiths I remember from my youth had enormous upper-body development from working at forges and resembled Longfellow's description in "The Village Blacksmith." Scott says that some blacksmiths in the medieval period, like Balian, knew how to make jewelry and find water, both of which Balian does. He immediately finds water on the barren land he has inherited from his father when the natives have apparently been incapable of finding it there for centuries. The problem in the film is not that Balian finds water there or makes jewelry, but that the viewer is never told how he managed it or how a blacksmith mastered the delicate work required for jewelry.

Old pro Liam Neeson is suitably muscular and stalwart as Godfrey of Ibelin. Indeed, he has had a patent on the role of the muscular warrior since playing Rob Roy in the 1995 film of the same name. The versatile Edward Norton is his usual effective self behind a golden mask. French actress Eva Green is both fragile and strong as Balian's romantic interest, and Marton Csokas is suitably obnoxious and arrogant as Guy de Lusignan. But the film's acting honors belong to Syrian actor Ghassan

Muslim Style: Eva Green as Sibylla in *Kingdom of Heaven* (2005).

Massoud as Saladin. Impeccably attired, honorable, courteous, dangerous and noble, he resembles Mark Strong's Hani, a different Muslim warrior in Scott's *Body of Lies*.

Kingdom of Heaven may be the most complex political film ever made. While it is certainly successful in communicating what Scott takes to be the complex reality of the Crusades, it is less successful as drama. It has many effective dramatic moments and a really big battle at the end, but lacks the dramatic force of the climax of *Gladiator*. What it does have is the visual splendor typical of Scott's films. Moment by moment, the film's images go by like a dream, and when we awaken, we remember those images, and not necessarily the whole in which they are embodied. The film convincingly presents a complex, plausible, ideological portrait of distant times. Such an expensive film would hardly have been possible in the past, but the advances in technology, the possibility of worldwide marketing, and the growth in subsidiary rights, especially television, DVD and Blu-ray, made it possible and, as it turned out, profitable.

On a production budget of $130,000,000, *Kingdom of Heaven* took in $47,398,413 domestically and $164,253,638 from the foreign markets for a gross of $211,632,051. Although the domestic return was disappointing, the foreign gross must have brought joy to the film's investors.

19

A Good Year (2006):
Postcards from Provence

Version. The only authorized text is the American release version available on DVD. The film was shot in anamorphic widescreen, 2.35:1, and runs 118 minutes. It also contains what the DVD calls "a feature-length hybrid of video featurettes" and audio commentary by Scott and writer Marc Klein. The result is both informative and entertaining and furnishes a DVD model which, unfortunately, does not seem to have become popular. Considering the beauty of the film, a Blu-ray edition is a desideratum.

In Peter Mayle's 2004 novel *A Good Year*, the author thanks Ridley Scott for the plot. According to Patrick Fahy, Scott and Mayle, old buddies in the advertising business, cooked up the plot over a bottle of wine. Mayle's earlier book *A Year in Provence* was filmed by the BBC in 1993 with John Thaw (best known for his portrayal of Inspector Morse) as the author. Much of *A Good Year* was shot within minutes of Scott's home and small vineyard. Scott worked on the screenplay with writer Marc Klein, but as usual did not claim a writing credit. For a while they considered featuring the ghost of Uncle Henry in the film but eventually decided in favor of using flashbacks to introduce each of the three acts. In the book, Max quits his job the day he inherits the vineyard, but that was, for obvious reasons, considered un-dramatic and was changed. Klein suggested Albert Finney for the role of Uncle Henry, and Scott, who had used Finney in *The Duellists* some thirty years earlier, readily agreed.

Scott's commentary, a film in itself, is entitled "Postcards from Provence," and follows the chronology of the movie: (1) The Chess Game, (2) On the Road, (3) The Swimming Pool, (4) The Tennis Match, (5) The Wine Cellar, (6) Fanny's Café, (7) The Dinner, and (8) A Good Life. It is a generic template for comedy.

"A few vintages ago," a boy named Max (Freddie Highmore) is about to return home after an idyllic visit in Provence with his Uncle Henry (Finney), who had instructed him in the mysteries of wine and of life. "Many vintages later," Max (Russell Crowe), now grown and the hard-driving head of a London brokerage firm, has just made a cold-blooded killing in the market when he receives word of his uncle's death. Uncle Henry has died intestate and left Max as the sole legatee to his estate in Provence.

After Max arrives in Provence, he rents a Mercedes-Benz Midget — dubbed "a lime-green roller skate" — which quickly becomes one of the more interesting characters in the film, and visits his new inheritance. He finds a run-down vineyard and a chateau which has appar-ently not been cleaned since some time before his uncle's

A Good Year (2006): Max (Russell Crowe) and Fanny (Mar-ion Cotillard) in love in Provence.

death. The caretaker, Francis Duflot (Didier Bourdon), and his sensual wife Ludivine (Isabelle Candelier) have supposedly been in charge of the place for decades, but have done little to keep either the vineyard or the chateau in repair. The pool is empty and the tennis court without a net.

Although Max's original intention is to sell the vineyard and chateau and take the next plane back to London, the viewer does not think for a minute that is what will happen. He does consult a lawyer, a beautiful woman with tattooed ankles, but fate conspires to prevent the sale. Max accidentally runs a woman (Marion Cotillard) on a bicycle into a ditch. Fanny Chenal seeks revenge, reappearing and confronting Max after he has managed to trap himself in the deep but fortunately empty swimming pool.

Max decides to take three days to revamp the place, and the trio goes to work. A vineyard tester, called an oenologue, arrives and the vineyard flunks the test. Young Christie Roberts (Abbie Cornish) shows up and claims to be Henry's illegitimate daugh-ter. (The viewer familiar with Scott's films will immediately recall a similar ploy in *Matchstick Men*.) There is a crisis back at the London brokerage film when a usurper works to supplant Max. And of course Max's romance runs into difficulty.

The denouement is improbable. Max, who has been shown as a child to be a perfect imitator of his uncle's handwriting, forges a will in which, among other good deeds, he acknowledges that Christie was legitimate. Max accepts a golden parachute (a check with a large number of zeroes in it), retires permanently to Provence, and presumably marries his sweetie and lives happily ever after.

The reviewers generally regarded *A Good Year* as a harmless respite for Scott while he prepared for more ambitious films. They called it pleasant and predictable, but few were enthusiastic. James Berardinelli wrote that the film was "a respectable retelling of the 'back to nature' narrative" showing a highly successful but selfish man being saved by the beauty of the countryside and a pretty woman with whom he falls in love. If the film is indeed a "back to nature" narrative, it is a very civilized version far removed from Jack London's "tooth and claw."

According to Patrick Fahy, the "jolly story" concocted by Scott and Mayle did not translate well into film. Mayle's use of local color, lightness of touch and observation of the gentle charm of Provence conflicts with Scott's talent for "the vivid realization of spectacularly violent worlds." Fahy does not believe that Crowe's character is convincing. He looks "ill-dressed and seedy" and his position as a captain of industry is "too contradictory to convince." In short, the film is "[b]usy and overblown when it should be playful and blithe."

Stephen Holden in the *New York Times* called it "an innocuous, feel-good movie" which is a far cry from the "triumphant metallic stomp" of *Gladiator*. Holden cites an unnamed British critic who called the film a "three-P movie: pleasant, pretty and predictable," and then (to show that he can be clever too) added "piddling." Like *Matchstick Men*, it is a periodic palate cleanser amid his string of "would-be blockbusters." Holden praises the beauty of the film, but blames the scriptwriter for its blandness.

Todd McCarthy, in *Variety*, called the film "a divertissement," an excuse for the filmmakers to spend some time in Provence and for the audience to spend some two hours there. Although he is unable to generate much enthusiasm for the film, he believes that it is good enough to generate "OK B. O. returns."

The template of *A Good Year* is boiler-plate romantic comedy. Over-achieving alpha male meets native girl and learns the joys of a simple life. Max is presented as a trading buccaneer who veers close to the edge of the law and presumably crosses the line occasionally. He has no other interest in life except making money for himself and what he calls his "lab rats." He controls the pretenders in his office as long as they support him, but when they betray him or the company, he treats them ruthlessly.

The supporting cast, especially the women, is top-flight. Talented romantic lead Marion Cotillard was to become a genuine star as Edith Piaf in *La môme* and as Billie Frechete opposite Johnny Depp's John Dillinger in *Public Enemies*. The real surprise, however, is the unknown Isabelle Candelier, who perfectly exemplifies middle-aged sensuality. Her husband, the caretaker, played by Didier Bourdon, is a literary type who quotes Proust: "Leave women to men without imagination." Considering his wife's sensual endowments, the quotation must surely be ironic, since there is nothing to indicate that the caretaker is not a flaming heterosexual. If he is not, she surely would have no difficulty finding a replacement.

Albert Finney, is in fine form as the old wine lover, and the other actors are all convincing enough. What happened? The brief answer is that Russell Crowe, although an outstanding dramatic actor, is not a strong comic or romantic actor. Tilt the film one way, and a young Buster Keaton would be perfect. Imagine what he could do leading the stock trading or attempting to get out of that swimming pool. Tilt it another and an older Cary Grant would be perfect. Imagine him as a wine-taster and sophisticate. Or even imagine Jim Carrey ruling the stock market and finding love in Provence.

A Good Year places itself in direct competition with some of the greatest French films ever made, especially the so-called Fanny trilogy directed by Marcel Pagnol from the novels of Jean Giono — *Marius* (1931), *Fanny* (1932) and *César* (1936) — as well as with their other collaborations, including *Harvest* (1937) and *The Baker's Wife* (1938). The old black-and-white films are largely stage-bound and primitive by today's standards, but the actors bring them to life. In mysterious ways, the characters seem to have sprung from the soil of Provence. Except for a few city films, American films, by contrast, seem to have no sense of place. Except for the caretaker and his wife, no one in *A Good Year* seems to belong. It can be argued that people today, including Scott, have lost their sense of place. Certainly, we can still feel a sense of that loss, and it is a measure of Scott's talent that we can feel that loss, at least intermittently, in *A Good Year*.

A Good Year was a box-office failure, and an investor in the film complained bitterly on television about the large amount of money he lost on the film. According to Box Office Mojo, against an estimated cost of $35,000,000, the film collected only $7,459,300 domestically. The foreign take, $34,604,805, hardly cushioned the considerable loss.

20

American Gangster (2007):
Cops Kill Cops They Can't Trust

Versions. The theatrical release of *American Gangster*, shot in anamorphic widescreen, 2.35:1, runs 156 minutes. The extended edition, which is not billed as a "Director's Cut" or a "Preferred Cut," runs 174 minutes. The most significant addition is a scene in which Richie tells Frank that he will "take care" of him. The scene adds little that is new and is probably better omitted.

The screenplay for *American Gangster* was written by Steven Zaillian, the screenwriter and sometime director who had previously worked with Scott on the screenplay of *Hannibal*. It is based upon "The Return of Superfly," a profile of gangster Frank Lucas in *New York* magazine by Mark Jacobson.

Black gangster films are an interesting but minor subdivision of black cinema. Although largely forgotten today except by film historians and followers of Curtis Mayfield, who did the popular score, *Superfly* (1972) is the story of an African-American drug dealer, played by Ron O'Neal. The film, called "corruptive" by Donald Bogle in his groundbreaking 1973 study *Toms, Coons, Mulattoes, Mammies & Blacks* (336), was directed by Gordon Parks, Jr., son of the famous photographer of the same name. *Superfly* was part of the wave of so-called blaxploitation films made after the coming of the Motion Picture Association of America's ratings system in 1967 allowed a generous helping of violence and nudity under the umbrella of an R rating. Superfly, the main character, is a corrupt Harlem cocaine dealer and sex machine, and the film is "a black fantasy picture almost devoid of any humanity or reflection" which "held things back" (Bogle, 337). Although the films may have been, in many ways, regrettable, it is not clear to the present writer, who remembers attending some of them in a theater in a small Louisiana town when he was the only white person present, how they "held things back." Blaxploitation films eventually became too expensive to justify making them for a predominantly black audience and the studios dropped them. As exemplars of their period, they deserve much more critical attention than they have received.

American Gangster is rich in narrative and details, but generically is the familiar story of the rise and ultimate fall of a gangster tracked down by the dogged persistence of an honest cop. The chief differences between *American Gangster* and mainstream gangster films are the skill with which the story is told and the fact that the gangster is black.

American Gangster tells the parallel stories of African-American gang boss Frank Lucas and white police officer Richie Roberts. Set in the late 1960s and early 1970s, it begins with the death of black gang leader Bumpy Johnson, Frank's mentor and idol; chronicles Frank's rise to power as a drug lord responsible for importing enormous amounts of nearly pure heroin into the United States; and concludes with the exposure of his criminality and his conviction, which coincides with the fall of Saigon in 1973. A pair of brief concluding sequences show now-lawyer Richie, opposed by a battery of criminal lawyers, successfully prosecuting the drug lord, and Frank turning informer for a reduced sentence, and Richie and Frank meeting after Frank's 1991 prison release. (It came as somewhat of a shock to at least one viewer to learn that working-class Richie — who seems at best to be only semi-literate in the film — turns out to be a hot-shot lawyer.)

The film opens with what is in effect an execution. Under the careful gaze of Bumpy Johnson, Frank Lucas fires up a cigar, sets a man on fire, and impassively shoots him. (Although Scott makes no mention of Wallace Stevens' "The Emperor of Ice Cream," which describes "death" as "the roller of big cigars," his DVD commentary has a long and interesting analysis of the virtues of big Cuban cigars. He might well have added cigarettes, considering the number smoked in his films.) The scene is important because it establishes immediately Frank's close relationship to Bumpy and his capacity for violence, if he considers it necessary. Like the godfather he is, Bumpy talks about respect, order and taking care of his "people." He hates "flash" in clothing, large corporations and lack of reserve. When Bumpy passes to his reward, if that is where he goes, Frank is fully prepared to do — and does — whatever is necessary to take his place.

Frank comes to the story fully formed. Aside from the fact of his apprenticeship to Bumpy, there is no indication concerning the formation of his character. At the height of his success, he is taking in about $1,000,000 a day. Ironically, he comes to the attention of the feds when his wife convinces him that he should wear an expensive chinchilla fur coat which she had bought for him to the Ali-Frazier championship fight in Madison Square Garden.

Frank achieves his success in classic American fashion by eliminating the middleman. He goes straight to the poppy fields of Cambodia to buy heroin and smuggles it into the U.S. hidden in the false bottoms of caskets carrying the bodies of dead Americans home for burial. All the other crooks want a "taste"; Frank wants it all. The engrossing scene with Armand Assante, as a Mafia don who wants his "fair share," is illustrative of both Frank's attitude and his methods.

When it appeared, Coppola's *Godfather* was criticized for its absence of the relationship between criminal corruption and family life; the justness of the criticism, if indeed it was just, was negated by the second film in which the face of Al Pacino's

Michael can be seen almost literally rotting before our eyes as both of his "families" disintegrate. While *American Gangster* hardly reaches that level of intensity, it clearly shows the corruption of both Frank's immediate and his large extended family.

After Frank becomes successful, he imports his family from South Carolina. Among the first to be corrupted is his nephew, Huey Lucas, a young athlete of exceptional promise as a baseball player. Frank gets him a tryout with the New York Yankees, but he turns it down in favor of doing what his uncle does. The plague brought by addiction, money and corruption eats through the entire family. The film is silent about Frank's feeling, if any, about this development. Scott and Zaillian might argue that the real Frank Lucas was not concerned with such niceties, and they might be correct, but Frank would certainly prefer a major league pitcher to another gangster in the family. Without a greater degree of self-knowledge than he is shown to possess in the film, Frank hardly qualifies as a tragic hero. The tragic hero always knows, at least at the end, the price he paid.

Finally, only Frank's mother, superbly played by Ruby Dee, stands above the carnage to mourn the wreckage. Frank Lucas may not have been nearly as interesting as Denzel Washington makes him out to be. Scott said that Lucas, who had served his time in jail and spent every day on the set, never admitted to feeling "regret or remorse"; a "failure of morality never entered his peripheral vision." Scott asks quietly, "What do you call that, a sociopath?" (Jacobson, 23).

Richie Roberts is another story. When he and his partner discover nearly $1,000,000 in mob money, he insists on doing the unthinkable: he turns it all in and becomes, at least to his fellow officers, a poor role model for police behavior. He is an honest man. The film, however, does not say that all policemen are corrupt, merely that they believe that they live in a violent world, are underpaid, and deserve the occasional perk which comes their way. The perks are drugs, women and money, and Richie navigates them at the expense of his family life, his marriage, and the fellowship of his fellow officers. Richie is, according to Scott's commentary, "a paragon of morality," but he is "immature" and has neither time nor money for his family. Or, to put it another way, he has all of the big virtues and none of the small ones.

Although present at least to some extent in earlier gangster films, the policeman who must make accommodations of one sort or another with informants and criminals has always been a player in the story. With film noir, the Dirty Harry movies, and gangster films in general, he became gradually much darker until finally, like Vic Mackey in the mesmerizing television series *The Shield*, it became almost impossible to tell him from the criminals. Richie, however, refuses to compromise and, so to speak, he pays the price. His family life is in shambles and he is mistrusted and harassed by his fellow officers. The good news is that, when a plague of nearly pure heroin, given the brand name "Blu-Magic" or "Blue Magic," hits the streets, and addicts began to die in record numbers, Richie, apparently one of the few honest men around, is chosen to track down the source of the drug. He is appointed head of a Special Investigations Unit (SIU) and allowed to pick his own men.

The problem with such a story is making the two parallel strands of the plot intersect without allowing the story of the gangster to predominate and leach interest from the subplot, if that is what it is or is allowed to become. Classical film theory would require at least three meetings, one at the beginning, one in the middle and one at the end. Of course, this could be adjusted somewhat, as in Sam Peckinpah's *Pat Garrett and Billy the Kid*, which begins with the last friendly meeting of the two old companions before flashing back to an earlier period.

The gangster story is likely to be so much more filled with complex characters, moral ambiguity, incidents, violence, drugs and sex, and, in the present case, racial questions, that a great deal of skill is required both from the writer and the director to keep the viewers' interest in the potentially much less interesting story of an honest law enforcement officer. "That was tricky," Zaillian says in his commentary. His solution, in effect, was to write two scripts, one told from Frank's point of view and the other told from Richie's, and then to blend them together. Although the success of the resulting script is a matter of opinion, a fair judgment is likely to be that the experiment succeeds at least reasonably well. True, the film is more than two hours old in the so-called "extended version" before the two main characters confront each other, and the viewer will either accept the story or reject it. It can be argued that the story, lacking the dramatic unity of *Alien* or *Black Hawk Down*, might have been better treated in a miniseries.

By any reasonable standard, *American Gangster* is an enormous film. It has 135 speaking parts and was shot on 360 locations. Critics familiar with New York occasionally complained of the way in which the location sites were mixed together at the expense of the verisimilitude of the story. But most viewers won't be aware of the mixture.

When *American Gangster* opened, reviewers took it seriously by comparing it to the great gangster films of the past, and although they found it wanting is some respects, they also found much to praise. Michael Wood, in the *London Review of Books*, called it "a stylish and intelligent contribution to the genre, a little overhaunted by past masterpieces ... but gripping and troubling all the way through." Wood argues that Scott wants to have "both grim facts and glamour," but glamour wins out in the end "and even turns into a kind of cosiness."

Wood has a point. After all the terrible deaths shown in the film, many of them unforgettable (a dead druggie mother with her infant, for example), Lucas turns state's evidence and, we are told, helps in convicting a multitude of offenders and recovering huge amounts of money. He spends fifteen years in prison, gets out; becomes close friends with the man responsible for his capture (who later even serves as his lawyer); then works as advisor, whether paid or not, on a film about his career; and expresses not an iota of remorse for any of his actions. Certain aspects of Lucas' life depicted in *American Gangster* are a matter of dispute, but Scott argues that the essential facts are correct. Scott calls him a sociopath, but whatever we call him, he is an evil man who, whether we believe in the death penalty or not, deserves a permanent seat in Hell. The fact that Denzel Washington makes him both likable and human is beside the point. After all, that's his job.

The ending seems to have bothered other critics as well. Owen Gleiberman in *Entertainment Weekly* called it "weirdly upbeat." Academy Award–winning producer Brian Grazer admitted to being uneasy when he met the real Frank Lucas, and said that he was still "a gangster.... He hasn't changed. He's still that person." For Gleiberman, the film is "a bit too controlled" and "not quite enthralling," but depicts the era well. While most critics praised Washington's performance, Gleiberman thought that Roberts's fixation on Frank has a "ghastly ingenuity." It is, at the very least, artistically unsatisfying to see a man who has, as the film argues, killed so many people, both directly and indirectly, hanging out on a movie set and being treated like royalty.

J. Hoberman argued in his *Village Voice* review that *American Gangster* has a "familiar argument," namely that organized crime is "outsider capitalism." He believes that Washington's "star quality — the circumspect badass" is well suited to the role, "a combination of ruthless thug and gentlemanly striver." Both the character's (real) ruthlessness and his (presumed) charity are clearly established at the beginning of the film.

According to David Ansen of *Newsweek*, the film announces its wish to take its place with the great seminal films of "criminal royalty" and "both glamorizes and condemns its hero." Of course, that is what gangster films have always done, at least the popular ones, since von Sternberg's *Underworld* (1927). Ansen believes that the film presents the "loathsome" Frank Lucas as a "triumphant example of black capitalism." The film has "great style," but lacks the "lurid atmosphere" of Brian De Palma's *Scarface* and the "intricate grasp of the criminal lifestyle" in Coppola and Scorsese. In brief, *American Gangster* has a great story which has "not been mined for all its potential." Ansen is hardly the first critic to point out that "a certain hypocrisy is built into the genre." This means that the cops are often more odious than the crooks, who have more style and kill many more people. They also, at least in the case of *American Gangster*, have better hairdos. But, then, Shakespeare's Macbeth had more style than the people he murdered; but unlike Frank Lucas, he also had, at some level, an active conscience.

David Denby, in a carefully considered review in *The New Yorker*, cites Lucas' treatment of "an insolent dude called Tango." Frank shoots him in the head, apparently for putting a damp glass down on a lacquered table, although for other reasons as well, since the killing occurs some time after the affront to etiquette. According to Denby, Washington's star power is the story here. To what extent this distorts the events depicted is open to question.

Brian Johnson, (*Maclean's*) finds Lucas a "warmly sympathetic portrait" of a mythic crime lord in the tradition of Don Vito Corleone or Tony Soprano," stressing the "old values of loyal allegiance and unbridled capitalism." Like others, Johnson thought the film too long, but great on details. In the end, both super-cop and super-criminal walk out as heroes. Johnson concludes that this could happen [only] in America," without apparently seeing much, if any, irony in the conclusion.

Ross Douthat in the *National Review* writes, perhaps ironically, that the film attempts to make up for the 1970s and to gain "African-American crime kingpins the respect they deserve." Douthat sees Lucas as a cross between the Mephistophelean cop Denzel Washington played in *Training Day* and his Malcolm X. He contrasts Lucas, not with Frank Lucas, as most critics and viewers did, but with slimy Detective Trupo (Josh Brolin). Lucas was, in reality, a "wilder, more self-aggrandizing personality" than his screen counterpart who, according to Douthat, battled bandits in the Thai jungle and smuggled drugs on the same plane with Henry Kissinger. Washington's performance shows Frank Lucas as more cautious, buttoned down and professional than he really was in life. Douthat concludes that the film would probably have been better if Washington had not played it so safe in his portrayal. While this may be true, it is unclear whether the choice was that of the actor or of the director.

Some critics regarded the story of Richie Roberts as weak. Peter Travers, in *Rolling Stone*, suggested that the custody battle with his wife should have been on the Lifetime network. Travers does admit that the long-postponed confrontation between the two characters has dramatic juice, but if it is a question of too little too late, then the film must be considered a failure.

Upon the first viewing of the film, the criticism appears to be true, but the story of Richie Roberts — and the integrity of Crowe's performance — grow upon successive viewings. The reason for the change is, at least partly, due to the superb performance of Josh Brolin as Trupo, whose confrontations with Richie serve as a stand-in for the confrontations with Frank Lucas to come. Brolin, big, arrogant with authority, sporting a mustache that seems to have originated on Mount Rushmore, bullies, threatens, throws his weight around and generally harasses Richie before finally, as he sees how the wind has shifted, attempting, after it is too late, to come to terms with him. Trupo believes that all men can be threatened or bought, and the film simply could not work without him.

Perhaps the chief criticism of the film was that it was too derivative of other gangster films. Ryan Gilbey in *Sight and Sound* argues that the film, unlike the Bangkok heroin, is cut "with any number of influences that dilute its potency" and cites, among others, *Scarface* (1983), *Goodfellas* (1990), *Carlito's Way* (1993), *Dead Presidents* (1995), *Blow* (2001) and the HBO series *The Wire*. Gilbey might also have mentioned that gang lord Bumpy Johnson (1905–1968) had already made it into films as a character in *Hoodlum* (1997) and in *The Cotton Club* (1984), played by Laurence Fishburne in both films.

Gilbey's list, although not as potent as it might have been, is certainly adequate for his point, but all big-budget dope movies pretty much work and rework the same material. If all the films are telling more or less the same story, the distinction then depends upon the cinematic style of the film, or the lack or it, and here, at least in the opinion of the present writer, Scott's cinematic style is certainly equal to or superior to that of any of the films cited; and Scott's content introduces racial and historical elements not treated in any of the other films. Scott's film expands to include many important historical elements, including Vietnam, the civil rights struggle, the migration of African-Americans to the cities of the North, and the destruction of the nuclear family which often followed. Only *The Wire*, which lasted 60 episodes, may reasonably be considered its superior in the comprehensive treatment of criminality.

Denzel Washington has won two Academy Awards playing angry men: Best Supporting Actor for *Glory* (1989) and Best Actor in a Leading Role for *Training Day* (2001). He also played Brutus in William Shakespeare's *Julius Caesar* on Broadway. His performance was adequate, but the present writer, who saw the play, believes that Washington is much more suited for the role of Marc Antony. Brutus is an intellectual man — you can almost see the ideas click into place when the role is well played — but Marc Antony is an angry one. Marlon Brando's sullen anger is almost palpable in Joseph Mankiewicz's *Julius Caesar* (1953).

D. W. Griffith's two-reeler *The Musketeers of Pig Alley* (1912) may be said to have started the gangster film and to have shown its great paradox: the complicity between the wanted gangster and the good white citizen who wants to do away with crime but who is in some way obligated to the gangster. In the New York ghetto of the film, crime exists because it provides at least some benefits to people when the law is distant and its benefits uncertain.

The idea of crime as outsider capitalism has been around for a long time. Traditionally, of course, at least in the films of the early 1930s which introduced a new violence, the gangsters were Italian city boys. Later, they became largely simply generic American types. "The Professor," an intellectual bank robber played by Sam Jaffe in John Huston's *The Asphalt Jungle,* defined crime as "a left-handed form of human endeavor." However, the Professor, a moralist of sorts, did not approve of violence and certainly would have disapproved of the traffic in hard drugs shown in Scott's film.

Typical black gangster films show what Mark A. Reid calls "the contemporary narrative convention and iconography of the Hollywood gangster film," but some evoke "a markedly ethnic-inflected difference" in the construction of law and order. Although this does not indicate a biological or racist fact, it does indicate the belief that the representation of race resists a strict definition of "law and order" and "a monolithic definition of blackness" (Reid, 457).

According to Reid, African American Oscar Micheaux, in *The Scar of Shame* (1927), accepts the idea that black Americans can achieve socio-economic success only if they adopt "European standards" or accept their essential "bad nigger" ways to survive in the ghetto. Faced with this choice, they can either deny their identity and accept the ways of the white man or reign in the ghetto. Like John Milton's Satan, they could either "reign in Hell" or "serve in Heaven." Like the Baltimore criminals of *The Wire*, they often choose to reign in Hell, or Harlem. Frank Lucas' church attendance does not indicate any moral sensitivity; it is simply a part of his "concern" for his people, a

way to show that he iden-
tifies with them and is
ready to help.

The film suggests an
element of racism involved
in Frank's easy advance-
ment up the criminal
ranks. The feds seemed to
believe, in spite of clear
evidence to the contrary,
that the Italians had a
monopoly upon large-scale
organized crime and
ignored any evidence to
the contrary. Apparently,
they felt that African-

Two corrupt men in *American Gangster* (2007), the crime lord (Denzel Washington) and the cop (Josh Brolin).

Americans were not intelligent enough to be crime bosses. This belief was the equivalent of an idea prevalent, at least in the South some fifty years ago, that black athletes were not intelligent enough to produce great quarterbacks in the National Football League.

In an interesting essay in *World Literature Today* analyzing *American Gangster*, J. Madison Davis argues that "the relationship of a dominated culture or sub-culture to the culture that dominates it" is "more complex than is generally recognized." Ironically, Frank Lucas' fall is occasioned by the gaudy display of dress — a chinchilla coat which his wife has given him and which he later burns — at a championship fight which brings him to the attention of the FBI. Why, they ask, does this guy have a better seat than the Mafia boss? By wearing the coat, he explicitly disobeys the dictum handed to him by his revered mentor, Bumpy Johnson, and pays the price. In the words of Davis, "Lucas's momentary lapse into the ghetto subculture has doomed him" (10). Davis's main point seems to be that money has no color in real life and does not worry about the color of the man who carries it. Real life has more context than the movies, although it seldom tells so good a story.

American Gangster was a hit. According to Box Office Mojo, the film grossed $130,164,645 domestically and $136,300,392 in the foreign markets. On an estimated production budget of $100,000,000, the film will eventually be a substantial earner, if it is not already one, when ancillary rights are included.

21

Body of Lies (2008): Closing Time

Version. The theatrical, the DVD and the Blu-ray versions run an identical 128 minutes. The extended high-definition version contains more than forty minutes of omitted material, the importance of which is discussed below. Scott has provided a thoughtful and particularly illuminating commentary.

The major portion of *Body of Lies* was filmed during nine weeks on location in Morocco, where Scott had already filmed scenes of *Gladiator, Black Hawk Down* and *Kingdom of Heaven*. Other scenes were shot in Washington, D.C., and Europe. The opening sequence, which takes place in Manchester, England, was filmed in Baltimore. Scott has often said that he likes shooting in Morocco, and children who have now grown to adolescence and beyond warmly welcomed him back.

Body of Lies is about the international fight against terrorism. The film opens with a quotation from W.H. Auden which asserts that all children who have evil done against them do "evil in return," followed by a raid in the industrial town of Manchester, against a cell of Muslim terrorists. Although military authorities catch the terrorists by surprise, they are prepared for such an eventuality and set off an explosion. It apparently kills all the terrorists and a substantial number of soldiers and innocent civilians.

From Langley, Virginia, we see American terrorist expert and family man Ed Hoffman (Russell Crowe) helpfully explaining to his spy on the ground in Iraq, American agent Roger Ferris (Leonardo DiCaprio), the meaning of the raid. Because the terrorists have largely abandoned modern technology and disappeared into the crowd, they are, according to Hoffman, nearly impossible to pin down. Ferris and his confederate meet with a potential turncoat who wishes to go to America. Because he knows too much, his superiors have asked him to undertake a suicide mission. Although Ferris agrees to help him, Hoffman, half a world away, turns down the deal and Ferris is forced to kill the man, in effect to "execute him." "You did what you had to do," Hoffman tells him, instead of the more exact, "You did what I told you to do." Needing help with surveillance, Ferris goes to the urbane head of Jordanian intelligence, apparently known only as Hani (Mark Strong), who becomes a major player in the rest of the film.

When Ferris goes in for a rabies shot, he becomes infatuated with a beautiful Muslim nurse named Aisha (Golshifteh Farahani). At the climax of the film, Ferris is told that the girl has been taken captive and, rather improbably, he dashes off into Syria to find her. He is picked up in the middle of the desert, but in the dust created by a number of identical cars, Hoffman, who is of course watching by satellite, is apparently unable to tell which car to follow. Ferris eventually meets the terrorist Al-Saleem and they have an interesting, if improbable, conversation about the correct interpretation of the Koran, before the torture of Ferris begins. He is rescued at the last minute through the combined efforts of Hani and Hoffman. At the conclusion of the film, Ferris leaves the agency, but decides to stay in the Middle East. He watches the nurse from afar, and disappears into the crowd. Hoffman, ever the realist, turns to the next operative.

The plot of *Body of Lies* reads like John Le Carré's *Tinker, Tailor, Soldier, Spy* on steroids. The conflict is simple enough, but as ever in Scott's films, its depiction is complex. When combined with Scott's complicated visuals and information overload about the ways of the world of intelligence and terrorists, it is difficult to work out the relationships, especially on a first viewing. Roger Ebert, always sympathetic to Scott, called *Body of Lies* "a James Bond plot inserted into today's headlines." Although the film "looks to be persuasive," the hero is a Lone Ranger who causes all sorts of mayhem and falls in love with a local beauty in his spare time. Generally speaking, Ebert likes its visual style and its acting and considers its depiction of character worthy of Le Carré, the gold standard for how spies think, while deploring the film's extreme violence and the absurdities of its plot, which he considers sensationally improbable. Among other absurdities, Ebert rightly ridicules the perfect cell phone communication across continents even during "perilous situations."

In an insightful essay, Simon Dalby examines *Gladiator, Black Hawk Down, Kingdom of Heaven* and *Body of Lies* as explorations of the morality and identity of warriors in "exotic landscapes and settings that emphasize the confrontation with danger as external and frequently unknowable" and "political violence ... as something which has both simple and very complicated geographies." What Dalby calls "the professional warrior" becomes "enmeshed in discourses of nationalities, rights, and 'just wars.'" As an analysis of the conflicting cross-currents of motives presented in Scott's epic films, this statement could hardly be bettered.

National Review's Ross Douthat had a low opinion of the political films made in Hollywood after 9/11 and regarded *The Kingdom* (2007), *Traitor* (2008), and *Body of Lies* as attempts to find a middle ground that would be both more fair and more commercial than films done in the immediate aftermath of the attack. Unfortunately, Scott's attempt to provide a more even-handed treatment of political revolution turns into a "straight-forward bang-pow actioner" which has only middling success in dealing with large issues. Douthat notes that W.H. Auden is said to have had doubts later about his poem quoted at the beginning of the film, which he had directed against the Nazis, and often refused permission to reprint it. Owen Gleiberman presented the negative case. He begins by denouncing the "tacky and meaningless title" and argues that Scott is fighting "the last war — the cold war." He describes Scott as a "veteran big-budget action painter" who uses "musty clichés" from the days when America was playing "nuclear chicken with the Russians." By this reading, Hoffman is a kind of idiot Goldfinger attempting to rule the Middle East by infallible cell phone calls from thousands of miles away.

Peter Travers, in *Rolling Stone*, had high praise for Russell Crowe's Hoffman's "killer

sense of mischief." Crowe, he writes, is "flabby, fifty-ish and friendly to a fault … lethally funny and dangerously scary." Travers, however, does not like the romance between Roger Ferris and the Jordanian nurse Aisha.

The problem with the romance is not that it is a "serpentine mind ben-

Mark Strong and Leonardo DiCaprio in *Body of Lies* (2008).

der," as Travers calls it, but that it is undeveloped in the film. In the omitted scenes, Scott is shown standing before "a kind of a storyboard" of the film containing Avid photographs with a brief statement of the action taken from each scene of the film, perhaps some two or three hundred in all. After the film is shot, the storyboard enables Scott to examine the film as a whole and "to move things around" for a greater dramatic effectiveness.

Among the more than forty minutes of "omitted material" placed to one side is a sequence of scenes showing a tryst on a beach between Ferris and Aisha. They hold hands, she fondles his face, discovers a small bone fragment (not his), and eases it through the skin, recognizes what it is and wonders who he is. When he takes her home, there is a series of confrontations with Arab youths playing soccer in the dirt who want to pick a fight with him, but, thinking of the girl and his mission, he avoids them. When Ferris is forced to defend himself in a fight in a bar, the nurse sees what is happening and turns away.

In his commentary, Scott says that the scene shows that Ferris is so immersed in the "body of lies" that, had the romance been kept in, "the ending wouldn't work in the film," and that it was better to leave the ending undecided. Perhaps, but the romantic scene is so moving and heartfelt that it somehow makes all the explosions and intricate plot maneuverings seem trivial. It should have been included even if it necessitated a re-jiggering of the ending, either tragic or romantic. Scott considers himself a realist and has little truck with romance in the context of a complicated political situation, but romance, both tragic and comic, has ever thrived in desperate circumstances. Still, nobody ever promised two lovers from different cultures eternal happiness without difficulties, and any problems facing them could hardly be worse than the ones they have already encountered.

When *Inception*, starring Leonardo DiCaprio, was released in 2010, at least one reviewer complained about DiCaprio's penchant for thrillers rather than romantic films and opined that the actor had somehow betrayed his audience. The romantic interlude cut from *Body of Lies* clearly indicates that the reviewer has a point. But then again, perhaps romantic films do not pay as well as international thrillers.

Although no one is ever likely to call *Body of Lies* an "actor's film," the acting is strong throughout. DiCaprio has long since lost the early bloom of his *Titanic* days and has become a dependable leading man, but Ridley Scott stalwart Russell Crowe, though often derided for his pudgy, non-heroic roles, has never been better. Crowe's Ed Hoffman forms a messy contrast with the dapper Jordanian intelligence head Hani, played by the gifted Mark Strong, who was to reappear as the chief villain in Scott's *Robin Hood*. Hani is sophisticated, elegant, in shape, a gourmet and a linguist. He is, also, like Hoffman, a realist, but a more civilized one. Although her best scene was cut from the release version, Golshifteh Farahani's performance as the helpless pawn in a doomed romance is moving and deserves particular notice.

According to Box Office Mojo, *Body of Lies* was hardly a failure and with revenues from DVD, television and other ancillary rights, may yet turn a profit. On a production budget of $70,000,000, the domestic take was $39,395,666 and the foreign receipts added an additional $75,702,620 for a combined total of $115,097,286. The totals proved, if any additional proof were needed, the importance of foreign receipts for Scott's big-budget films.

22

Robin Hood (2010):
The Outlaw Returns to History

Version. The theatrical version of *Robin Hood*, with an aspect ration of 2.40:1, is rated PG-13 and runs 141 minutes. The unrated version, billed as a "director's cut," runs 158 minutes. The Blu-ray also contains a number of fascinating extras, including storyboards and Ridleygrams.

Robin Hood is known the world over. Harlan Ellison has written that "children in Zaire" who do not know who Jay Gatsby, Hamlet, Raskolnikov or Emma Bovary is, "know these five: Tarzan, Superman, Mickey Mouse, Robin Hood and Sherlock Holmes" (Ellison, 146). What they know, of course, is what kind of a man he is. He is the man who has been described as "the archetypal philanthropist with a hands-on approach to redistributing wealth" (Hope-Jones, 30). Although only a few die-hard fanatics believe that a historical Robin Hood ever existed, stories about him continue to flourish in theaters and on television. Francis James Child, the great American scholar who published the pioneering *English and Scottish Popular Ballads* from 1892 to 1898, collected 38 Robin Hood ballads and their many variants.

Although the origins of the legendary figure of Robin Hood are lost in ballads and stories of the Middle Ages (they may date from as early as the ninth century) the modern story may, for our purposes, be said to begin with Sir Walter Scott's *Ivanhoe* (1820), in which, as Robin of Locksley, he is a minor figure. The central incident of the novel depicts Ivanhoe's return from the Third Crusade. In his successful attempt to regain his throne from his wicked brother Prince John, Richard the Lion Heart is assisted by Robin Hood and his band of outlaws.

The "look" of earlier Robin Hood films, particularly the dress and appearance of the outlaws, owes much to late nineteenth and early twentieth-century illustrators, particularly Howard Pyle, whose *The Merry Adventures of Robin Hood* (1883) had an influence on the visual representation of Hollywood films. The two actors whom many fans regard as the best swashbucklers of all time starred as the celebrated rogue of Sherwood Forest: Douglas Fairbanks (in the popular *Robin Hood* [1922], directed by Allan Dwan with Fairbanks looking over his shoulder) and Errol Flynn (*The Adventures of*

Robin Hood [1938], directed by William Keighley and Michael Curtiz and lavishly produced in Technicolor). None of the subsequent multitude of other films about the legendary bandit of Sherwood Forest has equaled their style, athleticism and sheer audience appeal.

Kevin Brownlow, in *The Parade's Gone By...*, has a fascinating account of the filming of Fairbanks' epic. Apparently, the castle set was so enormous that Fairbanks, upon seeing it, feared that he would be lost in its vastness. Director Dwan quickly showed him how he could use the scale to his advantage in his feats of derring-do. Impressed by the scale of the castle drawbridge, Charlie Chaplin is said to have wanted to use it in a gag. After the drawbridge is lowered, he planned to come out carrying a kitten, put the kitten down, pick up a bottle of milk and some mail, and saunter back inside the castle to the raising of the drawbridge. Unfortunately for the comic, Fairbanks refused permission (257).

For a brief period of time in the 1930s and early 1940s, the dashing Errol Flynn donned the mantle of Fairbanks and occasionally surpassed him. For masculine sexual appeal and athleticism, Flynn's Robin Hood has remained the standard for the better part of a century. Although totally absent of any degree of historical accuracy, *The Adventures of Robin Hood* has spirited direction, unrivaled Technicolor photography and several state-of-the-art mattes. In addition to Errol Flynn, it has a beautiful Olivia de Havilland as Maid Marian, Alan Hale as the definitive Little John, Eugene Pallette wondrous as Friar Tuck, and Basil Rathbone and Claude Rains suitably villainous as (respectively) Sir Guy and Prince John. The film was nominated for four Academy Awards and won three: Best Art Decoration (Carl Jules Weyl), Best Original Score (Erich Wolfgang Korngold) and Best Editing (Ralph Dawson). Unfortunately, Frank Capra's *You Can't Take It with You* almost unbelievably beat out *Robin Hood* for Best Picture.

Later Robin Hood films have not come close to matching these two early ones. Sony took advantage of the opening of Scott's film to re-release four Robin Hood films of the post-war period on DVD: *The Bandit of Sherwood Forest* (1946), *Prince of Thieves* (1948), *Rogues of Sherwood Forest* (1950) and *Sword of Sherwood Forest* (1960). (The 1950 film includes Alan Hale's third and last performance, finished just before his death, of his signature role as Little John, a role he had portrayed in both the Fairbanks and Flynn versions.) Perhaps the most moving of all the Robin Hood films is Richard Lester's *Robin and Marian* (1976), starring Sean Connery as an aging Robin Hood and Audrey Hepburn in the best of her later roles as his beloved Maid Marian. Mention should also be made of Kevin Costner's lavishly produced *Robin Hood: Prince of Thieves* and John Irvin's *Robin Hood*, notable for an early performance by Uma Thurman (both 1991). Mel Brooks' *Robin Hood: Men in Tights* (1993) is not usually considered one of Brooks' better films, but the story was, of course, fair game for Brooks' burlesque.

Critics admit that the Robin Hood story is "infinitely adaptable" and "constantly changing" (Puente). Certainly, the story has an obvious appeal both to the money men and to Ridley Scott. The screenplay was by veteran writer-director-producer Brian Hel-geland, doubtless in collaboration with Scott. Helgeland's recent work has included Tony Scott's *Man on Fire* (2004) and *Payback: Straight Up* (2006), which he also directed.

As usual, Scott paid close attention to the look of the film and wanted to move away from the bright greens and reds of the Technicolor of the 1938 film, *The Adventures of Robin Hood.* He sent DP John Mathieson to Brussels to view the winter landscapes of Brueghel and his followers. Unfortunately, the makers of the film were largely unable to get the landscapes they wanted because of production delays. As usual, Scott had several cameras going at the same time, sometimes as many as a dozen (Hope-Jones, 32). The viewer immediately recognizes that the film has a darker palette than any earlier Robin Hood film and that this Robin Hood is rather older than usual, especially for a film that may be intended as the first in a series. But then Fairbanks was no spring chicken when he made his version (he was nearly forty); and Sean Connery was even older when he played Robin. Apparently, Robin Hood ages well.

As the film opens, King Richard the Lion Heart (Danny Huston) is returning from the Crusades in a bad mood. He has no funds and is plundering his way home. Richard is injured raiding a castle and reported killed. (Although Richard has disappeared from the film and is spoken of as dead, a viewer does not have to be cynical to believe that he might reappear in a sequel.) The real Richard was killed in similar circumstances some four or five years after returning to his throne [Asbridge, 516]. Robin Longstride, a commoner and the future Robin Hood, heads for the court with a group of his con-federates, including Will Scarlet, Allan A'Dayle, and Little John. On their way home, they drive off attackers assaulting the party of Sir Robert Loxley, who had been assigned the duty of returning the king's crown to England for the new king, John. The dying Loxley entreats Longstride to deliver the crown to the king and his sword to his father, Sir Walter Loxley.

Because Longstride has no authority of his own, he poses as Loxley to board a ship to England, where he delivers the crown to the new king. Meanwhile, the villainous Godfrey (Mark Strong, in a strong performance) has secretly aligned himself with Prince John, who has long been plotting to replace his brother as king. When Godfrey returns from the Crusades, he is surprised to discover an imposter posing as the dead Sir Robert. The new king, John (Oscar Isaac), immediately replaces William Marshal (William Hurt), King Richard's chief adviser, with Godfrey, who curries favor with the new king by swearing to extract tribute from the Northern barons by all necessary means, includ-ing murder and pillage.

Robin and his three boon buddies go to Loxley Hall, where they meet Sir Walter's widow, Marion (Academy Award winner Cate Blanchett), who is, of course, no longer a maid, and her aged, blind but still feisty father, Sir Walter (Max von Sydow, half a century after his iconic performance in Ingmar Bergman's *The Seventh Seal*). The old man likes Robin and, for dynastic reasons, decides to palm him off as his son. Marion understands the reason for the ruse; with her husband dead, the estate will be forfeited to the crown. But she is hesitant to accept Robin as her husband. Her earlier marriage had lasted only a few days before her husband went away on a Crusade, and he probably smelled better than Robin, who, as Sir Walter tells him, stinks.

Discovering that the villagers lack grain for the approaching planting season, Robin and his men decide to steal back grain that had been exacted for the church and is being shipped to the bishop. Meanwhile, Godfrey has joined soldiers from France and led them into the North to plunder. He intends to divide the country by alienating the Northern barons against the new king. (This is improbable since it is likely that the Northerners would have quickly decided that they were fighting French and not English soldiers.) Marshal, who has discovered Godfrey's plot, warns King John and, at the meeting of the barons, Robin convinces them to unite with the king against their common enemy.

Robin returns home to find the villagers under attack and Marion under assault; Godfrey kills Sir Walter. The English, now united, go off to fight the French, and in a really big battle which includes fusillades of arrows, Prince John leads the charge and the French are defeated. After the battle, the perfidious King John immediately refuses to sign the Magna Carta and sentences Robin to death. It turns out that Robin's father had drafted the Magna Carta! Outlawed, Robin, Marion and the now Merry Men retreat to the forest, and the film ends with the statement that the legend is just beginning. This means that, if the need should arise, everyone will be back for another go-round. Everyone, that is, except for Godfrey, who took an arrow shot by Robin Hood high in the air and from a great distance directly through the neck. One of the questions of the film is how, among the zillions of arrows, we could know that it was Robin Hood's which did the deed. The credits at the end, presumably by Scott, are done in the style of the Scott Free logo and chronicle the film's story in high fashion.

In general, reviewers thought that the film was not up to its ambitions. They emphasized its differences from earlier Robin Hood films, but did not believe that the differences benefitted it. Rebecca Murray thought the film "disappointingly short on action." Considering the general violence and the elaborate battle sequence which concludes the film, this can only mean that the reviewer missed the derring-do of Flynn and Fairbanks, that is, leaping around from pillar to post while making clever remarks. Scott's liking for complex stories with many characters and subplots, although expected by viewers familiar with his epic films, was generally regarded as a liability. The plotting, however, is less complex and more coherent than, say, *Kingdom of Heaven* or *Body of Lies*.

In a long, jovial review, *The New Yorker*'s Anthony Lane regarded both the film and Crowe as dour, but expressed hope that the children shown in the forest at the beginning of the film might become the Merry Men of a sequel. Lane believes that the film suffers from "geographical unlikelihood," but apparently accepts the chronological unlikelihood of having King Richard apparently killed on his return from the Crusades, when, in actuality, he died in circumstances akin to those shown in the film some five years later. Of course, the charge of "geographical unlikelihood" has haunted other Scott films, especially *White Squall* and *American Gangster*. Some critics complained about improbable flora and fauna in the former and improbable New York location

Russell Crowe as Robin Hood.

scenes for gangland violence in the latter. In *Robin Hood*, it is absolutely impossible to believe that a large fighting force from Nottingham could arrive at Dungeness in Kent, a distance of more than two-hundred miles, in two days. Under the best of circumstances, even crack cavalry could not average more than twenty to twenty-five miles a day. And any number of critics have grumbled about the difficulty of figuring out the precise path of Thelma and Louise's journey around Western America.

On May 14, 2010, Stephen Crowder on Fox News argued that Robin Hood was the first Tea Party activist. He took from "an oppressive government that had taxed its citizens into poverty, and returned the wealth back to its rightful owners." Although scriptwriter Brian Helgeland, doubtlessly a confirmed liberal, argues stoutly against the interpretation—"no, no, that would not be good"—the question remains open and requires further analysis.

In an interesting on-line review, Peter Simek wrote that, in Scott's version, the "world of the past is a rougher, rawer, grittier, less pious, and more 'realist' than previous Hollywood generations have depicted it." Robin Hood, he asserts, emerges "as a Boston Tea Party Revolutionary who is the brains behind the Magna Carta," but the "charm and originality" of the film is lost in the derivative plot of the second half which concludes with the obligatory battle scene containing imagery improbably pilfered from World War II. The reference here is to the landing crafts used by the French invaders.

The director himself says that, without realizing it, "we'd devised a story that is about the forming of Robin Hood, the beginning of the legend and how he came to be as opposed to what people already know" (Carr). This is, of course, hardly surprising considering that this is Hollywood and that a sequel is always possible if the film is a commercial success. In more detail than is usual for a Scott film, *Robin Hood* deals with class and station. King John is an "ineffectual greedhead" in *Robin Hood*, but Robin

Longstride, as he is known in the film, and his band of outlaws go to war on the king's behalf "because he is what stands between England and the condescending French" (Carr). While Scott says that the country could run without a monarchy, "a monarchy is part of our institutional history," and adds, perhaps ironically, that the royal family is a business now and must be managed as such. In the film, the royals use henchmen, particularly the evil Sheriff of Nottingham, to shake up their subjects and exploit them while they stand largely aloof from the fray. Scott says, "In a sense you are watching Robin beginning to understand the corruption around him, whether it is King John or Philip of France…. And watching that forming of Robin Hood is the beginning of the legend of how he came to be" (Carr, 8). The advantage of this interpretation is that it clearly leaves room for a sequel.

Under the title "This Robin Hood robs from the filmgoers," *USA Today*'s Claudia Puig reported that the film is glum and lacking in charm and romance. And whatever happened to the Merry Men and robbing from the rich and giving to the poor? The plot, she reports, is gloomy, complicated and uninvolving. And Crowe's "distinctive quality of contained ferocity" is lost in the muddle. Puig *does* like the photography and offers modest praise for some of the actors. According to Puig, the result is tedious and shameless and, worst of all, a back-story for a projected second film. John Wirt in the *Baton Rouge Advocate* was more sympathetic and considered the film "better or even above the veteran director's best work."

Probably the most negative, and certainly the most unfair review was by David Edelstein for *New York*; he calls the film "a pompous hash rich in bogus historical context." His chief complaint, as with the variety of reviewers who disliked the film, is that it is not merry or funny like the ballad he quotes or like Flynn's film and that all the historical references muddy up the film. His most telling riposte, which is fair enough, is to poke fun at the finale in which Marion shows up on the beach to battle the evil French and attempt to do in Godfrey for killing her father. Certainly, in many respects, the film's rousing finale seems to be attempting to play catch-up on the excitement quotient with a rousing battle scene.

One aspect of the film apparently not mentioned by the reviewers is the ease with which Robin assumes the identity of Loxley. In fact, the switch would not have been as difficult as it might seem nowadays. In the days before photography, such deception was much easier than it would be today, especially in cases in which some years passed before the imposter appeared. Some years after the disappearance of a rich French peasant named Martin Guerre in the sixteenth century, an imposter appeared, was taken to bed by Guerre's wife and accepted, albeit with some controversy, as the real Martin. The return of the true Martin and the resulting trial are chronicled in fiction and film, most notably in the film *The Return of Martin Guerre* (1983), which starred Gérard Depardieu and which Scott surely has seen.

The acting of *Robin Hood* is strong. Although some critics complained that Crowe was getting long in the tooth for heroics, he was generally praised. Cate Blanchett is a plausible Marion and furnishes a surprising amount of erotic heat. Middle-aged sex has seldom looked better. Mark Strong, with his head shaved, is admirably villainous and Max von Sydow is a hoot bragging about his morning erection. While the critics complained that Robin's Merry Men were not merry enough, they are a rough and boisterous bunch and will doubtless become more merry on Blu-ray.

The makers of *Robin Hood* emphasized what they called its "political vision." Robin "actually starts a revolution and brings the people together," not to mention his sponsorship of the Magna Carta, which his father is said to have written. If so, it was indeed "the beginning of all our democracies, in a way" (Hope-Jones, 90).

The castle warfare and the violence of the period is, in general, convincingly represented, but some actions are totally unbelievable. In an opening scene, Marion, in the middle of the night, shoots a flaming arrow at a masked teenage bandit. Thatch, straw and flammable materials are everywhere, and the whole setting would likely have gone up in flames immediately. Even leaving aside the implausibility of the French landing crafts, bows and arrows were costly and difficult to manufacture and the unknown thousands of arrows shown in the concluding battle are not only fictional, but impossible. (See Reid, *Warfare, passim*, for many fascinating details.)

The previews and advance advertisements widely shown on the Internet and on television are a blatant imitation of the action and visual style of *Gladiator*, Scott's biggest hit. Such advertising sometimes indicates that the producers believe that their film is problematic and faces an uncertain future at the box office, at least in relationship to its cost. Scott's *Robin Hood* opened the Cannes Film Festival on May 13, 2010, and in U.S. theaters the following day. *Robin Hood* was an expensive film. According to Universal Studios, who co-financed it with Relativity Media, the film cost $155,000,000; however, according to the TheWrap.com, an internet web site which covers the media, the actual cost was closer to $200,000,000 even after tax breaks. According to Box Office Mojo, the domestic box office was $105,269,730, and the foreign box-office added $205,399,810 for a total of $310,669,540. While this total was hardly enough to encourage the sequel which the makers of the film had hopefully allowed for in the plotting, it was, with DVD, Blu-ray and television added in, hardly a disaster.

Filmography

Unless otherwise stated, credits and times are for original American theatrical releases. The complete credits of several of these films run for pages and may be found on the Internet Movie Database. The IMDb credits are usually, but not always, both complete and correct. Running times are for the American theatrical release versions.

Boy and Bicycle (1962) British Film Institute. *Director-Producer:* Ridley Scott. *Theme Music:* John Barry. *Incidental Music:* John Baker. *Sound Recording:* Brian Hodgson, Murray Marshall. *Cast:* Tony Scott (Boy). *Running Time:* 27 minutes.

Adam Adamant Lives! "The League of Uncharitable Ladies" (1966). *Screenplay:* John Penington. *Camera:* Charles Parnell. *Editor:* Valerie Best. *Telerecording Editor:* Paddy Wilson. *Designer:* Mary Red. *Production:* Verity Lambert. *Cast:* Gerald Harper (Adam Adamant), Juliet Harmer (Georgina Jones), Jack May (William E. Sims), John Carson (Randolph), Amelia Bayntun (Charity), Gerald Sim (Jarrot), Larry Noble (Harry Marshall), Geraldine Moffatt (Prudence), Sheila Grant (Hope), Lucy Griffiths (Faith), Jean Gregory (Mrs. Lightfoot), Joan Paton (Mrs. Jarrot), Eve Gross (Abstinence), Pauline Loring (Mrs. Winter), Joyce Carpenter (Mrs. Tudor), Betty Cardno (Mrs. Wright). Broadcast on September 8, 1966. Running Time: 50 minutes.

Of the three episodes of *Adam Adamant* directed by Scott, "League" is the only one which survives. The complete series, minus the three episodes which were erased, is available on BBC Region 2 DVD along with an excellent informative booklet.

The Duellists (1977). Paramount. *Director:* Ridley Scott. *Screenplay:* Gerald Vaughan-Hughes, based on Joseph Conrad's story "The Duel." *Producer:* David Puttnam and Ivor Powell. *Music:* Howard Blake. *Photography:* Frank Tidy. *Editor:* Pamela Power. *Art Director:* Bryan Graves.

Cast: Keith Carradine (D'Hubert), Harvey Keitel (Feraud), Cristina Raines (Adele), Edward Fox (Colonel), Robert Stephens (Treillard), John McEnery (Commander), Albert Finney (Fouché), Diana Quick (Laura). Running Time: 99 minutes. MPAA Rating: PG.

Alien (1979). 20th Century–Fox release of a Brandywine–Ronald Shusett Production. *Producers:* Gordon Carroll, David Giler and Walter Hill. *Director:* Ridley Scott. *Executive Producer:* Ronald Shusett. *Screenplay:* Dan O'Bannon. *Music:* Jerry Goldsmith. *Photography:* Derek Vanlint. *Editor:* Terry Rawlings. *Production Design:* Michael Seymour. *Art Directors:* Les Dilley, Roger Christian. *Special Effects:* Brian Johnson and Nick Allder. *Costumes:* John Mollo. *Assistant Director:* Paul Ibbetson. *Music:* Jerry Goldsmith. *Cast:* Tom Skerritt (Dallas), Sigourney Weaver (Ripley), Veronica Cartwright (Lambert), Harry Dean Stanton (Brett), John Hurt (Kane), Ian Holm (Ash), Yaphet Kotto (Parker). MPAA Rating: R. Running Time: 124 minutes.

Filmography

Blade Runner (1982). The Ladd Company, Warner Brothers. *Director:* Ridley Scott. *Screenplay:* Hampton Fancher and David Peoples, based on the novel *Do Androids Dream of Electric Sheep?* by Philip K. Dick. *Music:* Vangelis. *Sets:* Lawrence C. Paull. *Art Director:* David Snyder. *Visual Futurist:* Syd Mead. *Photography:* Jordan Cronenweth. *Cast:* Harrison Ford (Deckard), Rutger Hauer (Batty), Sean Young (Rachael), Edward James Olmos (Gaff), M. Emmet Walsh (Bryant), Daryl Hannah (Pris), William Sanderson (Sebastian), Brion James (Leon), Joe Turkel (Tyrell), Joanna Cassidy (Zhora), James Hong (Chew), Morgan Paull (Holden), Kevin Thompson (Bear). MPAA Rating: R. Running Time: 117 min.

Legend (1985). Universal Pictures. *Producer:* Arnon Milchan. *Director:* Ridley Scott. *Screenplay:* William Hjortsberg. *Photography:* Alex Thomson. *Production Designer:* Assheton Gorton. *Editor:* Terry Rawlings. *Special Makeup:* Rob Bottin. *Music:* Tangerine Dream. *Cast:* Tom Cruise (Jack), Mia Sara (Princess Lily), Tim Curry (Darkness), David Bennent (Gump), Alice Playten (Blix), Billy Barty (Screwball), Cork Hubbert (Brown Tom), Peter O'Farrell (Pox), Kirah Shah (Blunder), Annabelle Lanyon (Oona), Robert Picardo (Meg Mucklebones), Tina Martin (Nell). MPAA Rating: PG. Running Time of Original U.S. Release: 89 minutes.

Someone to Watch Over Me (1987). Columbia Pictures Corporation. *Director:* Ridley Scott. *Producers:* Thierry De Ganay and Harold Schneider. *Screenplay:* Howard Franklin. *Photography:* Steven Poster. *Editor:* Claire Simpson. *Music:* Michael Kamen. *Sound:* Gene Cantamessa. *Production Design:* Jim Bissell. *Set Decorator:* Linda DeScenna. *Cast:* Tom Berenger (Mike Keegan), Mimi Rogers (Claire Gregory), Lorraine Bracco (Ellie Keegan), Jerry Orbach (Lt. Garber), John Rubinstein (Neil Steinhart), Andreas Katsules (Joey Venza), Tony DiBendetto (T.J.), James E. Moriarty (Koontz), Mark Moses (Win Hockings), Daniel Hugh Kelly (Scotty), Harley Cross (Tommy Keegan). MPAA Rating R. Running Time 106 minutes.

Black Rain (1989). Paramount and Pegasus Film Partners. *Director:* Ridley Scott. *Producers:* Stanley R. Jaffe and Sherry Lansing. *Executive Producers:* Craig Bolotin and Julie Kirkham. *Screenplay:* Craig Bolotin and Warren Lewis. *Casting:* Dianne Crittenden. *Music:* Hans Zimmer. *Costumes:* Ellen Mirojnick. *Editor:* Tom Rolf. *Production Designer:* Norris Spencer. *Photography:* Jan De Bont. *Cast:* Michael Douglas (Nick), Andy Garcia (Charlie), Kate Capshaw (Joyce), Ken Takakura (Mashahiro), Yusaku Matsuda (Sato), Tomisaburo Wakayama (Sugi), Shigeru Koyama (Ohashi), John Spencer (Oliver), Luis Guzman (Frankie). MPAA Rating: R. Running Time: 129 minutes.

Thelma & Louise (1991). MGM, Pathé and Percy Mann. *Director:* Ridley Scott. *Producers:* Mimi Polk, Callie Khouri, Dean O'Brien and Ridley Scott. *Writer:* Callie Khouri. *Costume Designer:* Elizabeth McBride. *Music:* Hans Zimmer. *Editor:* Thom Noble. *Production Designer:* Norris Spencer. *Photography*: Adrian Biddle. *Cast:* Susan Sarandon (Louise), Geena Davis (Thelma), Michael Madsen (Jimmy), Christopher McDonald (Darryl), Stephen Tobolowsky (Max), Brad Pitt (J.D.), Timothy Carhart (Harlan), Lucinda Jenney (Lena the Waitress), Jason Beghe (State Trooper), Marco St. John (Truck Driver). [St. John is listed at the beginning of the film but not at the credits at the end.] MPAA Rating: R. Running Time: 129 minutes.

1492: Conquest of Paradise (1992). Légende Enterprises, France 3 Cinéma du West. *Director:* Ridley Scott. *Producers:* Alain Goldman and Ridley Scott. *Screenplay:* Roselyne Bosch. *Photography:* Adrian Biddle. *Music:* Vangelis. *Production Design:* Norris Spencer. *Cast:* Gérard Depardieu (Columbus), Armand Assante (Sanchez), Sigourney Weaver (Queen Isabella), Frank Langella (Luis), Loren Dean (Older Fernando Columbus), Fernando Rey (Antonio). MPAA Rating: PG-13. Running Time: 154 minutes.

White Squall (1996). Hollywood Pictures, Largo Entertainment and Scott Free. *Director:* Ridley Scott. *Producers:* Mimi Polk Giflin and Rocky Lang. *Associate Producer:* Terry Needham. *Executive Producer:* Ridley Scott. *Co-Producer:* Todd Robinson and Nigel Wooll. *Screenplay:* Todd Robinson.

Casting: Louis Di Giaimo. *Special Effects:* Joss Williams. *Music:* Jeff Rona. *Costumes:* Judianna Makovsky. *Editor:* Gerry Hambling. *Production Designers:* Peter J. Hampton and Leslie Tomkins. *Photography:* Hugh Johnson. *Cast:* Jeff Bridges ("Skipper" Sheldon), Caroline Goodall (Alice Sheldon), John Savage (McCrea), Scott Wolf (Chuck), Jeremy Sisto (Frank Beaumont), Ethan Embry (Tracy), Ryan Phillippe (Gil Martin), David Lascher (Robert March), Julio Mechoso (Gerard Pascal), David Selry (Francis Beaumont), Jason Marsden (Shay Jennings), Eric Michael Cole (Dean Preston), Balthazar Getty (Tod). MPAA Rating: PG-13. Running Time: 129 minutes.

G.I. Jane (1997). Hollywood Pictures. Scott Free/Moving Pictures Production. *Director:* Ridley Scott. *Producers:* Roger Birnbaum. *Screenplay:* David Twohy and Danielle Alexandra, from a story by Danielle Alexandra. *Music:* Trevor Jones. *Casting:* Louis Di Giaimo and Brett Goldstein. *Photography:* Hugh Johnson. *Production Designer:* Arthur Max. *Editor:* Pietro Scalia. *Costumes:* Marilyn Vance. *Cast:* Demi Moore (Jordan O'Neill), Anne Bancroft (Lillian DeHaven), Viggo Mortensen (Master Chief John Urgayle), Jason Beghe (Royce), James Caviezel (Slovnik), John Michael Higgins (Chief of Staff), Kevin Gage (Instructor Pyro), David Warshofsky (Instructor Johns), David Vadim (Cortez), Scott Wilson (C. O. Salem). MPAA Rating: R. Running Time: 125 minutes.

Gladiator (2000). DreamWorks Pictures and Universal Pictures. *Director:* Ridley Scott. *Executive Producers:* Laurie MacDonald and Robin Shenfield. *Producers:* Douglas Wick, David Franzoni, and Branko Lustig. *Screenplay:* David Franzoni, John Logan and William Nicholson, from a story by David Franzoni. *Photography:* John Mathieson. *Production Designer:* Arthur Max. *Editor* Pietro Scalia. *Costumes:* Janty Yates. *Visual Effects:* John Nelson. *Music:* Hans Zimmer and Lisa Gerrard. *Cast:* Russell Crowe (Maximus), Joaquin Phoenix (Commodus), Connie Nielsen (Lucilla), Oliver Reed (Proximo), Richard Harris (Marcus Aurelius), Derek Jacobi (Gracchus), Djimon Hounsou (Juba), David Hemmings (Cassius), David Schofield (Falco), John Shrapnel (Gaius). MPAA Rating: R. Running Time: 155 minutes.

Black Hawk Down (2001). Revolution Studios, Jerry Bruckheimer Films and Scott Free. *Director:* Ridley Scott. *Executive Producers:* Mike Stenson, Chad Oman, Branko Lustig and Simon West. *Producers:* Jerry Bruckheimer and Ridley Scott. *Screenplay:* Ken Nolan, based on the book by Mark Bowden. *Music:* Hans Zimmer. *Photography:* Slawomir Idziak. *Editor:* Pietro Scalia. *Production Designers:* Arthur Max. *Sets:* Elli Griff. *Cast:* Ewan McGregor (Grimes), Eric Bana (Hoot), Jason Isaacs (Steele), Orlando Bloom (Blackburn), Ian Virgo (Wedell), Gabriel Casseus (Kurth), Sam Shepard (General Garrison), Josh Hartnett (Eversmann), Hugh Dancy (Schmid), Jeremy Piven (Wolcott), Nikolaj Coster-Waldau (Gordon), Johnny Strong (Shugart), Ron Eldard (Durant), Brian Van Holt (Steuker).

Hannibal (2001). MGM, Universal and Scott Free. *Director:* Ridley Scott. *Executive Producer:* Branko Lustig. *Producers:* Dino De Laurentiis and Martha De Laurentiis. *Screenplay:* David Mamet and Steven Zaillian, based on the novel by Thomas Harris. *Casting:* Louis DiGiaimo. *Costume Designer:* Janty Yates. *Music:* Hans Zimmer. *Editor:* Pietro Scalia. *Production Designer:* Norris Spencer. *Photography:* John Mathieson. *Cast:* Anthony Hopkins (Hannibal Lecter), Julianne Moore (Clarise Starling), Gary Oldman (Mason Verger), Ray Liotta (Paul Krendler), Frankie R. Faison (Barney), Giancarlo Giannini (Pazzi), Francesca Neri (Allegra Pazzi), Zeljko Ivanek (Doemling), Hazelle Goodman (Evelda), David Andrews (Agent Pearsall), Francis Guinan (Noonan), Enrico Lo Verso (Gnoco), Mark Margolis (perfume expert), Ivano Marescotti (Carlo), Fabrizio Gifuni (Matteo), Ennio Coltorti (Ricci).

Matchstick Men (2003). Warner Brothers, Scott Free, Image Movers, Live Planet and HorsePower Entertainment. *Executive Producer:* Robert Zemeckis. *Producers:* Sean Bailey, Ted Griffin, Jack Rapke, Kathy Scott and Steve Starkey. *Director:* Ridley Scott. *Co-Producers:* Charles J.D. Schlissel and Geannina Facio. *Casting:* Debra Zane. *Costume Designer:* Michael Kaplan. *Music:* Hans Zimmer. *Editor:* Dody Dorn. *Production Manager:* Tom Foden. *Photography:* John Mathieson. *Screenplay:*

Nicholas and Ted Griffin, *based on the novel by* Eric Garcia. *Cast:* Nicolas Cage (Roy Waller), Sam Rockwell (Frank Mercer), Alison Lohman (Angela), Bruce Altman (Dr. Harris Klein), Bruce McGill (Chuck Frechette), Sheila Kelley (Kathy), Beth Grant (Laundry Lady), Jenny O'Hara (Mrs. Schaffer), Steve Eastin (Mr. Schaffer), Melora Walters (Heather). MPAA Rating: PG13. Running Time: 116 minutes.

All the Invisible Children: "Jonathan" (2005). *Directors:* Ridley Scott and Jordan Scott. *Producers:* Maria Grazia Cucinotta, Chiara Tilesi and Stefano Veneruso. *Script:* Jordan Scott. *Photography:* James Whitaker. *Production Designer:* Ben Scott. *Music:* Ramin Djawadi. *Cast:* David Thewlis, Kelly Macdonald, Jordan Clarke, Jack Thompson, Joshua Light. Running Time: 17 minutes.

Kingdom of Heaven (2005). 20th Century–Fox, Scott Free, Choca Productions, Dritte Babelsberg and Inside Track 3. *Producer-Director:* Ridley Scott. *Executive Producers:* Branko Lustig, Lisa Ellzey and Terry Needham. *Screenplay:* William Monahan. *Photography:* John Mathieson. *Production Designer:* Arthur Max. *Editor:* Dody Dorn. *Music:* Harry Gregson-Williams. *Costumes:* Janty Yates. *Music Supervisor:* Marc Streitenfeld. *Cast:* Orlando Bloom (Balian de Ibelin), Eva Green (Sybylla), Jeremy Irons (Tiberias), David Thewlis (Hospitaler), Brendan Gleeson (Reynald de Chatillon), Michael Sheen (Gravedigger), Liam Neeson (Godfrey de Ibelin), Edward Norton (King Baldwin), Ghassan Massoud (Saladin). MPAA Rating: R. Running Time: 144 minutes.

A Good Year (2006). *Producer-Director* Ridley Scott. *Executive Producers:* Branko Lustig, Julie Payne and Lisa Ellzey. *Screenplay:* Marc Klein, based on the book by Peter Mayle. *Photography:* Philippe Le Sourd. *Cast:* Russell Crowe (Max Skinner). Albert Finney (Uncle Henry), Marion Cotillard (Fanny Chenal), Abbie Cornish (Christie Roberts), Didier Bourdon (Francis Duflot), Tom Hollander (Charlie Willis), Freddie Highmore (Young Max), Isabelle Candelier (Ludivine Duflot). MPAA Rating: PG-13. Running Time: 118 minutes.

American Gangster (2007). Universal. *Director:* Ridley Scott. *Producers:* Brian Grazer, Ridley Scott. *Executive Producers:* Nicholas Pileggi, Steven Zaillian, Branko Lustig, Jim Whitaker, and Michael Costigan. *Screenplay:* Steven Zaillian, based on an article by Mark Jacobson. *Photography:* Harris Savides. *Production Designer:* Arthur Max. *Editor:* Pietro Scalia. *Music:* Marc Streitenfeld. *Costume Designer:* Janty Yates. *Cast:* Denzel Washington (Frank Lucas), Russell Crowe (Richie Roberts), Chiwetel Ejiofor (Huey Lucas), Josh Brolin (Detective Trupo), Lymari Nadal (Eva), Ted Levine (Lou), Armand Assante (Dominic Cattano), Ruby Dee (Mama Lucas), Cuba Gooding, Jr. (Nicky Barnes). MPAA Rating: R. Running Time: 156 minutes.

Robin Hood (2010). *Director:* Ridley Scott. *Producers:* Russell Crowe, Brian Glazer and Ridley Scott. *Screenplay:* Brian Helgeland. *Story:* Brian Helgeland, Ethan Reiff and Cyrus Voris. *Photography:* John Mathieson. *Music:* Marc Streitenfeld. *Editor:* Pierre Scalia. *Production Designer:* Arthur Max. *Cast:* Russell Crowe (Robin Longstride), Cate Blanchett (Marion Loxley), Max von Sydow (Sir Walter Loxley), William Hurt (William Marshal), Mark Strong (Godfrey), Oscar Isaac (Prince John), Danny Huston (King Richard the Lion Heart), Eileen Atkins (Eleanor of Aquitaine), Mark Addy (Friar Tuck), Matthew Macfadyen (Sheriff of Nottingham), Kevin Durand (Little John), Scott Grimes (Will Scarlet), Alan Doyle (Allan A'Dayle), Douglas Hodge (Sir Robert Loxley), Léa Seydoux (Isabella of Angoulême). MPAA Rating PG-13 Aspect Ratio 2.35:1 Running Time 140 minutes.

Bibliography

Reviews

ALIEN

"Har.," *Variety*, 5/23/1979.
Canby, Vincent, *New York Times*, 5/25/1979, p. C19.
Kroll, Jack, *Newsweek*, 5/28/1979, pp. 101–103.
Rogerebert.com, 10/26/2003.
Strick, Philip, *Sight and Sound*, 1979, pp. 258–259.
Wood, Robin, *Film Comment*, 8/1979, 28–32.

AMERICAN GANGSTER

Ansen, David, *Newsweek*, 11/12/2007, p. 77.
Denby, David, *New Yorker*, 1/5/2007, p. 77.
Douthat, Ross, *National Review*, 11/19/2007, p. 63.
Gilbey, Ryan, *Sight and Sound*, vol. 18, no. 1, 1/2008, p. 56–57.
Gleiberman, Owen. *Entertainment Weekly*, 10/31/2007.
Hoberman, J., *Village Voice*, 10/22/2007.
Jacobson, Harlan, *Film Comment*, 11/2007, pp. 22–23.
James, Nick, "Dealing Dope and Death," *Sight and Sound*, vol.17, no. 12, 12/2007, 36–40.
Korman, Klein, *Sight and Sound*, 5/2008, p. 76.
Morgenstern, Joe, *The Wall Street Journal*, 11/12/2007, p. W1.
Wood, Michael, *London Review of Books*, vol. 29, no. 4, 12/13/2007, p. 18.

BLACK HAWK DOWN

Clark, Mike, *USA Today*, 12/28/2001.
Denby, David, *The New Yorker*, 12/31/2001, p. 124.
Ebert, Roger, rogerebert.com 1/18/2002.
Graham, Bob, *San Francisco Chronicle*, 1/18/2002.
Hoberman, J., *Village Voice*, 12/25/2001.
Jacobson, Harlan, "Bad Day at Black Rock," *Film Comment*, 38, no. 1, 01/02/2002, 28–31.

Mitchell, Elvis, *New York Times*, 3/24/2002, p. E22.
Schickel, Richard, Time, Approx. 12/31/2001.
Strick, Philip, *Sight and Sound*, 21/2002, pp. 40–41.
Thomas, Evan, "Arts and Culture in the Bush Era," *Newsweek*, 12/22/2008, p. 54.

BLACK RAIN

Bernard, Jami, *New York Post*, 9/22/1989, p. 27.
Brown, Georgia, *Village Voice*, 10/3/1989, p. 71.
Canby, Vincent, *New York Times*, 9/22/1989, p. C12.
Combs, Richard, *Monthly Film Bulletin* 1/1990, p. 8.
Corliss, Richard, *Time*, 10/2/1989, p. 90.
Denby, David, *New York*, 10/2/1989, p. 66.
Grant, Edmond, *Films in Review*, 1–2, 1990, p. 40.
Kauffmann, Stanley, *New Republic*, 10/16/1989, p. 31.
Kempley, Rita, *Washington Post*, 9/22/1989, p. 81.
"Mac.," *Variety*, 9/20/1989.
McGrady, Mike, *Newsday*, 9/22/1989, Part III/p. 3.
Moore, Suzanne, *New Statesman and Society*, 2/3/1990, p. 44.
Wilmington, Michael, *Los Angeles Times*, 9/22/1989, *Calendar*/p. 1.

BLADE RUNNER

Asahina, Robert, *New Leader*, 7/12/1982, p. 27.
Bernard, Jami, *New York Post*, 9/1/1992, p. 29.
"Cart.," *Variety*, 6/18/1982, p. 15.
Coleman, John, *New Statesman*, 9/10/1982, p. 54.
Denby, David, *New York*, 6/28/1982, p. 10.
Gelmis, Joseph, *Newsday*, 9/11/1992, Part II/p. 64.
Hoberman, J., *Village Voice*, 9/15/1992, p. 61.
Howe, Desson, *Washington Post*, 9/11/1992, Weekend, p. 42.

Bibliography

Kempley, Rita, *Washington Post*, 9/11/1992, p. 81.

Osmond, Andrew, "Definitely Maybe," *Sight and Sound*, Jan, 2008, vol. 18, no. 1, p. 92.

Romney, Jonathan, *New Statesman* & Society, 11/27/1992, p. 33.

Sarris, Andrew, *Village Voice*, 7/6/1982, p. 147.

Wilmington, Michael, *Los Angeles Times*, 9/1/1992, *Calendar*, p. 6.

BODY OF LIES

Clarke, Roger, *Sight and Sound* 12/2008, p. 55.

Dalby, Simon. *Political Geography* 5/2008, Issue 4, pp. 439–455.

Denby, David, *New Yorker*, 10/13/2008, pp. 151–153.

Douthat, Ross, *National Review*, 11/3/2008, p. 57.

Ebert, Roger, *Body of Lies*, rogerebert.com, 10/8/2008.

Edelstein, David, *New York*, 10/13/2008, pp. 62–63.

Gleiberman, Owen, *Entertainment Weekly*, 10/17/2008, pp. 74–75.

Travers, Peter, *Rolling Stone*, 10/16/2008, pp. 82–86.

THE DUELLISTS

Byron, Stuart, "The Keitel Method," *Film Comment*, 14, 1, 1–2/1978, p. 39.

Davis, Roderick, "Conrad Cinematized: *The Duellists*," *Literature/Film Quarterly*, Vol. 8, no. 2, 1980, pp. 125–132.

"Mosk." *Variety*, 6/01/1997.

1492: CONQUEST OF PARADISE

Aspden, Peter, *Sight and Sound*, 1/11/1992, pp. 41–42.

Anderson, John, *Newsday*, 10/9, 1992, II/p. 71.

Bernard, Jami, *New York Post*, 10/9/1992, p. 36.

Canby, Vincent, *New York Times*, 10/9/1992, p. C1.

Denby, David, *New York*, 10/19/1992, p. 122.

Garcia, Maria, *Films in Review*.

Hoberman, J., *Village Voice*, 10/20/1992, p. 53.

Kroll, Jack, *Newsweek*, 10/19/1992, p. 68.

McCarthy, Todd, *Variety*, 10/12/1992.

Romney, Jonathan, *New Statesman*, 10/23/1992, p. 37.

Sragow, Michael, *New Yorker*, 10/19/1992, p. 11.

Strick, Philip, *Sight and Sound*, 11/1992, p. 41.

Turan, Kenneth, *Los Angeles Times*, 10/9/1992, *Calendar*, p. 1.

Wollen, Peter, *Sight and Sound*, 11/11/1992, pp. 19–23.

G. I. JANE

Anderson, John, *Newsday*, 8/22/1997, pt II, p. 85.

Denby, David, *New York*, 9/19/1997, p. 47.

McCarthy, Todd, *Variety*, 8/11/1997, reprinted in Sammon, *Making*, pp. 149–151.

Medved, Michael, *New York Post*, 8/22/1997, p. 37.

Schickel, Richard, *Time*, 8/25, 1997, p. 72.

Taubin, Amy, *Village Voice*, 8/26/1997, p. 73.

Turan, Kenneth, *Los Angeles Times*, 8/2/1997, *Calendar*, p. 1.

GLADIATOR

Corliss, Richard, *Time*, 5/8/2000, p. 83.

Felperin, Leslie, *Sight and Sound*, 6/2000/p. 33, 44.

Foreman, Jonathan, *New York Post*, 5/5/2000, p. 51.

Hoberman, J., *Village Voice*, 5/9/2000, p. 129.

Lane, Anthony, *New Yorker*, 5/8/2000, p. 125; reprinted in *Nobody's Perfect* NY: Knopf, 2002, pp. 309–312.

McCarthy, Todd, *Variety*, 4/24–30/2000, p. 27.

Mitchell, Elvis, *New York Times*, 5/5/2000, p. E1.

Rainer, Peter, *New York*, 5/15/2000, p. 68.

Seymour, Gene, *Newsday*, 5/5/2000, Part II/p. 83.

Sterritt, David, *Christian Science Monitor*, 5/5/2000, p. 15.

Turan, *Los Angeles Times*, 5/5/200, Calendar, p. 1.

A GOOD YEAR

Berardinelli, James, *reelviews.net*, n.d.

Fahy, Patrick, *Sight and Sound*, 16, no. 12, 12/2006, 55.

Stephen Holden, *New York Times*, 11/10/2006.

McCarthy, Todd, *Variety*, 9/10/2006.

HANNIBAL

Anderson, John, *Newsday*, 2/9/2001, part II/p. 83.

Anson, David, *Newsweek*, 2/12/2001, p. 96.

Corliss, Richard, *Time*, 2/12/2001, p. 84.

Foreman, Jonathan, *New York Post*, 2/19/2001, p. 49.

Hoberman, J. *Village Voice*, 2/13/2001, p. 127.

Newman, Kim, *Sight and Sound*, 4/2001, p. 48.

Rainer, Peter, *New York*, 2/19/2001, p. 182.

Sammon, Paul M., "Feeding Hannibal," *Fangoria*, 3/2001, pp. 34–39.

Sterritt, David, *Christian Science Monitor*, 2/16/2001, p. 15.

Turan, Kenneth. *Los Angeles Times*, 2/19/2001, Calendar, p. 1.

Bibliography

KINGDOM OF HEAVEN

Corliss, Richard, *Time,* 10/3/2004.
Dabashi, Hamid, "Warriors of Faith," *Sight and Sound,* 5/2005, 27, vol. 15, no. 5, p. 27.
Ebert, Roger, *Kingdom of Heaven, rogerebert.com,* 5/6/2005.
Jones, Nick, *Sight and Sound,* 15, no. 6, 6/2005, 64–65.
Metzger, Scott, "The Kingdom of Heaven: Teaching the Crusades," *Social Education* 9/2005, pp. 256–260.

LEGEND

Coleman, John, *New Statesman,* 12/18/1985, p. 30.
Corliss, Richard, *Time.* 5/12/1986, p. 98.
McGrady, Mike, *Newsday,* 4/18/1986, Part iii/p. 3.
Newman, Kim, *Monthly Film Bulletin,* 12/1985, p. 380.
Reed, Rex, *New York Post,* 4/18/1986, p. 25.
Sterritt, David, *Christian Science Monitor,* 4/25/1986, p. 30.
"Strat.," *Variety,* 8/21/1985.
Thomas, Kevin, *Los Angeles Times,* 4/18/1986, Calendar, p. 4.

MATCHSTICK MEN

Anonymous, *moviegazette.com,* n. d.
Berardinelli, James, *reelviews.net,* n. d.
Ebert, Roger, *Chicago Sun–Times,* 10/12/2003.
Graham, Renee, *Boston Globe,* 9/12/2003. *boston. com.*
Sterritt, David, *Christian Science Monitor,* 10/12/2003.
White, Rob, *Sight and Sound,* 11/2003, p. 54.

ROBIN HOOD

Carr, David, *New York Times,* 5/9/2010, *Arts,* pp. 1, 8.
Edelstein, David, *New York,* 5/24/2010, p. 72
Lane, Anthony, *The New Yorker,* 5/24/2010, pp. 82–83.
Murray, Rebecca, *About.com/Hollywood Movies,* 5/14/2010.
Puente, Maria, *USA Today,* 5/10/2010, p. 3D.
Puig, Claudia, *USA Today,* 5/13/2010, p. 6D.
Wirt, John, *Baton Rouge Advocate,* 5/14/2010, *Fun,* p. 22.

SOMEONE TO WATCH OVER ME

Ansen, David, *Newsweek,* 10/2/1987, p. 84B.
Canby, Vincent, *New York Times,* 10/9/1987.
Corliss, Richard, *Time,* 10/12/1987, p. 84.
Cunliffe, Simon, *New Statesman,* 3/11/1988, p. 38.

Ebert, Roger, 10/9/1987, p. 31.
Hoberman, J., *Village Voice,* 10/20/1987, p. 68.
"Lor.," *Variety,* 9/30/1987.
Kael, Pauline, *The New Yorker,* 11/28/1987, p. 140.
Magill, Marcia, *Films in Review,* 12/1987, p. 61.
Petley, Julian, *Monthly Film Bulletin,* 4/1988, p. 118.
Wilmington, Michael, *Los Angeles Times,* 10/19/1987, *Calendar,* p. 1.

THELMA & LOUISE

Abrams, Janet, *Sight and Sound,* 7/1991, p. 55,
Bernard, Jami, *New York Post,* 5/24/1991, p. 27.
Billison, Anne, *New Statesman & Society,* 7/12/1991, p. 33.
Carlson, Margaret, *Time,* 6/24/1991, p. 57.
"Daws.," *Variety,* 5/13/1991.
Denby, David, *New York,* 6/10/1991, p. 55.
Grant, Edmond, *Films in Review,* 8/1991, p. 258.
Hoberman, J. *Village Voice,* 5/28/1991, p. 51.
Kroll, Jack, Newsweek, 5/27/1991, p. 59.
"The Many Faces of *Thelma & Louise,*" *Film Quarterly,* Winter, 1991–92, reprinted in *Film Quarterly: Forty Years—A Selection, Berkeley:* University of California Press, 1999, pp. 542–560. Contains essays by Harvey A. Greenberg, "Thelma & Louise's Exuberant Polysemy; Carol J. Clover, "Crossing Over"; Albert Johnson, "Bacchantes at Large"; Peter N. Chumo II, "*Thelma & Louise* as Screwball Comedy"; Brian Henderson, "Narrative Organization"; Linda Williams, "What Makes a Woman Wander"; Leo Braudy, "Satire into Myth"; and Marsha Kinder, "*Thelma & Louise* and *Messidor* as Feminist Road Movies."
Maslin, Janet, *New York Times,* 5/24/1991.
_____. *New York Times,* 6/18/1991.
Mason, M. S., *Christian Science Monitor,* 7/19/1991, p. 11.
Mathews, Jack, *Newsday,* 5/24/1991, part II/p. 65.
Schickel, Richard, 5/27/1991, p. 64.
_____. *Time,* 6/24/1991, p. 52.
Sterritt, David. *Christian Science Monitor,* 6/17/1991, p. 11.
Turan, Kenneth, *Los Angeles Times,* 5/24/1991, Calendar/p. 1.

WHITE SQUALL

Brown, Georgia, *Village Voice,* 2/6/1996, p. 48.
Denby, David, *New York,* 2/12/1996, p. 53.
Kermode, Mark, *Sight and Sound,* 5/1996, p. 64.
Kroll, Jack, *Newsweek,* 2/5/1996, p. 65.
Lowry, Brian, *Variety,* 1/29, 1996, reprinted in Sammon, *Making,* pp. 147–148,
Mathews, Jack, *Los Angeles Times,* 2/29/1996, Calendar, p. 14.

Medved, Michael, *New York Post*, 2/2/1996, p. 42.

Pearson, Harry, Jr., *Films in Review*, 5/6/2996, p. 65.

Schickel, Richard, *Time*, 2/12/1996, p. 79.

Books and Articles

Andrew, Dudley. *Concepts in Film Theory*. New York: Oxford University Press, 1984.

Andrew, Geoff, ed. *Film: The Critics' Choice*. New York: Watson-Guptill, 2001.

Armstrong, Stephen B. *Picture About Extremes: The Films of John Frankenheimer*. Jefferson, NC: McFarland, 2007.

Asbridge, Thomas. *The Crusades*. New York: Ecco, 2010.

Ashton, Dore. *The Delicate Thread*. Tokyo: Kodanska International, 1997.

Aumont, Jack. *Aesthetics of Film*. Trans., rev., and ed. Richard Neopert et al. Austin: University of Texas Press, 1992.

Balio, Tino. *United Artists: The Company That Changed the Film Industry. Vol. 2, 1951–1978*. Madison: University of Wisconsin Press, 2009.

Bogle, Donald. *Toms, Coons, Mulattoes, Mammies, & Bucks*. New York: Bantam Books, 1974.

Bowden, Mark. *Black Hawk Down*. 2nd ed. New York: Penguin, 2000.

Brooker, Will, ed. *The Blade Runner Experience*. London: Wallflower Press, 2005.

Brunel, Pierre, ed. *Companion to Literary Myths, Heroes and Archetypes*. London: Routledge, 1996.

Bukatman, Scott. *Blade Runner*. London: British Film Institute, 1997.

Burroughs, William S. *Blade Runner, A Movie*. Berkeley, CA: Blue Wind Press, 1989.

Carnes, Mark C., ed. *Past Imperfect: History According to the Movies*. New York: Henry Holt, 1995.

Clarke, David B., ed. *The Cinematic City*. London: Routledge, 1997.

Clarke, James. *Ridley Scott*. London: Virgin Books, 2002.

Collins, Jim, Hilary Radner, and Ava Preacher Collins, eds. *Film Theory Goes to the Movies*. New York: Routledge, 1993.

Conrad, Joseph. *The Complete Short Fiction of Joseph Conrad*. Ed. Samuel Hynes. 4 vols. New York: The Ecco Press, 1992.

Cook, Pam, and Philip Dodd, eds. *Women and Film: A Sight and Sound Reader*. Philadelphia: Temple University Press, 1993.

Crowther, Bruce. *Film Noir: Reflections in a Dark Mirror*. New York: Continuum, 1988.

Cubitt, Sean. *The Cinema Effect*. Cambridge, MA: MIT Press, 2005.

Dalle Vache, Angela. *Cinema and Painting: How Art Is Used in Film*. Austin: University of Texas Press, 1996.

Dante. *Dante's "Vita Nuova."* Trans. Mark Musa. 2nd ed. Bloomington: Indiana University Press, 1973.

Dargis, Manohla. "How Oscar Found Ms. Right." *New York Times*, Arts 3/14/2010.

_____. "The Land and the Tradition of the Male Road Movie." In Cook and Dodd, eds., *Women and Film: A Sight and Sound Reader*. Philadelphia: Temple University Press; 1993), pp. 86–92.

Davis, J. Madison. "Living Black, Living White: Cultural Choices in Crime Films." *World Literature Today* 82, issue 3, May-June 2008, pp. 9–11.

Deeley, Michael. *Blade Runners, Deer Hunters, & Blowing the Bloody Doors Off: My Life in Cult Movies*. New York: Pegasus Books, 2009.

Delbrück, Hans. *History of the Art of War*. Trans. Walter J. Renfroe, Jr. 4 vols. Lincoln: University of Nebraska Press, 1995.

Dick, Philip K. *Do Androids Dream of Electric Sheep?* In *Four Novels of the 1960s*. New York: The Library of America, 2007.

Ellison, Harlan. *Harlan Ellison's Watching*. Foreword George Kirgo. Intro. Leonard Maltin. Milwaukee: M Press, 2008.

Eyman, Scott. *Empire of Dreams: The Epic Life of Cecil B. DeMille*. New York: Simon & Schuster, 2010.

_____. *Print the Legend: The Life and Times of John Ford*. New York: Simon & Schuster, 1999.

Finke, Laurie A., and Martin B. Shichtman. *Cinematic Illuminations*. Baltimore: Johns Hopkins University Press, 2010.

Fisk, Robert. "Why Ridley Scott's Story of the Crusades Struck Such a Chord in Lebanese Cinema." *Washington Report on Middle East Affairs* 24, issue 6, 8/2005, *POV* 15–16. Originally published in *The Independent*, UK; 6/4/2005.

Giger, H. R. *Portfolio*. 2nd ed. New York: Barnes and Noble, 2008.

Gladiator: The Making of the Ridley Scott Epic. Foreword by Waler Parkes. Intro. Ridley Scott. New York: Newmarket Press, 2000.

Grant, Barry Keith, ed. *Film Genre Reader II*. Austin: University of Texas Press, 1995.

Griggers, Cathy. "*Thelma and Louise* and the Cultural Generation of the New Butch-Femme." In Collins, Rodner, and Collins, eds., *Film Theory Goes to the Movies*. New York: Routledge, 1993, pp. 129–141.

Guerin, Frances. *A Culture of Light: Cinema and*

Technology in 1920s Germany. Minneapolis: University of Minnesota Press, 2005.

Hardy, Phil. *The Encyclopedia of Science Fiction Movies.* London: Woodbury Press, 1984.

Hayward, Susan. *Key Concepts in Cinema Studies.* London: Routledge, 1996.

Higham, Charles. *Cecil B. DeMille.* New York: Scribner's, 1973.

Hope-Jones, Mark. "*Slings and Arrows.*" *American Cinematographer* 91, no. 6. 6/2010, pp. 30–42.

Hopp, Glenn. *VideoHound's Epics: Giants of the Big Screen.* Detroit: Visible Ink, 1999.

Houston, David. "Directing *Alien* Through an Artist's Eye." *Starlog* 26, 9/1979.

_____. "H.R. Giger, Behind the *Alien* Forms." *Starlog* 26, 9/1979.

Humphrey, Robert. *Stream of Consciousness in the Modern Novel.* Berkeley: University of California Press, 1954.

Jacobson, Harlan. "Ridley Scott, an Overachieving Underachiever." *Film Comment*, 11–12/2007, pp. 22–23.

Jeffords, Susan. "The Big Switch: Hollywood Masculinity in the Nineties." In Cook, and Dodd, eds., *Women and Film.* Philadelphia: Temple University Press, 1993, pp. 196–208.

Johnson, Rachael. "Playing Fathers and Monsters: The Classical Appeal of Anthony Hopkins." *CineAction*, Issue 55, no date, pp. 24–30.

Kael, Pauline. *Taking It All In.* New York: Holt, Rinehart and Winston, 1984.

Kaes, Anton. "*Metropolis* (1927): City, Cinema, Modernity." In Isenberg, ed., *Weimar Cinema: An Essential Guide to Classic Films of the Era.* New York: Columbia University Press, 2009.

_____. *Shell Shock Cinema: Weimar Culture and the Wounds of War.* Princeton, NJ: Princeton University Press, 2009.

Karl, Frederick R. *Joseph Conrad: The Three Lives.* New York: Farrar, Straus and Giroux, 1979.

Keegan, Rebecca. *The Futurist: The Life and Films of James Cameron.* New York: Crown, 2009.

Kerman, Judith B. *Retrofitting "Blade Runner."* 2nd ed. Madison: University of Wisconsin Press, 1997.

Kingdom of Heaven: The Ridley Scott Film and the History Behind the Story. Intro. Ridley Scott. New York: Newmarket Press, 2005

Klein, Marc, and Rico Torres. *A Good Year: Portrait of the Film Based on the Novel of Peter Mayle.* New York: Newmarket Press, 2006.

Knapp, Laurence F., and Andrea F. Kulas. *Ridley Scott Interviews.* Jackson: University Press of Mississippi, 2005.

Kuhn, Annette, ed. *Alien Zone: Cultural Theory and Contemporary Science Fiction Cinema.* London: Verso, 1992.

Lapsley, Robert, and Michael Westlake. *Film Theory: An Introduction.* Manchester, UK: Manchester University Press, 1988.

Leab, David J. *From Sambo to Superspade: The Black Experience in Motion Pictures.* Boston: Houghton Mifflin, 1975.

Levy, David. *Love + Sex with Robots: The Evolution of Human-Robot Relationships.* NY: Harper, 2007.

Lindsay, Jack. *Blast-Power and Ballistics: Concepts of Force and Energy in the Ancient World.* New York: Barnes & Noble, 2009.

Louvish, Simon. *Cecil B. DeMille: A Life in Art.* New York: St Martin's Press, 2007.

Maltin, Leonard. *151 Movies You've Never Seen.* New York: HarperCollins, 2010.

"The Many Faces of *Thelma & Louise.*" In Henderson and Martin, eds., *Film Quarterly: Forty Years — A Selection.* Berkeley: University of California Press, 1999, pp. 542–560.

Martin, Les. *Blade Runner.* New York: Random House, 1982.

McCarthy, Todd. *Howard Hawks: The Grey Fox of Hollywood.* New York: Grove Press, 1997.

McGilligan, Patrick. *Fritz Lang: The Nature of the Beast.* New York: St. Martins Press, 1997.

McKendry, Rebekah. "Fondling Your Eyeballs: Watching Doris Wishman." In Cline and Weiner, eds., *From the Arthouse to the Grindhouse.* Lanham, MD: Scarecrow Press, 2010.

McLynn, Frank. *Marcus Aurelius: A Life.* Cambridge, MA: Da Capo Press, 2009.

Martin, Michael. "Meditations on *Blade Runner.*" *Journal of Interdisciplinary Studies* 17 issue 1–2, pp. 105–122.

Michalczyk, John J. *The French Literary Filmmakers.* Cranbury, NJ: Associated University Presses, 1980.

Minden, Michael, and Holger Bachmann, eds. *Fritz Lang's "Metropolis": Cinematic Visions of Technology and Fear.* New York: Boydell & Brewer, 2000.

Mitry, Jean. *The Aesthetics and Psychology of the Cinema.* Trans. Christopher King. Bloomington: Indiana University Press, 1997.

Morton, Andrew. *Tom Cruise: An Unauthorized Biography.* New York: St. Martin's Press, 2008.

Motion Picture Guide. Ed. Jay Robert Nash and Stanley Ralph Ross. 10 vols. Chicago: Cinebooks, 1985.

Muller, Eddie. *Dark City: The Lost World of Film Noir.* New York: St. Martin's Press, 1998.

Neumann, Dietrich, ed. *Film Architecture: Set Designs from "Metropolis" to "Blade Runner."* Munich: Prestel-Verlag, 1997.

O'Brien, Geoffrey. *The Phantom Empire*. New York: W.W. Norton, 1993.

Ott, Frederick W. *The Films of Fritz Lang*. NY: Citadel Press, 1980.

Parrill, William B. *European Silent Films on Video: A Critical Guide*. Jefferson, NC: McFarland, 2006.

Pastorino, Gloria. "The Death of the Author and the Power of Addition" in *Naked Lunch* and *Blade Runner*." In Sayer, and Moore, eds., *Science Fiction, Critical Frontiers*. New York: St. Martin's Press, 2000, pp. 100–115.

Phillips, Carla Rahn, and William D. Phillips, Jr. "Christopher Columbus." In Carnes, ed., *Past Imperfect: History According to the Movies*. New York: Henry Holt, 1997, pp. 60–65.

Phillips, Gene D. *Conrad and Cinema: The Art of Adaptation*. New York: Peter Lang, 1997.

Pyle, Forest. "Making Cyborgs, Making Humans: Of Terminators and Blade Runners." In Collins, Radner, and Collins, eds., *Film Theory Goes to the Movies*. New York: Routledge, 1993, pp. 227–241.

Pynchon, Thomas. *Gravity's Rainbow*. New York: Viking Press, 1973.

Raw, Laurence. *The Ridley Scott Encyclopedia*. London: Scarecrow Press, 2009.

Redmond, Sean. *Studying "Blade Runner."* Leighton Buzzard, UK: Auteur, 2008.

Reid, Mark A. "The Black Gangster Film." In Grant, *Film Genre Reader*. Austin: University of Texas Press, 1995, pp. 456–473.

Reid, Peter. *A Brief History of Medieval Warfare*. London: Running Press, 2009.

Riley-Smith, Jonathan, ed. *The Oxford Illustrated History of the Crusades*. Oxford: Oxford University Press, 1995.

Ringgold, Gene, and DeWitt Bodeen. *The Complete Films of Cecil B. DeMille*. Secaucus, NJ: Citadel Press, 1969.

Robb, Brian J. *Ridley Scott*. Harpenden, UK: Pocket Essentials, 2005.

Robinson, Jeremy Mark. *"Blade Runner" and the Cinema of Philip K. Dick*. Maidstone, Kent, UK: Crescent Moon, 2009.

Said, Lawrence H. *Guts & Glory: The Making of the American Military Image in Film*. Rev. ed. Lexington: University Press of Kentucky, 2002.

Sale, Patrick. *The Conquest of Paradise: Christopher Columbus and the Columbian Legacy*. New York: Knopf, 1990.

Sammon, Paul M. *Future Noir: The Making of "Blade Runner."* New York: Harper, 1996.

_____. *Ridley Scott Close Up: The Making of His Movies*. New York: Thunder's Mouth Press, 1999.

Sanders, James. *Celluloid Skyline: New York and the Movies*. New York: Alfred A. Knopf, 2001.

Santosuosso, Antonio. *Barbarians, Marauders, and Infidels: The Ways of Medieval Warfare*. New York: MJF Books, 2004.

Sarris, Andrew. *The American Cinema: Directors and Directions: 1929–1968*. New York: Da Capo Press, 1996.

_____. "Notes on the Auteur Theory in 1962." In Gerald Mast. Marshall Cohen and Leo Braudy, eds., *Film Theory and Criticism*. 4th ed. New York: Oxford University Press, 1992, pp. 585–605.

Scanlon, Paul. *The Book of "Alien."* Illus. Michael Gross. New York: Simon & Schuster, 1979.

Schwartz, Richard A. *The Films of Ridley Scott*. Westport, CT: Praeger, 2001.

"Scott, Ridley." *1991 Current Biography Yearbook*, pp. 511–514.

Solomon, Jon. *The Ancient World in the Cinema*. Rev. ed. New Haven: Yale University Press, 2001.

Staiger, Janet. "Taboos and Totems: Cultural Meanings of *The Silence of the Lambs*." In Collins, Rodner, and Collins, eds., *Film Theory Goes to the Movies*. New York: Routledge, 1993, pp. 142–154.

Stern, Lesley. *The Scorsese Connection*. London: British Film Institute, 1995.

Stern, Richard. "Studs: WFMT; April 7, 1995." In *What Is What Was*. Chicago: University of Chicago Press, 2002, pp. 28–41.

Stuart, Keith. "Sigourney Weaver: The Individualist." *Filmstar*, 10/2009, pp. 152–157.

Sturken, Marita. *Thelma and Louise*. London: British Film Institute, 2000.

Suvin, Darko. "Novum Is as Novum Does." In Sayer and Moore, eds., *Science Fiction, Critical Frontiers* New York: St. Martin's Press, 2000, pp. 3–22.

Szunskyj, Benjamin. *Essays on the Novels of Thomas Harris*. Foreword by Daniel O'Brien. Jefferson, NC: McFarland, 2008.

Tayler, Christopher. "Gender Bait for the Nerds." *London Review of Books* 23, no. 10, 5/2003, p. 34.

Telotte, J. P. *Replications: A Robotic History of the Science Fiction Film*. Urbana: University of Illinois Press, 1995.

Thomson, David. *Have You Seen...?* New York: Knopf, 2008.

_____, and Ian Christie, eds. *Scorsese on Scorsese*. Intro. Michael Powell. London: Faber & Faber, 1996.

Weller, Sheila. "The Ride of a Lifetime," *Vanity Fair*, March 2011, pp. 316-327, 350-351.

Willett, John. *The Theatre of the Weimar Republic*. New York: Holmes & Meier, 1988.

Bibliography

Willis, Sharon. "Hardware and Hardbodies, What Do Women Want? A Reading of *Thelma and Louise*." In Collins, Radner, and Collins, eds., *Film Theory Goes to the Movies*. New York: Routledge, 1993, pp. 120–128.

Williams, Linda. "What Makes a Woman Wander." In Henderson and Martin, eds., *Film Quarterly: Forty Years: A Selection*. Berkeley: University of California Press, 1999, pp. 554–555.

Winkler, Martin M., ed. *Gladiator: Film and History*. Malden, MA: Blackwell, 2005.

Wyke, Maria. *Projecting the Past: Ancient Rome, Cinema, and History*. New York: Routledge, 1997.

Index

Numbers in **bold italics** indicate pages with photographs.

Index

Index

Index

Index

Index

Index